THE
CRUISING GUIDE
TO THE
VIRGIN ISLANDS

Dedicated to the ones we've lost...
Roger & Jana Downing, and Dean Morgan.
Tortola doesn't feel the same without you.

16TH EDITION
2013-2014

by Nancy and Simon Scott

A Complete Guide
for Yachtsmen, Divers and Watersports Enthusiasts

THE CRUISING GUIDE TO THE
VIRGIN ISLANDS

16TH EDITION
2013-2014

by Nancy and Simon Scott

A Complete Guide
for Yachtsmen, Divers
and Watersports Enthusiasts

Cruising Guide Publications, Inc. is a special-interest publisher of sailing guides to cruising in various areas around the world and other publications of nautical interest. CGP endeavors to provide comprehensive and invaluable materials to both inveterate sailors and less experienced seafarers seeking vital vacationing tips and navigational information relative to the journey to and the enjoyment of their destinations.

The Cruising Guide to the Virgin Islands is intended for use in conjunction with either U.S. National Ocean Survey charts, U.S. Hydrographic Office charts, N.V. Charts, or British Admiralty charts. Every effort has been made to describe conditions accurately. However, the publisher makes no warranty, express or implied, for any errors or omissions in this publication. Skippers should use this guide only in conjunction with the above charts and/or other navigational aids and not place undue credence in the accuracy of this guide. **The Cruising Guide to the Virgin Islands** is not intended for use for navigational purposes.

For regular V.I. information updates
see our website:
www.CruisingGuides.com

Anchoring in coral is
STRICTLY PROHIBITED
in both the U.S. and B.V.I.

Published by
Cruising Guide Publications, Inc.

P.O. Box 1017, Dunedin, FL 34697-1017
Telephone: (727) 733-5322
(800) 330-9542
Fax (727) 734-8179

Email: info@cruisingguides.com
www.CruisingGuides.com

By Nancy & Simon Scott

Art Direction
Julie L. Johnston
Carol Design, Inc.
Affinity Design
A.E. Sabo

Advertising/Marketing Director
Maureen Larroux

Editor/Production Manager
Ashley Scott

Administration
Pat Kozemski

Illustrations
Roger Burnett
Roger Bansemer

Photography
A.J. Blake   Simon Scott
Diane Butler   Chris Simmons
Aragorn Dick-Read   Dougal Thornton
Marc Downing   USVI Tourist Board
Walker Mangum   VI National Park
Julian Putley   Yacht Haven Grande
Jim Scheiner   Yacht Shots BVI

Contributing Writers
Carol Bareuther
Julian Putley
William Stelzer
Neil Whitehead, PhD

Copyright © Maritime Ventures, Ltd. 2012
Sixteenth Edition
Printed in China

Front Cover Photography:
Dougal Thornton and Yacht Shots BVI
Foxy

ISBN: 978-0-944428-95-5

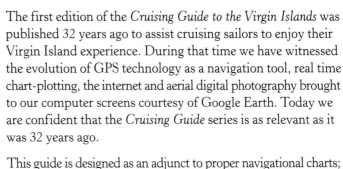

INTRODUCTION

The first cruising sailor to visit the Virgin Island chain was Christopher Columbus in 1493 with his fleet of 17 boats chartered in Spain. Since that time, cruising sailors from around the world have discovered for themselves the near perfect tradewind conditions that dominate Virgin Island weather the year round.

The first edition of the *Cruising Guide to the Virgin Islands* was published 32 years ago to assist cruising sailors to enjoy their Virgin Island experience. During that time we have witnessed the evolution of GPS technology as a navigation tool, real time chart-plotting, the internet and aerial digital photography brought to our computer screens courtesy of Google Earth. Today we are confident that the *Cruising Guide* series is as relevant as it was 32 years ago.

This guide is designed as an adjunct to proper navigational charts; not a substitute. All the necessary navigational equipment that one would normally utilize is still required. For sailors discovering the islands aboard a chartered vessel, the charter fleet operators all prepare skippers with an area briefing outlining the individual restriction to the cruising area. This guide will help prepare you for that briefing. It includes information on planning your cruise, what to expect upon arrival, medical facilities, etc. All of the frequently-utilized anchorages are discussed in detail and supported with both detailed harbor charts and aerial photography. In addition, there are updated sections on diving and dive facilities, marine parks and conservation, GPS waypoints, suggested itineraries, restaurants and ferry services.

Conditions are constantly changing; shifts on the sea bed, natural growth and intervention by human forces constantly produce new and varied situations. We have made every effort to describe accurately the conditions in the anchorages listed; however, the authors and publisher assume no responsibility for possible errors in the charts, soundings or accompanying text that may be contained in the *Guide*.

Welcome to the Virgin Islands!

Simon & Nancy Scott
Publishers

TABLE OF CONTENTS

TABLE OF CONTENTS

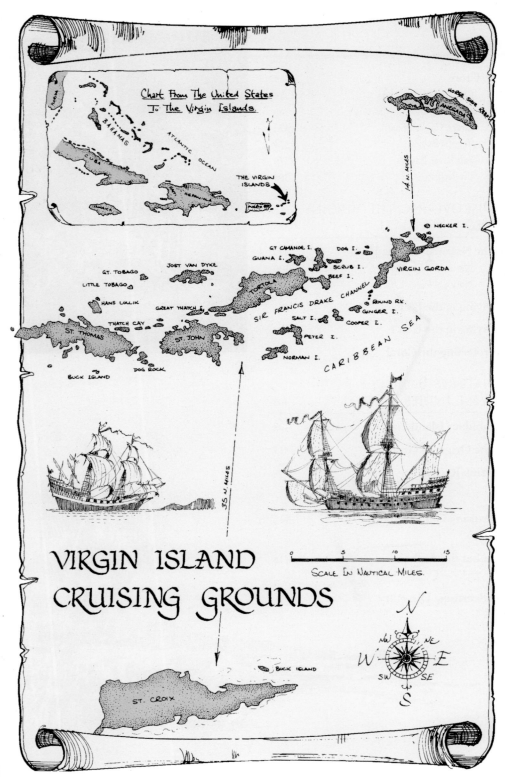

VIRGIN ISLAND
CRUISING GROUNDS

IMAGINE

THIS IS YOUR PARADISE

...spoilt Caribbean paradise. Unforgettable relaxation.
...is the British Virgin Islands. As uniquely welcoming as they are
...quil and private, these 60 islands offer you a true escape. Ride the
...d aboard a sailboat, windsurfer or kite board. Explore a century-old
...wreck or a timeless coral reef, or just lose yourself amidst the
...ceful sounds of the sea.

60 Islands. 1 Unforgettable Experience.
Visit www.bvitourism.com or **Call** 1.800.835.8530

THE
BRITISH
VIRGIN ISLANDS
NATURE'S LITTLE SECRETS®

VIRGIN ISLANDS HISTORY

Nothing has influenced the history of the Virgin Islands more profoundly than their geography and physical makeup. Situated at the high point of the curving archipelago that swings from Trinidad to Florida, they survey strategically all of the Americas, and, with their steady trade winds and numerous sheltered harbors, it is not surprising that they rapidly became a center for sea routes to every point of the compass, providing a welcome pause in the lengthy trade lines between Europe and the riches of south and Central America. Having been described as "the place on the way to everywhere," they have long been desirable for both trading and military advantage, from the days when Spaniards sailed through carrying Mexican and Peruvian bullion to Spain until this century when the United States paid $25 million to buy the US Virgin Islands from Denmark in order to forestall any unfriendly foreign power from parking on her doorstep.

Sailors and sailing have therefore been at the core of Virgin Islands history from the moment the first Amerindians brought their kanawa (canoes) from the South American mainland and populated the Antilles.

The various migrations that occurred into the Caribbean from South America over the last thousand years have been identified with various archaeological complexes such as the Ciboney, Arawak and Caribs. However, the relationship amongst these different archaeological traditions remains obscure, although the old story of fierce and cannibalistic Caribs eating their way across the islands at the expense of the peaceable Arawaks is now seen as rather more the lurid colonial fantasy than a credible anthropological reconstruction of the early Caribbean.

Native words were adopted directly into European languages, as with canoe, tobacco, barbecue, potato, hurricane and, notoriously, cannibal.

reclining woman with a protruding belly. As Spanish settlements increased so did Carib resistance which only provoked Emperor Charles V to order that the Indians "should be treated as enemies and given no quarter." Nevertheless, Carib military resistance to the Europeans lasted in one form or another until the start of the nineteenth century – and there was even a minor Carib War with the British in the 1930s.

Columbus discovered the Virgin Islands in 1493, on his second voyage to the New World. He anchored off Salt River Bay in St. Croix for fresh water and then was driven by unfavorable winds to Virgin Gorda. Seeing the numerous islands, he named them "the Virgins" in honor of St. Ursula and the 11,000 virgins who, threatened by the marauding Huns in 4th-century Cologne, sacrificed their lives rather than submit to a fate worse than death. Virgin Gorda may have got its name (fat virgin) because Columbus, viewing it from seaward, thought that it resembled a

Piracy arose in general because various European nations who were unable to challenge Spanish dominance in the region directly, gave these pirates unofficial backing, in the form of letters of marque, to follow private enterprise or to indulge in smuggling, piracy and the harassment of Spanish settlements. Even a famous personage like Sir Walter Raleigh was therefore known to the Spanish as "El Pirata Ingles."

This combination of privateering and piracy (the distinction between the two wearing very thin at times) was to continue for several hundred years. A vast array of colorful and bizarre characters paused in the Virgin Islands, among them the well-known pirate Henry Morgan and the legendary Sir John Hawkins, who visited the area four times.

As the power of Spain waned, other countries began to colonize the West Indies more seriously, although piracy continued for a while, the struggling settlers being happy to trade their agricultural produce and materials for a share of the Spanish gold.

Eventually, however, the bullion treasures from America dried up and a process of colonization for commercial profit emerged. The Danes formally took possession of St. Thomas and, later, St. John; the English ousted the Dutch and gained a firm foothold in Tortola and Virgin Gorda; and the French settled in St. Croix but later sold it to the Danish West India Company.

The Spaniards continued to raid occasionally from their strongholds in Puerto Rico and Hispaniola through the late 1600s and piracy flared up intermittently in the early 1700s. Considerable cleaning up and law enforcement took place as the casual farming that had begun, merely in order to colonize the islands and break the Spanish monopoly, gave way to serious plantations which,

unsubsidized by stolen Spanish gold, needed to trade at a steady profit.

Following the example of the original Spanish settlers, early plantation owners brought slaves from Africa. When the introduction of sugar cane production in the 1640s required a large, cheap and stable labor force, the number of slaves began to increase. For some time the colonies thrived. Sugar and cotton were valuable commodities and the plantations diversified into the production of indigo, spices, rum, maize, pineapples, yams and coconuts. In 1717 the first census taken in Virgin Gorda showed a population of 625, about half of whom were black. By the mid-1700s this population had grown to nearly 2,000 and the proportion of slaves throughout the Virgin Islands had increased dramatically.

Life on the plantations was extremely hard for the slaves and, as their majority on the islands increased, so did the restrictions

on them and the severity of the punishments meted out to them for the breaking of these. Conflict over the slave trade was increasing; it had been outlawed in England in 1772 and the impetus for its abolition was growing.

The obstacles to plantation life increased, several hurricanes and droughts ravaged the islands, and the American Revolution and Napoleonic wars created a revival of enemy raids, piracy and fighting within the islands. The slaves suffered as a result and, as news of abolition elsewhere began to filter through to the West Indies, they began to make use of their by now considerable majority to rebel.

The slave rebellions coincided, more or less, with the introduction of the sugar beet in Europe, which dealt a fatal blow to the once great "trade-triangle" based on West Indian cane. By the mid-1800s the slaves were free and the white population had deserted the colonies.

For almost 100 years the Virgin Islands dozed peacefully, the freed slaves living quietly off the land and sea, though with some difficulty in years of drought and famine. Government was minimal. The islands struggled on with tottering economies. Virgin Gorda was visited briefly by Cornish miners who reopened the old Spanish mine in search of copper. An earthquake leveled all the churches in Tortola and the R.M.S. Rhone was wrecked off Salt Island. As late as 1869 the steamship Telegrafo was detained in Tortola and charged with piracy. Labor riots and rebellions occasionally protested the hardships. The United States began to show an interest in buying the Danish

islands, afraid that they would be sold to a hostile nation such as Germany.

The islands moved into the 20th century without much change. An agricultural station was established in Tortola in 1900 in hopes of boosting the faltering economy, various homestead projects were begun throughout the island with little effect and the parent governments of each colony were forced to accept financial responsibility for the islands, which were fast becoming a liability.

The first world war was tightening the purse strings further, and by 1917 the Danes were happy to sell their Virgin Islands to the United States, which was eager to have a military outpost in the Caribbean. St. Thomas had long been a useful coaling station and harbor for steamships and was well positioned to defend the approaches to the Panama Canal.

Over the first half of the 20th century there was gradual social reform and progress towards local government. This process began to speed up as the tourist trade, boosted by the increasing ease of casual travel, began to grow. Situated conveniently close to the United States and blessed with a warm climate and a beautiful, unspoiled environment, the Virgin Islands rapidly became popular with tourists. This is an industry which needed only the natural resources of the islands to sustain their economies, and responsible tourism will also ensure that sustainability continues.

With the charter industry becoming the backbone of the islands, particularly in the BVI, sailors continue to make use of one of the finest sailing areas in the world. The quiet coves where Drake, Columbus and Blackbeard used to anchor are once more havens for fleets of sailing vessels and the modern adventurers who come to explore the Virgin Islands.

With thanks to Neil Whitehead, PhD

destination
ST. MAARTEN
the Marine Center of the Caribbean

Make St. Maarten your Caribbean base. Our little island wonderland is hands down the best place in the Caribbean to berth, provision, repair, and explore.

Just about everything is designed to make getting things done easier: a sheltered lagoon with several marinas and plenty of anchoring room; easy check-in procedures; duty-free status; large international airport with direct flight to the Americas & Europe; and a world-class marine service sector ready to cater to your every need.

Our selection of marine parts and supplies, hardware, food & beverages, household goods and consumer electronics is unparalleled anywhere in the Caribbean. With no import taxes or Customs red tape, prices are lower than anywhere in the neighborhood. What is not stocked locally can be sourced and shipped in quickly by air, or economically by ocean freight.

Provisioning is a delight, with our melting-pot of cultures resulting in food from all corners of the world readily available.

Best of all – most of what you'll need is within reach of a dinghy dock. When hired help is needed, dozens of world-class professionals - shipwrights, mechanics, sailmakers, riggers, fabricators, electricians, electronics technicians, refrigeration specialists, painters and many others – are a service call away for a quick repair or a big job.

Our great air connections make it easy to get away for a quick trip home, or fly in friends, family or charter guests.

And, while getting your boat repaired in an exotic location, there's plenty to do: From numerous bars, restaurants, nightclubs and casinos to beaches, watersports, land activities, movies and music. Once the boat is ready to go, check out our relaxing anchorages and cruise our neighboring islands.

www.yachtingstmaarten.com

Pirates of the Caribbean

As long as men have transported anything of value across the ocean, there have been others willing to relieve them of it. Even the Bible speaks of "princes of the sea." Julius Caesar had first-hand experience of these – he was kidnapped and held for ransom by them, and his invasion of Britain was partly in order to subdue the Veneti pirata and their British crews.

For several hundred years the Vikings made annual raids along the coasts of Western Europe, and in the Middle Ages, as trade and travel by sea expanded, piracy got underway with a vengeance.

"Privateering" also came into vogue at this time. A pirate called Eustace The Monk, who was believed to have black magic powers, did well plundering French ships on behalf of England's King John. Privateering was basically government-sponsored piracy – tacit approval given to raids on the ships of potential enemies. Privately owned vessels manned by civilians were commissioned with "letters of marque" as auxiliaries to the Royal Navy. They were used mainly against merchant shipping and were actively encouraged by monarchs in times of war or hostility. (As the 16th and early 17th centuries saw Europe in a fairly constant state of turmoil, this meant that they were encouraged most of the time.) Since a healthy percentage of the "purchase" went to the Crown, there was an added incentive for Royalty to turn a blind eye to the often extreme actions of the privateers and a deaf ear to the whining and complaining of the Ambassadors from semi-hostile nations.

Having laid claim to all of the Americas and the West Indies, Spain was the most powerful nation in the world at this time. Other nations, though afraid to challenge the monopoly directly, were happy to see pirates siphoning off funds intended for the Spanish Reformation by intercepting the treasure ships loaded with Aztec gold. The increasing number of privateers also provided a handy pool of trained sailors who could be called upon in times of outright conflict.

Numerous ex-pirates played an important role in the eventual defeat of the Spanish Armada. In times of covert hostility they could go back to being privateers (the "legality" made visiting ports for supplies easier), and in the infrequent and uneasy intervals of peace they resorted to plain piracy – their status was largely dependent upon the diplomatic label given to it at the time.

In reality their lives changed very little. If press-ganged into the Navy they could expect long voyages, harsh discipline, vile food and a good chance of an early demise – all for a pathetic pittance which would be cut off abruptly in peacetime. As pirates, their conditions at sea were little better but were offset by a freer democratic lifestyle, a similar chance of survival and the possibility of vast financial reward. As Bartholomew Roberts, one of the most successful pirates of the early 18th century, commented, "In an honest service there is thin rations, low wages and hard labor; in this, plenty and satiety, pleasure and ease, liberty and power; and who would not balance creditor on this side, when all the hazard that is run for it, at worst, is only a sour look or two at choking. No, 'a merry life and a short one' shall be my motto."

The defeat of the Armada intensified the harassment of Spanish merchant ships and allowed English, French and Dutch colonies to germinate in the now undefended West Indies.

Some of the first colonists were the inerrant French boucaniers who settled on Hispaniola. They made a meager living barbecuing beef in smokehouses called boucans and selling it to passing vessels. Foolishly the Spaniards drove them off the island; in revenge they took to the sea where, instead of hunting wild cattle, they went after Spanish ships.

"Buccaneer" became a new and fearful term for "pirate", and their ranks swelled as out-of-work naval crews drifted to the new world. New colonies struggling desperately to gain a foothold were a willing market for plundered goods. The governors of these new settlements gained a 10% commission for issuing letters of marque to privateers and, as a result, Jamaica's Port Royal became one of the richest towns in the hemisphere because of pirate gold. It also became known as "the wickedest city in the world," but it was largely due to the transient population of fighting sailors that the British were able to keep Jamaica. As late as 1774, historian Edward Long wrote, "It is to the bucca-neers that we owe possession of Jamaica to this hour."

So the pirates were a vital part of the colonization of the West Indies. Henry Morgan, for example, dealt terrible blows to Spanish dominance when he attacked Spanish shipping, ransomed Puerto de Principe in Cuba, assaulted Porto Bello and burned Panama City to the ground. Despite a new treaty with Spain, neither Morgan nor the governor who issued the commission was ever punished, possibly because of the shares received by the King and his brother, the Duke of York.

The Spanish meted out their own punishment if they caught pirates or privateers. They made no distinction between the two except that privateers were sent to the gallows with their commissions tied around their necks. Hanging was the usual end for captured pirates, although, if they were unlucky enough to fall into the hands of the Inquisition, they might receive a more drawn-out demise on the rack.

"Going on the account" was the term used when a man signed up for a career in piracy; this basically meant "no prey, no pay," but all the crew were shareholders in the "company" and part owners of the ship. The company typically

began with a very modest vessel – some of the early buccaneers used dug-out canoes – but after a few killings on the market, they would generally acquire more suitable headquarters.

The ideal pirate vessel was small and fast. Bermudan sloops were felt to be ideal because of their speed (over 11 knots) and maneuverability, and could carry up to 75 men. A bigger company might go for a brigantine, a two-masted vessel that could carry either a square or fore-and-aft rig or a versatile combination of the two.

This was often how pirates made their assaults, sneaking out from the coast in poor light to spring upon a sluggish merchantman. The Virgin Islands made an excellent hunting ground with their myriad coves and passages. Situated right on the treasure route from South America to Europe, the area was visited by many notorious Caribbean pirates such as Edward England, whose kind treatment of prisoners so disgusted his crew that he was deposed; Charles Vane, who Defoe reported, "died in agonies equal to his villainies but showed not the least remorse for the crimes of his past life;" Calico Jack, well known for his romance with lady pirate Anne Bonny; Bartholomew Roberts, who became one of the greatest

pirates of all "for the love of novelty and change alone;" and the formidable Blackbeard, who would go into battle with slow-burning matches alight in his beard and behind his ears to enhance his devilish resemblance.

As the colonies in the island began to stabilize, law and order made the pirates less welcome as members of the community. Many of them set off for the North American mainland, where the newer colonists, already muttering about Independence, were quite pleased to help the newcomers harass British shipping magnates. Others headed for the Orient, the Red Sea, the Indian Ocean and Madagascar.

PLANNING
THE
CRUISE

CRUISE PLANNING LOGISTICS

Each year thousands of sailors from both sides of the Atlantic converge on the Caribbean to explore the thousands of coves and anchorages and discover the many wonderful cultures and colors that it offers. Many will arrive by air from the U.S. or Europe, to charter a boat, while others will make the passage aboard their own vessels.

When contemplating a cruise around the Virgin Islands there are myriad questions and issues to be asked and answered. We have tried to address some of the more germane issues here and a visit to our website will offer an enhanced reference guide for those looking to cruise the waters of the Virgin Islands.

The considerations for information are somewhat different depending upon which of the above options is chosen. The cruiser will require a deeper understanding of the Caribbean weather patterns on a seasonal basis, while the charterer will require a different set of data points. We have tried to strike a reasonable balance in this regard.

CRUISING YOUR OWN BOAT TO THE ISLANDS

Cruisers en route to the Virgin Islands from North America have three distinct options when contemplating a winter in the Caribbean; they can migrate their way down the east coast, or intra-coastal waterway, to Florida and then embark on the "Thorny Path" to the Virgin Islands. The Thorny Path as the name implies is a long, sometimes difficult path that routes them across the Bahamas where they will encounter the affects of the easterly trade winds as they enter the tropics en route to the Virgin Islands. Bruce Van Sant, in his book *A Gentleman's Guide to Passages South* describes this route in detail and offers excellent advice on how to avoid many of the difficulties. (Available at CruisingGuides.com)

For those contemplating making the offshore passage of some 1500 miles, from the US they will typically depart from ports like Newport, RI or Virginia Beach at the mouth of the Chesapeake Bay during early November in order to catch the short weather window between the end of the hurricane season (October 31st) and the start of the winter gales in December. This is a real blue water offshore experience; the passage time is approximately 10 days during which you will encounter some challenging weather conditions.

The Caribbean 1500 Rally for Cruisers departs from Virginia Beach around the first week of November and attracts a fleet of about 70 yachts of various sizes. This is an excellent way to make the passage in the company of other cruisers and with the added confidence of knowing that there is a support system close at hand. The rally organizers also conduct excellent safety seminars on offshore passage making and boat safety during the weeks prior to departure.

There is always the option of having your vessel shipped to the Virgin Islands, thereby saving the wear and tear on your yacht.

Dockwise Yacht Transport departs from Fort Lauderdale in late October and then Newport, RI in early November and onto St. Thomas at a cost of about $11,000 (Ft. Lauderdale) to $14,500 (Newport) for a typical 40' sailboat.

Caribbean bound sailors departing Europe and the Mediterranean before the onset of winter will be able to take full advantage of the northeast trade winds on their passage across the Atlantic. The ARC rally departs annually from the Canary Islands in late October, with a fleet of 60-70 vessels ending on the island of St. Lucia in the Windward Islands. After cruising the Windwards the boats generally work their way north through the Leeward Islands and then onto the Virgin Islands. Some consideration needs to be given as to where the vessel will be at the start of the next year's hurricane season. Many yachts will be heading back to Europe via Bermuda or heading to the east coast of the USA.

Customs Considerations:
The British Virgin Islands: Yachts visiting the BVI for the first time will be required to pay an Annual Tonnage Fee, which is based on your yacht's net tonnage up to a limit of $55. If the vessel is to remain in the BVI for more than one month, there is a fee of $200 to temporarily import the yacht for up to one year. When arriving in the British Virgin Islands you must immediately proceed to a port of entry and clear customs and immigration. The skipper may present him/herself on behalf of the entire crew

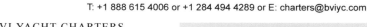

CRUISE PLANNING LOGISTICS

with passports, ships documentation and proof of clearance from the last port of call. If you are arriving after hours, raise the yellow Q flag and if possible notify customs by phone. In some instances it is possible to arrange for after hours clearance. Overtime fees will be applied. Guns of any kind are not allowed in the BVI. You must declare them and the police will take them and give you a receipt so that you can pick them up on your way out of the BVI.

In addition to the fees above, see the section Customs, Immigration & Formalities for details on Cruising Permit & National Parks fee structure.
BVI Customs: 284-494-3475

The US Virgin Islands: Vessels arriving in the USVI, regardless of flag or crew nationality, are required upon entry into US waters, to contact (via telephone) the nearest designated location and provide:
- Name, DOB and citizenship including passport number
- Name of vessel and documentation number
- CBP user fee number if applicable (see note)
- Homeport and current location
- Return contact number

Then (unless instructed to the contrary) proceed to the nearest port of entry, where the captain and crew are required to present themselves in person with documentation.

Yachts over 300 gross tons must send Advance Notice of Arrival to the U.S. Coast Guard 24 hours prior to arrival or they will not be admitted into the USVI. (Check nvmc.uscg.gov/nvmc/default.aspx for details of Advance Notice of Arrival "NOA.") Non-USA crew or guests must have the requisite visas. For yachtsmen already in the Caribbean, U.S. visas can be obtained from the U.S. Embassy in Barbados after first obtaining an appointment.

Cruising permits are not required in the USVI, however, vessels remaining six months or more are required to register with the Department of Planning & Natural Resources Environmental Enforcement Office (340-774-3320).

Vessels traveling between the BVI and USVI must clear out of BVI waters at one of the ports of entry (West End ferry dock, Road Town, Jost Van Dyke, St. Thomas Bay Virgin Gorda, and Yacht Club Costa Smeralda marina in North Sound Virgin Gorda) and clear into U.S. waters either at Cruz Bay, St. John or Charlotte Amalie, St. Thomas, or Gallows Bay, St. Croix.

When arriving into the U.S. Virgin Islands from the B.V.I. you must go to customs and immigration first. If you arrive at night you should hoist the yellow quarantine flag and wait until customs and immigration are open in the morning and not leave the boat before clearing in with the officials. U.S.V.I. customs and immigration offices: Cruz Bay, St. John- Charlotte Amalie, St. Thomas- Redhook, St. Thomas- Gallows Bay, St. Croix.
USVI Customs: 703-526-4200

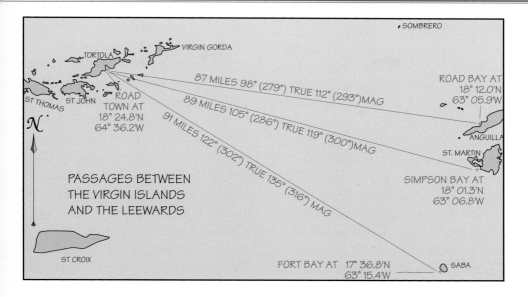

SOMBRERO

TORTOLA   VIRGIN GORDA

87 MILES 98° (279°) TRUE 112° (293°)MAG

ROAD BAY AT
18° 12.0'N
63° 05.9'W

ST THOMAS   ST JOHN   ROAD
TOWN AT
18° 24.8'N
64° 36.2'W

89 MILES 105° (286°) TRUE 119° (300°)MAG

91 MILES 122° (302°) TRUE 135° (316°) MAG

ANGUILLA

ST. MARTIN

PASSAGES BETWEEN
THE VIRGIN ISLANDS
AND THE LEEWARDS

SIMPSON BAY AT
18° 01.3'N
63° 06.8'W

ST CROIX

FORT BAY AT   17° 36.8'N
63° 15.4'W

SABA

South to the Leeward Islands

The northern most islands of the Leeward Islands, Anguilla, St. Martin and Saba, lie around 80-90 miles east of the Virgin Islands and getting there entails crossing the Anegada Passage. A current from half a knot to a knot and a half usually flows in a westerly to northwesterly direction. The trade winds blow from the easterly quadrant. All of this makes it really easy to sail from the Leewards to the Virgin Islands; it is downwind and downcurrent. Conversely, the trip from the Virgins is tough, with both wind and current on the nose. Unless the wind is way in the northeast, you are unlikely to be able to lay even Saba on one tack, so unless you like heavy weather beating in short seas, avoid the strong Christmas winds. Approaching cold fronts can be preceded by calm days,

which could provide a weather window if a 90 mile motor sail works for you. If schedule dictates that you must sail south during periods of strong north-easterlies, an alternative course would take you southeast from the Virgin Islands to Saba (passing west of the Saba Bank) and onto St. Kitts before heading east.

When conditions are favorable, it is best to depart the Virgin Islands from the most northerly point in order to deal with the wind and current. The BVI departure points would be via the Round Rock Passage, south of Virgin Gorda, or the Necker Island Passage, north of Gorda Sound. A late afternoon departure should get you into St. Martin by mid-day.

The Leeward Islands are covered in the *Cruising Guide to the Leeward Islands*, by Chris Doyle, available from the bookstore at www.CruisingGuides.com.

CHARTERING A YACHT

TIME OF YEAR

As the first blasts of cold arctic air make their way across Canada and the northeast of the USA, many sailors start contemplating a Caribbean sailing holiday during the months of January through March. Because of the popularity of these (high season) months, the rates are appreciably higher and availability limited so early planning is essential. The trade winds are also highest during this period and therefore one can expect generally settled weather with gusty wind and sea conditions (18-25 knots). The shoulder seasons are reflected with lower rates, but keep in mind that school holidays are often busy and demand drives cost. Thanksgiving and Easter holidays fill quickly, so make your plans as early as possible.

During the spring and summer months, the rates are generally lower and the anchorages less crowded as sailors launch and sail their vessels in home waters. We have always enjoyed the month of May, when the weather is settled, the charter rates reasonable and the anchorages are not crowded. Hurricane season officially starts in June, however early hurricane activity is very rare. Chartering continues through August with an appreciable drop off during September and early October when school holidays come to an end. Charter rates at this time are at their lowest. Temperatures throughout the Virgins remain stable year round with the coolest temperatures during the winter months between a low of 74°F and a high

of 84°F during the day. During the months of June, July and August the temperature will increase to a low of 79°F at night with daytime temperatures around 89°F.

SELECTING A CHARTER COMPANY

Choosing a bareboat, captained, or fully crewed sailing charter can seem a bewildering experience, especially if it's your first time. You will have to choose among different sailing locations, models and sizes of boats, provisioning plans and equipment options, not to mention the additional services of a sailing instructor, land accommodation, etc.

Before you are able to select the right charter company for your sailing vacation you will have to answer a few questions and establish criteria for decision-making: catamaran or monohull? Being traditionalists ourselves, we enjoy short handed cruising on a monohull, but when we have a group of friends or family sailing together and partying in the Virgins, a catamaran offers additional accommodation and specifically outside living area which makes it our favorite choice.

Determine the crew size, level of expertise, general appetite for activity and available budget. A charter holiday is logically comprised of airfare, provisioning, personal expenses and charter fee. Before you sign on the dotted line make sure that you have all the details and know what your overall costs are.

Look on the websites of the various charter operators listed in the back of the major

sailing publications and familiarize yourself with the individual offerings. Another route is to call an independent charter broker. Charter brokers can help charterers find the perfect yacht and crew for their trip. Selecting a crewed charter can be difficult and a broker can help match your needs to a specific crew or type of vessel as well as provide quotes from several different companies. They are paid by the ship's owners or operating companies, so their services are available at no cost to the traveler. The two most common charter broker trade organizations are the American Yacht Charter Association (AYCA) and Charter Yacht Broker's Association (CYBA).

Your available budget will often determine both the size and age of the vessel and associated equipment, therefore it is imperative that your budget and expectations are aligned. Leading brand companies such as The Moorings, Sunsail, Marine Max Vacations or Horizon who offer charter fleets all over the world, will typically keep a vessel in service four to five years. These

CHARTERING A YACHT

vessels are pre-specified with the builder, and have identical equipment in order to keep the logistics of maintenance under control.

Other fleet operators like TMM, BVI Yacht Charters or CYOA manage and charter yachts for individual owners. They are likely to have different types of vessels available with owner-customized equipment. Footloose Charters as well as Conch Charters and Pro Valor specialize in taking yachts out of the tier one fleets at the end of their initial term and offering them at substantial discounts. The important thing to consider is more the level of maintenance than the actual age of the vessel.

Whichever way you decide to go, make sure that you compare offerings and understand the total costs and trade-offs involved. Ask about sailing restrictions, chase boat coverage, service guarantees and before and after charter procedures and briefings. Do not be reluctant to ask the questions. There are also online postings, such as www.CharterAdvisors.com that can offer feedback from recent charterers.

WHAT TO EXPECT

When you book your charter vessel, the charter company will send you a packet of material, or in some cases, have you download it from their website. This will include a charter contract, sailing resume, provisioning and beverage preference list, inventory list, passenger list and projected arrival information. This information will be sent back to your charter company or broker so that appropriate arrangements for provisioning and transportation can be put in place prior to your arrival on the island.

Upon arrival at the airport or ferry, there will be a taxi or bus from the company waiting to take you to the marina.

Upon arrival at the marina, depending upon boarding time, you will be taken to the yacht and a staff member will set up a time for both an area chart briefing and a boat check out. The sooner you can get your gear put away, provisions stowed, beer chilled and briefings complete, the sooner you can cast off and get into the rhythm of the islands. Check all gear and inventory thoroughly and ask as many questions as you need to at the briefing.

The charter companies will give you copies of Cruising Permits and Parks Permits where applicable, along with contact numbers for communication. Unless specified differently, your vessel will be provided with a navigation chart and basic navigation tools. In many cases there will be an electronic chart plotter aboard also. Don't forget to take your copy of the *Cruising Guide!*

We highly recommend that you make the first overnight anchorage a relatively short sail from the base. A one to two hour sail gets you to a nearby anchorage where everyone can finish unpacking, get the boat organized, take a dive over the side and share a drink in the cockpit before firing up the grill for dinner.

Making Memories.
Charting New Waters.

For more than 30 years CYOA Yacht Charters has been creating Virgin Island vacation memories for sailors wanting to stay off the beaten path.

Our late model fleet of cats and monohulls, most with generator and air conditioning, is your launch platform for memories of a life time.

Let our caring staff prepare your boat now – call or email for reservations.

CYOA is enviro-friendly and 100% holding tank equipped.

CYOA

YACHT CHARTERS

Frenchtown | St Thomas USVI
800-944-2962 | 340-777-9690
www.cyoacharters.com | info@cyoacharters.com

Sail Cats | Power Cats
Monohulls | Trawlers
Bareboat | Skippered

British Virgins 7-day cruise from Road Town or Nanny Cay

Day 1: Depart charter base at noon and sail to Cooper Island or Little Harbour, Peter Island. Cooper Island has mooring balls available and the Beach Club serves dinner. Little Harbour has no moorings and no services, just wonderful solitude.

Day 2: If you are anchored at Little Harbour, motor over to Pelican Island and the Indians for a morning snorkel. From Cooper Island, motor across to Salt Island and snorkel over the wreck of the RMS Rhone. Sail on up the channel to Virgin Gorda and the Baths. Explore and snorkel before sailing across the channel to Marina Cay or Trellis Bay for the evening.

Day 3: Explore the Trellis Bay arts and crafts village before setting sail for the Dogs where you can stop for lunch or a snorkel before continuing on to Gorda Sound for the evening. Pick up a mooring at Saba Rock or Bitter End or visit Leverick Bay at the other end of the Sound.

Day 4: This should be a kick back day. Snorkel the reefs surrounding Eustatia Sound, book a dive tour or rent a small sailing boat or windsurfer from the Bitter End. Hike the trails or book a scenic tour. Try another anchorage for the evening.

For enthusiasts wanting to pack everything into seven days, an early morning departure to Anegada will get you enough time for some quick exploration and a lobster dinner at Neptune's Treasure or Anegada Reef Hotel.

Day 5: If you get an early start from Gorda Sound (or Anegada) through the Camanoe Passage, a lunch stop and snorkel at Monkey Point, Guana Island can be taken before heading for Cane Garden Bay.

At Cane Garden Bay, visit the old Callwood Rum Distillery, or Myett's Sea Spa for the ladies. Pick up some supplies. Spend the evening ashore and hopefully catch up on some live local music.

Day 6: Sail to Sandy Cay or Green Cay and spend the morning snorkeling. After lunch continue on to Little Jost Van Dyke, Little Harbour or visit Foxy's Bar or Corsairs in Great Harbour.

Day 7: Take the boat around to White Bay, snorkel, walk the beach or enjoy a Painkiller at the Soggy Dollar Bar.

Sail over to Soper's Hole, West End for lunch at Pusser's before heading up the channel to the Bight at Norman Island and a snorkel at the caves at Treasure Point. Visit the Willy-T for drinks, or head ashore for a final night celebration.

Day 8: Get the boat organized, depart by 9.30am in order to be back at the base by 11am in time to clean up the boat, and get ready to depart.

TYPICAL SAILING ITINERARIES

When planning your Virgin Island sailing trip it is important to determine the right balance between sailing, snorkeling, exploring etc. How experienced is the crew? What is the general appetite for enthusiastic trade wind sailing? Are there divers aboard? Do you and the crew want to eat ashore every night? All of these factors will impact the way you plan your sailing adventure.

One thing is clear, you should plan an itinerary with a blend of activities to suit everybody aboard and not try to fit everything into a seven-day cruise. The real pleasure of a vacation is having the freedom to change plans, stay in a beautiful anchorage for an extra day, or keep sailing when the conditions are perfect.

The first day is critical and should be planned so that you get the crew to an anchorage; into the water and relaxed as soon as possible. Allow them to get accustomed to the environment and de-stress. Don't overdo it with a long sail to weather.

Anegada and the U.S. Virgins:

For planning purposes; to add Anegada to

Typical Sailing
Itineraries

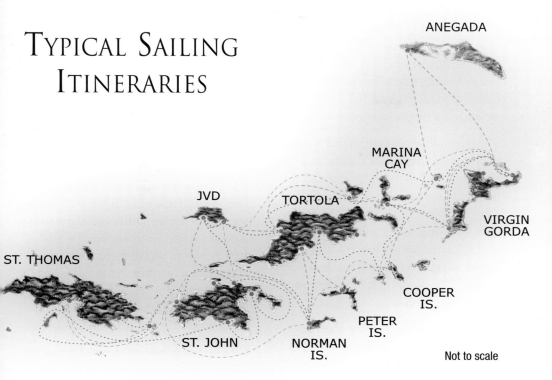

ANEGADA

MARINA CAY

JVD

TORTOLA

VIRGIN GORDA

ST. THOMAS

COOPER IS.

PETER IS.

ST. JOHN

NORMAN IS.

Not to scale

BVI, Nanny Cay - 10 Days

Day	Anchorage
1	Treasure Pt. / Norman Island
2	Pelican Is. / Jost Van Dyke
3	Sandy Cay / Little Jost Van Dyke
4	Bubbly Pool / Cane Garden Bay
5	Monkey Point / Marina Cay
6	The Baths / Gorda Sound
7	Anegada
8	Anegada / Gorda Sound
9	The Dogs / Cooper Island
10	Salt Is. / Peter Island

USVI, Charlotte Amalie / BVI - 10 Days

Day	Anchorage
1	Christmas Cove, Gt. St. James
2	Caneel / Leinster Bay, St. John
3	Annaburg Ruins / Jost Van Dyke
4	Marina Cay / Trellis Bay
5	Gorda Sound, Virgin Gorda
6	The Baths / V.G Yacht Harbour
7	Salt Is. / Peter Island
8	The Indians / Norman Is.
9	Hawksnest Bay, St. John
10	Charlotte Amalie, St.Thomas

BVI, Road Town - 7 days

Day	Anchorage
1	Cooper Is.
2	Marina Cay / Trellis Bay
3	The Baths / Gorda Sound, VG
4	The Dogs / Cane Garden Bay
5	Sandy Cay / Jost Van Dyke
6	White Bay/ Norman Is.
7	The Indians / Peter Is.

USVI / Benner Bay - 7 Days

Day	Anchorage
1	Hawksnest Bay, St. John
2	Leinster Bay, St. John
3	Coral Bay, St. John
4	Lameshur Bay, St. John
5	Water Is. St. Thomas
6	Christmas Cove, Gt. St. James
7	Benner Bay

your itinerary when sailing from the British Virgins, you will need 10 days. Likewise to add St. John and St. Thomas we suggest a 14-day charter.

The possibilities are endless and we offer the suggested itineraries as a starting point only. When planning your sailing holiday, make sure that you allow at least a day on both ends for travel. Depending upon your originating point and time of arrival, you may want to consider a first night hotel stay or, when available, a sleep-aboard. Your charter agent can help you with this decision.

For my own part, it takes me three days to de-stress and stop worrying about the office. After that I need seven days minimum to sail and explore the islands. More time is better of course but try not to pack so much into your time in the islands that the crew feels that they are on a European tour bus vacation. Determine a loose itinerary and allow it to evolve on a daily basis with input from your crew.

We offer the suggested itineraries for planning purposes only, the actual route and timing should be adjusted based upon the prevailing weather conditions. Visit our website at CruisingGuides.com for additional itineraries.

WHAT TO BRING FOR YOUR TRIP

At the top of the list is to bring any prescription medications you are taking along with some medication for sea sickness. Although, there are good pharmacies in the Virgins, it might be difficult to replace if you forget to bring them. It is also good to bring along your own toiletries and bug spray.

Some charter companies supply fins, masks and snorkels, however, I always bring my own snorkel.

The days in the tradewinds and sun are very comfortable and it is tempting when you live in the far north to go home with a gorgeous tan. However, bring a good sunscreen with you, and a hat and you will still return with a tan, but not a peeling red sunburn. Wicking shirts are a good idea as they help evaporate perspiration while protecting you from the sun's rays.

Polarized sunglasses are a must for keeping the glare from water and sun away. They also enable you to see through the water so that sometimes you may be able to avoid a rock or sand bar or be lucky enough to see a sea turtle under the surface.

Make sure to bring your camera along with extra camera batteries! There will certainly be images that you will always want to see again and remind you of a great adventure.

CURRENCY AND CREDIT CARDS

The U.S. dollar is the local currency in both the U.S. and British Virgin Islands. Since you will be spending a lot of time on small islands, it is a good idea to keep traveler's checks in smaller denominations. Major credit cards are honored at most USVI stores and hotels and the larger BVI establishments, but do not expect to use them at small restaurants during your cruise. Personal checks are not accepted anywhere. There are a few ATMs in more populated areas. Most of the mooring balls you may pick up in many anchorages cost around $25-$30 (check first). The preferred payment is cash, so you may want to include cash in $10 and $20 denominations to cover that. Before leaving call your bank and the credit card companies you plan to use and notify them that you will be traveling out of the country to the U.S. and British Virgin Islands. This way they will be less likely to hold up any transactions of the cards you use, thinking that your card may have been stolen.

WHAT NOT TO BRING

(A) Scuba gear – Bring your own regulator, face mask, etc., but don't bring weight belts and tanks. They are available for rent throughout the islands.

(B) Food items – Unless you have special dietary needs, these items are readily available.

(C) Surfboards and windsurfers – These items present a problem for the major airlines and a nightmare for the smaller commuter airlines. They are available for rent. Make prior arrangements with the appropriate charter company or agent.

Remember that you will probably purchase a few items while in the islands and some allowance should be made for such purchases when packing.

The ideal amount of luggage to bring on a sailing holiday should fit in a duffel bag above your airline seat. This will save your worrying about checking bags and waiting with baited breath to see if they show up on the other end.

FIREARMS

Some cruisers feel more secure with guns aboard for protection. If you are bringing firearms on your vessel into the U.S. Virgin Islands, the firearms must be licensed. When clearing Customs, all firearms and ammunition must be declared to Customs. Before arriving in the U.S. Virgin Islands call Customs first to ensure the regulations have not changed.

Firearms in the British Virgin Islands are prohibited and must be declared to Customs when you enter the British Virgin Islands. Customs will confiscate the firearms, leave them at Police Headquarters, and give the owner a receipt. When leaving the BVI the guns may be claimed from Police Headquarters with the receipt. Please check with BVI Customs before arriving with guns in the event that regulations have changed.

AIR SERVICE

Traveling to and from the Virgins is very straight forward. Most of the larger bareboat companies have travel agents who work closely with them and are in touch with special air fares and hotel accommodations. San Juan, Puerto Rico is the main routing for passengers destined to the BVI, St. Thomas and St. Croix. There are numerous non-stop flights from major U.S. gateways with ample local connections. American Airlines is one of the main airlines that provides service the San Juan Airport. There are other airlines from the US, Europe, the UK and Canada, but with the changes taking place in the aviation industry due to fuel prices, it is best that you check online or with your travel agent.

There are plenty of good hotels throughout the islands and it is advisable to plan a one night stay before checking in at the appropriate marina. This will enable you to "acclimatize" slowly, watching the sun set and sipping a rum punch while the frustrations of the day's travel diminish to insignificance.

The Virgins are an extremely popular tourist destination not only for sailors, but for all sorts of tourists and water sports enthusiasts; consequently, air travel and hotel accommodations should be reserved well in advance.

ISLAND AIR TRAVEL

The following airlines service the BVI:

Air Sunshine
284-495-8900

American Eagle
284-495-2559

Cape Air
284-495-2100

Caribbean Sun
284-494-2347

Caribbean Wings (charter)
284-495-6000

Fly BVI (charter)
284-495-1747

Island Birds (charter)
284-495-2002

LIAT
284-495-1187

The following airlines service the USVI:

Air Center Helicopters (charter)
340-775-7335

Air Sunshine
888-879-8900

American Airlines
800-474-4884

American Eagle
800-474-4884

Bohlke International Airways (charter)
340-778-9177

Cape Air
800-352-0714

Caribbean Sun
800-744-7827

Continental
800-231-0856

LIAT
340-774-2313

Seaborne Aviation Inc.
340-773-6442

Spirit Airlines
800-772-7117

Sun Country
800-359-6786

United Airlines
800-864-8331

U.S. Airways
800-428-4322

Many of the airlines that fly in to the British Virgin Islands also fly to the U.S. Virgin Islands. Also check with your tourist agency and online for the latest information

If you are planning to travel between the islands, there are numerous methods available to you.

FERRY SERVICE

When traveling from one island to another, or between the British and U.S. Virgin Islands, ferries are a quick and convenient way to go when not using your yacht. The following telephone numbers should allow you to confirm schedules before making your plans, as schedules are subject to change. Most itineraries are scheduled at convenient times, and most ferries travel several times back and forth daily.

FERRIES

Road Town Fast Ferry 284-495-2323
RoadTown/Virgin Gorda/Anegada

New Horizon Ferry 284-495-9278
Tortola/Jost Van Dyke/ Tortola

North Sound Express 284-495-2138
Tortola (Beef Island)/Virgin Gorda (the Valley) And Leverick Bay

Bitter End Ferry 284-494-2746
Gun Creek/ Bitter End Yacht Club

Speedy's 284-495-5240
Government jetty (next to Virgin Gorda Yacht Harbour); Road Town/Charlotte Amalie

Road Town Fast Ferry 284-495-2323
Tortola /Virgin Gorda/and Anegada

Native Son 284-495-4617
Tortola/Charlotte Amalie, St. Thomas/ Red Hook

Inter Island 284-495-4166
West End Tortola/Cruz Bay

SmithsTortola Fast Ferry 284-495-4495
Road Town, West End, Charlotte Amalie, St. Thomas

TRANSPORTATION

New Horizon Ferry 284-495-9278
Tortola/Jost Van Dyke

North Sound Express 284-495-9278
Tortola (departs from Beef Island)/
the Valley Virgin Gorda/Leverick Bay,
Virgin Gorda

Bitter Island Ferry 284-494-2746
Gun Creek/Bitter End

Saba Rock 284-495-7711
Gun Creek/Saba Rock

Scrub Island 284-440-3440
Trellis Bay/Scrub Island

Peter Island Ferry 284-495-2000
Baughers Bay, Road Town/Peter Island

Marina Cay 284-494-2174
Trellis Bay/Marina Cay

Norman Island Ferry Service 284-494-0093
Hannah Bay, Tortola/Pirates Restaurant,
Norman Island

CAR RENTAL

Both the British and the U.S. Virgin
Islands have developed adequate car
rental agencies to cope with the needs of
the growing tourist industry.

Prices are slightly higher than on the U.S.
mainland, but considering the high cost of
freight and the limited life expectancy that
vehicles enjoy in the island environment,
the differential is not excessive. Most of
the major car rental companies have local

branches throughout the Virgins and advance reservations can be made through your travel agent.

In addition, many locally owned and operated companies are also represented. If you are chartering during the peak months (December-April), try to reserve well in advance to avoid delays. In both the U.S. and British Virgins, remember to drive on the left.

Taxi Service

All points of debarkation are more than adequately serviced by taxis. The airports and ferry docks are often lined with taxis with the drivers pushing hard to capture their share of the market.

It is common in the islands to see open safari buses, which can carry up to 20 passengers in natural "air-conditioned" comfort. Taxi fares tend to be expensive throughout the islands and taxis are not metered! However, there are official taxi rates in both the British and U.S. Virgin Islands, and the prudent traveler should inquire of the rate beforehand so that there are no misunderstandings.

The major charter-boat companies will arrange transportation to pick you up upon arrival at the airport, but, such service should be arranged at the time of booking the charter.

Sample Taxi Fares in the BVI and USVI

The following fares are from selected destinations to give you an idea of what the range in fares can be. Prices are subject to change. Always ask how much a fare will be before getting in the taxi. For good service a gratuity is appreciated.

Sample fares in the BVI
From Beef Island Airport to Road Town:
1 person $27; 2 people $14 each; 3+ people $12 each

From Road Town to Cane Garden Bay:
1 person $24; 2 people $12 each; 3+ people $8 each

From Road Town to West End:
1 person $27; 2 people $14 each; 3+ people $12 each

From Road Town to Nanny Cay:
1 person $15; 2 people $8 each; 3+ people $6 each

Sample fares in the USVI
St. Thomas
From Charlotte Amalie to Compass Point:
1 person $12; $9 extra for 2 people

From Charlotte Amalie to Magen's Bay:
1 person $10; $7 extra for 2 people

From Charlotte Amalie to Ritz Carlton Resort:
1 person $10; $7 extra for 2 people

SAFETY, HEALTH & EMERGENCIES

SUN PROTECTION

Although it may seem difficult to comprehend as you dig your car out of the snow to get to the airport, the tropical sun is hot, especially on pale bodies that have been kept undercover throughout a northern winter.

The constant trade breezes keep the temperature pretty much ideal, but be careful not to spend too long out in the sun, as the combined effect of overhead tropical sun and reflection from both sails and water can cause severe sunburns.

Most charter yachts are equipped with bimini tops; however, it is still a good idea to bring along a pair of lightweight pants and tops. These will enable you to cover up without getting too hot.

If you are fair, then perhaps you should think about a wide-brimmed hat.

Suntan lotions are available throughout the islands. Heed the warnings of dermatologists regarding excessive sun exposure and do not go out into the sun without using an appropriate sun block or cover-up. Start with at least SPF-15. If you are careful, you will gradually develop a rich, golden tan without suffering a painful and potentially dangerous sunburn.

SAFETY IN THE ISLANDS

As with any destination in the world, there is always a chance of having something of value targeted by a thief. If you take precautions in advance, then you can enjoy your holiday with less worry. If you are chartering a bareboat, direct any specific questions to your charter company.

The following are some suggestions to help keep your possessions safe from petty crime:

Valuables: Expensive jewelry can be left at home. It is too easy to lose rings, earrings etc. when swimming, beaching and sailing. The islands are very informal for the most part, beach bars are casual and it's unlikely you would want to wear anything fancy. If you can't leave it behind, insure it.

Passports: You can keep your passport with you or put it in a very safe place when leaving the vessel. We suggest using waterproof pouches that can be worn around the neck under a shirt that will fit a passport, some cash and credit cards. Leave your passport number with someone at home so that if you do lose it, it will be easier for Immigration to help you.

Cash: Of course you'll need some cash, but there are more and more ATMs located throughout the islands. Credit cards can be replaced if lost or stolen. Just make sure you have left your credit card number with someone at home and bring the telephone number listed on the card to call and report a lost or stolen card. Traveler's checks are always a good idea.

Cameras: About all you can do when leaving your camera behind on board is to lock your boat and put the camera out of sight.

Leaving your vessel: Most boats can be locked at the companionway hatch after dogging the portholes.

Dinghies: Most charter boats are equipped with metal cables and locks. When going ashore, lock your dinghy to the dock to avoid having it "borrowed." Also, at night or when leaving the dinghy with the boat make sure you lock it to the boat. Vessels with dinghy davits should raise the dinghy out of the water at night or when leaving the dinghy and the boat.

Nights aboard: When sleeping at night, many people leave the hatches open to enjoy sleeping with the trade winds lulling them to sleep. If you prefer, lock the companionway, close the large hatches and leave the portholes open to capture the breeze.

For your personal safety, the usual rules apply. Don't go anywhere where you feel uncomfortable, especially alone. Use caution as you would anywhere else. After several rounds of rum punch, anyone can become more vulnerable to crime, and it is not safe to be operating motor vessels after having a few too many.

The Virgin Islanders are very warm, friendly and helpful. The environment is mostly benign. As you would anywhere in the world, take a few simple precautions, relax, and enjoy your stay.

WATER SAFETY

The waters of the Virgin Islands are essentially a benign area. When people think of tropical waters, man-eating sharks, barracuda and giant moray eels come to mind. The truth of the matter is that more injuries are sustained by cuts from coral or by stepping on sea urchin spines than by encounters with underwater predators.

It is against BVI law to import jet skis. If you have a jet ski aboard you must declare it at customs when entering the BVI. Jet skis can be rented from local rental shops in certain locations.

Jet Skis are forbidden in the National Park Service waters in St. John and St. Croix.

Sharks: There are many large sharks around the waters of the Virgins, but they remain largely in deep water. It is highly unlikely that you will ever see a shark during your cruise.

Barracuda: You will, without doubt, see numerous barracuda of various sizes while snorkeling the reefs. They are curious fish and are likely to stay almost motionless in the water watching your movements. They will not bother you, and it is best to show them the same courtesy.

Moray Eels: These creatures are shy by nature and make their homes in rocks and crevices in the reef. They will protect themselves from perceived danger, so do not reach into caves or crevices unless you can see inside.

BVI BEACH SAFETY FLAGS

Red & Yellow Flags - mark areas of water that are patrolled by Lifeguards. These are the safest places to swim.

Black & White Chequered Flags - mean an area of water that has been marked out for use by craft, for example wind surfing, surf boards or dinghies. For your safety do not swim in this zoned area.

Red Flags - these indicate danger. **_Never swim when the Red Flag is flying._** At the Baths, Devils Bay & Spring Bay the Red Flag also indicates that the Yachts are prohibited from using the mooring field.

Yellow Flags - these indicate that you should take <u>caution:</u> weak swimmers are discouraged from entering the water. At the Baths, Devils Bay & Spring Bay the Red Flag also indicates that the Yachts should take caution when using the mooring field.

Purple Flags - indicate a marine life warning, for example Jelly Fish. The purple flag may also be flown with Yellow or Red Flags.

For More Information Visit: www.bvidef.org

Coral: Exercise extreme caution around all coral as cuts and scratches can become infected quickly. Familiarize yourself with the various types of coral and remember to stay well clear of the fire coral. To preserve the reefs, do not touch the coral, with your fins, your hands or anything. *Take only pictures, leave only bubbles.*

Sea Urchins: These black, spiny creatures are found in abundance throughout the islands. They can be seen on sandy bottoms and on reefs and rocks. If you stand on one or inadvertently place your hand on one, it is likely that one or more of the spines will pierce your skin and break off. Do not try to dig the spines out of your skin. Call a doctor for assistance.

Don'ts:

If you observe the following basic rules on water safety, you will add to your enjoyment of the cruise:

1. Don't swim at night.
2. Don't swim alone.
3. Don't swim in heavy surf.
4. Don't dump refuse in the water — it is illegal and attracts sharks.
5. Don't wear jewelry when swimming or diving.
6. Don't reach into crevices or caves.
7. Don't spear a fish and leave it bleeding in the water or in a bag at your waist.
8. Take no marine life without a permit!
9. Don't touch or anchor in coral under any circumstances.

SEASICKNESS

One of the downsides of a sailing holiday can be, of course, seasickness. This is one of the few times you can feel so badly that you are afraid that you won't die! Although the Virgin Islands have relatively little wave action there are those who just look at a boat and turn green. It can happen at the most unpredictable times, and seasickness is always every bit as embarrassing as it is miserable for the victim.

Over the years we have seen and heard all kinds of remedies, and have tried most of them. Here is a list of products to help you prepare for your trip and act like an old salt:

1. One favorite is Sea Bands. These elastic wrist bands have a small, plastic button that when placed in the right acupressure point on the inside of your wrist, helps to relieve symptoms. The bands come with easy instructions. They have no side effects, and are comfortable to wear. You may purchase them at drug stores. There are also other similar brands available. We have tried these numerous times with people who suffer from motion sickness at the slightest movement and have found them very successful.

2. An old, natural remedy that again, has no side effects and is safe to use is ginger capsules. Ginger has a settling effect on the stomach. These capsules are available in most health food stores.

3. Dramamine, Marezine, and Bonine are the old stand-by, over the counter antihistamines. Dramamine in particular can make you very, very drowsy. You can miss some good times if you are sleeping the days away, however, it is better than being sick.

4. For a prescription drug, ask your physician for Transderm Scop. This is only sold as a prescription, and can have some side effects. It does have some restrictions and is not safe for everyone. Transderm Scop comes in the form of a medicated patch that is worn behind the ear for three days at a stretch.

Avoid reading and going below when you are underway. The fresh breeze can help, and also remember to look at the horizon instead of the waves passing next to the boat. Good luck, and let us hear from you if there are any other miracle cures around.

Never overload dinghies

TROPICAL FISH POISONING

Ciguatera, also known as tropical fish poisoning, is a disease which can affect people who have eaten certain varieties of tropical fish.

The results of such poisoning can be very serious and, although seldom resulting in death, can cause severe discomfort. Victims of ciguatera poisoning are often ill for weeks and some symptoms may persist for months.

Ciguatera occurs only in tropical waters and in the Atlantic area, predominantly in the waters of south Florida and the islands of the Caribbean.

One problem with fish poisoning is that it is impossible to differentiate between toxic and nontoxic fish. The fish itself is not affected by the toxins and therefore appears quite normal and edible. The toxins cannot be tasted and washing, cooking or freezing will not render them harmless.

Many tales exist throughout the Caribbean on how to tell toxic from nontoxic fish, including cooking silver coins with the fish and if the coin turns black, it is toxic.

Another is that flies will not land on a piece of toxic fish. While such homespun ideas are interesting bits of Caribbean folklore, they do not work and should not be relied upon.

Symptoms of Ciguatera

In most cases, the symptoms will appear within three to ten hours after eating the toxic fish. The first signs are nausea, vomiting, diarrhea and stomach cramps.

Later, the patient may also start to suffer from a wide variety of neurological ailments, including pains in the joints and muscles, weakness in the arms and legs, and/or a tingling sensation in the feet and hands. A tingling sensation around the lips, nose and tongue is also common.

At the onset of any of the above symptoms, the patient should ask him- or herself, "Have I eaten any fish today?" If the answer is "yes," seek medical attention.

Types of Fish Carrying Ciguatera

The fish most likely to carry the toxins are the larger predatory fish associated with coral reefs. These include barracudas, grouper, snapper, jacks and parrotfish. It should be noted that only certain species in each family are associated with the toxins. Therefore, it is a good idea to check with a local fisherman before eating your catch.

The fish that are considered safe are offshore fish such as tuna, wahoo, swordfish, marlin, and dolphin. Others include sailfish, Spanish mackerel, small king mackerel and yellowtail snapper.

Hospitals and Health Clinics

TORTOLA

B&F Medical Complex
Open daily from 7:00am
Mill Mall Bldg., Wickham's Cay I
284-494-2196

Dr. June Samuel
Picsmith Medical Center
Road Town
284-494-3330

Bougainvillea Clinic
Cutless Bldg.
284-494-2181

Eureka Medical Clinic
Omar Hodge Bldg., Wickham's Cay I
284-494-2346

JOST VAN DYKE

Jost Van Dyke Clinic
284-495-3239

ST. JOHN

Cruz Bay Family Practice
340-776-6789
Emergency and Family Practice
Open 24 hours daily

Morris Keating Smith Community Clinic
340-776-8900

ST. THOMAS

Schneider Regional Medical Center
Sugar Estate, St. Thomas
340-778-8311

Pavia Hospital Information Center
Grand Hotel Bldg.
340-715-1190

**Governor Juan F. Luis Hospital
and Medical Center**
4007 Est. Diamond Ruby
340-778-6311

ST. CROIX

Governor Juan F. Luis Hospital
340-778-8311

There are two health clinics in Virgin
Gorda, one in Jost Van Dyke and one in
Anegada. Ask ashore for directions.

Emergencies

BVI

For Police, Fire or Ambulance:
Dial 999 or 911

**Virgin Island Search and Rescue
(VISAR)** VHF channel 16 or dial 767
(SOS) from any telephone

USVI

**Emergency 24 Hour, Police, Fire,
Ambulance** 911

U.S. Coast Guard
VHF 16 or dial 340-776-3497

SCUBA Emergencies

There is a re-compression chamber in St.
Thomas at the hospital (340) 776-2686

Divers Alert Network: (919) 684-8111

PROVISIONING

Most charter companies in and around the Virgin Islands offer the charter party a choice of provisioning programs or other options.

The original concept was designed to cope with the lack of supermarkets. But in recent years, both in the U.S. and British Virgin Islands, the selection of goods has increased tremendously. Therefore, your provisioning options are as follows:

A) Allow the charter company to provision for you from a pre-selected plan to save on sailing time. The main plans are full provisioning, which includes 3 meals a day, or the popular split program, which eliminates some evening meals so you can eat ashore. If you are considering this, ask the charter company for a sample menu.

B) Provision yourself from one of the local markets or delicatessens. This is a good idea if you have specific dietary needs, but it is time-consuming, and when analyzing costs, taxi fares and sailing time should be considered. However, many of the local markets have a surprisingly sophisticated array of products.

C) Have an independent provisioning company prepare your provisions in advance and have them delivered to the boat or swing by and pick them up. Provisioning lists can be faxed or emailed in advance, allowing you the luxury of choosing your provisioning from home.

RESTOCKING ALONG THE WAY

However you provision your vessel you will probably wish to augment your supply at some point along the cruise. Major items are available in Road Town, Nanny Cay, Soper's Hole, Cane Garden Bay, Trellis Bay, Maya Cove and East End in Tortola. Provisioning is available in Virgin Gorda Yacht Harbour, the Bitter End, and Leverick Bay in Virgin Gorda. In the U.S. Virgins you will be able to provision in Cruz Bay, Redhook, Charlotte Amalie, and in Christiansted, St. Croix.

Boatside delivery from Good Moon Farm, Trellis Bay

TORTOLA

ROAD REEF
Dockmaster's Deli
Tel:284-494-5188

WICKHAM'S CAY
Riteway
Tel: 284-494-2263

One Mart
Tel: 284-494-6999

TICO (Liquor)
Tel: 284-494-2211

EASTERN TORTOLA

FAT HOG'S BAY
Riteway East End Food
Market
Tel: 284-495-1682

Sailors Ketch Seafood
Market
Tel: 284-495-1100

TRELLIS BAY
Trellis Bay Market
Tel: 284-495-1421

Good Moon Farm
Fresh farm produce
Tel: 284-495-1849

Cyber Café
Tel: 284-495-2447

CANE GARDEN BAY
Bobby's Market
284-495-9971

Rhymer's Beach Bar &
Shop
284-495-4639

NANNY CAY
Bobby's Market
Tel: 284-494-2894

WEST END
Harbour Market
Tel: 284-495-4423

Ample Hamper Too
284-495-4684

Zelma's Courtesy
Grocery and Snack Bar
Tel: 284-495-4211

CHANNEL ISLANDS

Deliverance
Boat-to-boat delivery
Tel: 284-542-2181

VIRGIN GORDA

BITTER END
Provision Emporium
284-494-2745

LEVERICK BAY
Chef's Pantry
Supermarket/Deli
Open 8am to 5:50pm
Tel: 284-495-7372

Bucks Marketplace
Tel: 284-495-7368

ANEGADA

Lil'Bit Taz
Tel: 284-495-9932

JOST VAN DYKE

GREAT HARBOUR
Rudy's Superette
Tel: 284-495-9282

JVD Grocery Store
Tel: 284-495-0249

WHITE BAY
White Bay Superette

ST. JOHN

CORAL BAY
Lily's Gourmet Market
Tel: 340-777-3335

CRUZ BAY
Starfish Market
340-779-4949

Gallows Point Resort
340-693-5820

ST. THOMAS

CROWN BAY
Provisioning at Dock Walk
340-774-5280

Gourmet Galley
340-776-1595

Marina Market
Tel: 340-779-2411

RED HOOK
Cost U Less
340-777-3545

Marina Market
340-777-8806

ST. CROIX

CHRISTIANSTED
Cost U Less
Tel: 340-692-2220

Food Town
Tel: 340-718-9990

Plaza Xtra East
Tel: 340-778-6240

Pueblo Supermarket
Tel: 340-773-0118

Schooner Bay Market Place
Tel: 340-773-3232

FREDERIKSTED
Plaza Extra West
Tel: 340-719-1870

CRUISING
INFORMATION

HOW TO USE THIS GUIDE

The Cruising Guide to the Virgin Islands has been designed to incorporate both detailed information regarding a given anchorage and a quick visual guide to the cruising sailor, both with aerial photography and detailed anchorage charts.

The anchorage section of the guide is broken down by individual islands or groups of islands and color coded accordingly (see opposite page).

At the front of each section the reader will find a brief history or overview of the area, including a chart that is further broken down by individual anchorages shown by dotted red lines. A list of the relevant charts covering the area and the appropriate waypoints are also shown.

Turning to the individual anchorages; at the beginning of the text they are all identified with a *waypoint* location where applicable. *Navigation* gives the reader a quick fix on relevant distance to the anchorage and *Services* offers a one line overview on what is available.

The accompanying text is broken down by overview, followed by *Navigation and Piloting*, then *Anchoring* and finally detailed information on what to find *Ashore*.

At the back of each section, we have included a section entitled *Island Connections*. These pages are all sand colored and provide the reader with contact information for all the bars, restaurants and marine businesses around the islands.

The charts are accurate interpretations of the specific anchorages. They have been designed for vessels drawing about 6-6.5 feet and all water less than six feet is shown in yellow; once again allowing the skipper a quick reference for safety.

The *Guide* starts at Road Town, Tortola and continues counter clockwise around all of the anchorages in close proximity. This section is then followed by the Channel Islands east to Virgin Gorda and Anegada to then back west to Jost Van Dyke.

We have taken the liberty of starting the U.S. Virgin Islands at St. John, since that is a logical route for a vessel in transit to from the BVI.

The information in this Guide has been collected over numerous years of living and cruising in the islands in addition to a formal annual area audit. The authors have made every attempt to keep the guide updated but acknowledge that sea conditions change and buoys may be misplaced, lost or off station. Use caution, be vigilant and keep us informed of any changes that should be posted on our website for fellow sailors.

CHART INFORMATION

Our charts are interpretive and designed for yachts drawing about 6.5 feet. Deeper yachts should refer to the depths on their charts.

 LAND HILLS  ROADS PATHS

LAND HEIGHTS ARE IN FEET AND APPROXIMATE

 WATER TOO SHALLOW FOR NAVIGATION OR DANGEROUS IN SOME CONDITIONS

 SURFACE REEF

 ROCKS DEEPER REEF

 NAVIGABLE WATER

60	
	9
DEPTHS ARE IN FEET AND APPROXIMATE

 1.5 KNOTS CURRENT ✝ CHURCH AERIAL

 MANGROVES ⚓ ANCHORAGE

⚓ PICK UP MOORING ONLY

WRECKS DAY STOP ANCHORAGE

 GREEN BEACON
GREEN BUOYS (PORT)

N
W ⊕ E
S
IALA B MARKS SHOWING DIRECTION OF DANGER (BUOYS & BEACONS)

 RED BEACON
RED BUOYS (STARBOARD)

 ISOLATED SHOAL BEACONS & BUOYS

 YELLOW BUOYS

 RED & GREEN DIVIDED CHANNEL BUOYS

MOORING OR OTHER BUOY

 SECTOR
 WHITE (W)
GREEN (G)
YELLOW (Y)
RED (R)

LIGHTS

FL = FLASHING, F = FIXED, L = LONG, Q = QUICK, M = MILES
LIGHT EXPLANATION:
FL (2) 4S, 6M
LIGHT GROUP FLASHING 2 EVERY FOUR SECONDS, VISIBLE 6 MILES

NAVIGATION

PAPER CHARTS

It is possible to navigate through the U.S. and British Virgin Islands with a single paper chart, such as NIMA 25640 and our cruising guide. Many of the charter companies have duplicated this chart in one form or another as a handout for each charter group. If you're chartering, be sure to ask your charter company in advance which charts they'll provide you, when you'll receive them and whether the charts are yours to keep. Then take a careful look at the areas you intend to cruise and determine any additional chart coverage you may want. In many instances the company will provide a waterproof version of the area chart aboard the vessel as part of its permanent inventory.

Your own charts will allow you to plan your trip in advance and will also serve as a nice memento of your trip. Complete paper chart coverage of the Virgin Islands will range from about $50.00 to several hundred dollars, especially if you include electronic charts which are now very popular. Charts can be hard to obtain in the Virgin Islands, so taking your own charts is the best way to be sure you have the coverage you're comfortable with.

The following paper charts, or chart kits cover the Virgin Islands and surrounding areas and they are available from our web site or larger chart agents in the U.S., Canada and Europe.

British Admiralty Leisure Folio:

5640   The U.S. & British Virgin Islands
Kit contains 11 individual charts
5640-(1-11)

National Image & Mapping Agency (NIMA):

25609   St.Thomas to Anegada
25610   Virgin Gorda Sound
25611   Road Harbour
25640   St.Thomas to Tortola
25641   Virgin Gorda to St.Thomas & St.Croix

IMRAY-Iolaire:

A23   The Virgin Islands
A232   St.Thomas to Virgin Gorda
A232   Tortola to Anegada
A234   Northeast Coast of St.Croix

NV Charts (Nautical Publications GmbH):

The Virgin Islands (St.Thomas to Anegada)
Chart Pack – The Virgin Islands
Pack contains: 13 individual charts

ELECTRONIC CHARTS & GPS

Used in combination with GPS and paper charts, electronic charts have become extremely popular in the Caribbean, though they remain hard to purchase in the islands.

Many of the charter fleets are now equipped with chart plotters pre-loaded with software. Before purchasing any electronic charts, ask your charter company or agent what equipment and supporting software is aboard.

Personal smart-phones preloaded with navigation apps should be used with caution, since you will no doubt be roaming on a network outside of your plan and therefore subject to high roaming rates.

The following electronic charts cover the Virgin Islands (and beyond) and are available from selected chart agents and marine electronic dealers in the U.S., Canada and Europe.

Maptech:	Companion CD charts
Admiralty Leisure:	Electronic versions of the Leisure Folio
NV Charts:	Companion CD charts
C-Map:	NAC501 Cuba to Trinidad
Garmin:	US030 Southeast Caribbean
Navionics:	3XG: Central and South America
Navionics:	Mobile App: Caribbean and South America

NAVIGATION

GPS (GLOBAL POSITIONING SYSTEM) & WAYPOINT GUIDE

Navigation throughout the Virgin Islands is mostly line of sight. It is of course mandatory to have updated charts aboard, both paper and electronic, but it is essential that you not rely on any one piece of information for the overall safety of your vessel. Your authors are not proponents of listing waypoint information that might be relied upon to take you through a narrow entrance in a reef. We have established waypoints outside of the anchorage and listed a suggested course. When necessary, post a lookout on the bow and never be complacent. Take visual sightings, depth readings and proceed with caution.

GPS has been known to fail, software has been known to give false readings. There have been reports of navigators finding themselves a couple of miles away from where they expected in places where the GPS showed good correspondence. Occasional errors are a possibility.

The Cruising Guide to the Virgin Islands has adopted the following system of waypoint identification:

The British Virgin Islands carry a designator of BV (British Virgins) while in the U.S. Virgins they will be designated as UV (U.S. Virgins).

They are further broken down by island or island group:

Tortola, BVI	100
Jost Van Dyke	200
The Channel Islands (Norman, Peter, Salt & Cooper)	300
Virgin Gorda and Anegada	400
St. John, USVI	500
St. Thomas	600
St. Croix	700

The waypoints pertaining to a particular section of the guide are listed on the leading pages and the entire waypoint list is also copied onto the free planning chart included with this guide. Virgin Island Waypoints can also be downloaded from our website.

WAYPOINTS

WAYPOINT	DESCRIPTION	LATITUDE	LONGITUDE
Tortola		**North**	**West**
101	Road Town	18°24.80'	64°36.20'
102	Road Town/Kingston	18°24.50'	64°35.00'
103	Buck Island	18°25.10'	64°33.20'
104	Fat Hog	18°25.95'	64°33.20'
105	Beef Island	18°25.30'	64°30.90'
106	Marina Cay/Trellis	18°27.30'	64°31.50'
107	Cam Bay	18°28.55'	64°31.50'
108	Camanoe North	18°30.00'	64°32.40'
109	Guana Sound	18°27.70'	64°33.20'
110	Monkey Point	18°27.70'	64°35.00'
111	Guana North	18°30.00'	64°35.00'
112	Anderson/Rough Point	18°27.20'	64°39.80'
113	Cane Garden Bay	18°25.65'	64°40.20'
114	Soper's Hole N	18°23.70'	64°43.30'
115	West Point (Great Thatch)	18°22.80'	64°45.50'
116	Frenchman's Cay (S)	18°22.70'	64°41.90'
117	Nanny Cay	18°23.00'	64°38.50'
Jost Van Dyke			
201	Little Jost Van Dyke	18°26.60'	64°42.75'
202	Little Harbour	18°25.90'	64°43.05'
203	Great Harbour	18°26.10'	64°45.00'
204	White Bay	18°26.30'	64°45.80'
205	Tobago South	18°26.00'	64°49.50'
206	Tobago North	18°26.75'	64°50.00'
The Channel Islands			
301	Flannigan's Passage	18°20.60'	64°38.50'
302	Peter Island West Point	18°21.40'	64°37.00'
303	Dead Chest	18°22.00'	64°34.60'
304	Cooper Island	18°23.50'	64°31.00'
305	Round Rock Passage N	18°24.10'	64°28.20'
306	Round Rock Passage S	18°23.30'	64°27.10'
307	Carrot Rock, Peter Island	18°18.92'	64°34.25'
308	Peter/Norman Channel	18°20.00'	64°35.70'
309	Benures Bay	18°19.63'	64°36.40'
310	Pelican/Norman	18°19.70'	64°37.40'
311	The Bight, Norman Island	18°19.30'	64°37.50'
Virgin Gorda/Anegada		**North**	**West**
401	Baths	18°26.00'	64°27.00'
402	St. Thomas Bay	18°27.20'	64°26.90'
403	Great Dog	18°28.42'	64°26.80'
404	Dogs North	18°30.00'	64°29.20'
405	Cows Mouth	18°30.40'	64°25.20'
406	Mosquito Rock	18°31.30'	64°23.10'
407	Eustatia Passage	18°30.50'	64°18.70'
408	Necker Island Passage	18°32.20'	64°15.00'
409	N/A		
410	Anegada Setting Point	18°42.40'	64°24.50'

WAYPOINT	DESCRIPTION	LATITUDE	LONGITUDE
St. John			
501	Johnson's Reef	18°22.15'	64°46.70'
502	Windward Passage	18°21.50'	64°47.80'
503	Cruz Bay	18°20.30'	64°48.78'
504	Chocolate Hole	18°18.50'	64°47.70'
505	Dog Rocks	18°17.30'	64°48.75'
506	Lameshur Bay	18°18.30'	64°43.80'
507	Rams Head	18°17.60'	64°41.70'
508	Coral Bay Entrance	18°19.40'	64°40.30'
509	Hurricane Hole	18°20.30'	64°41.90'
St. Thomas		**North**	**West**
601	Redhook	18°20.00'	64°50.00'
602	Cabrita Point	18°19.30'	64°49.60'
603	Cow & Calf	18°18.20'	64°51.30'
603a	Jersey Bay	18°18.50'	64°51.50'
603b	The Lagoon	18°18.86'	64°52.06'
604	Packet Rock	18°17.60'	64°53.40'
605	St. Thomas Harbor	18°18.60'	64°55.60'
606	Saba Is.	18°18.10'	64°59.00'
607	Sail Rock	18°16.80'	65°06.30'
608	Salt Cay Passage	18°22.00'	65°04.20'
609	Lizard Rock	18°23.40'	64°59.65'
610	Omen Rock	18°23.40'	64°57.50'
611	Little Hans Lollik	18°24.75'	64°55.00'
612	Hans Lollik	18°23.40'	64°53.70'
613	Middle Passage	18°21.50'	64°50.70'
St. Croix			
701	Central Navigation Point	17°48.00'	64°42.00'
702	Christiansted Hbr	17°46.00'	64°41.90"
703	Scotch Bank/Green Cay	17°46.60'	64°40.10'
704	Buck Island N	17°48.50'	64°38.00'
705	Coakley Cut	17°46.50'	64°38.50'
706	Salt River	17°47.80'	64°45.00'
707	West Point	17°45.00'	64°55.00'
708	East Point	17°45.00'	64°32.00'

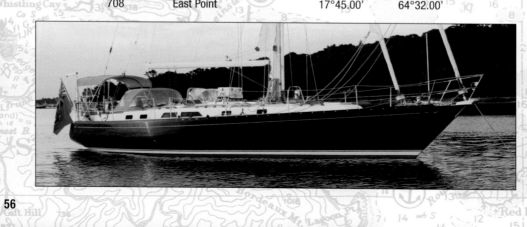

moor seacure limited

THE OTHER ALTERNATIVE

Tired of straining the old back? Tired of waking up all night worrying about your anchor dragging, thinking that THIS is supposed to be a vacation? WELL, now there is an alternative... Located throughout the British Virgin Islands at most popular anchorages there are professionally maintained moorings available for overnight use. The small fee for the mooring use is well worth the good night's sleep it affords.

Here are a few tips on picking up and leaving a mooring...

1. As in anchoring, approach the mooring area slowly with your dinghy pulled on a short line.
2. Have a crew member ready with a boat hook at the bow to direct you and to pick up the mooring pennant.
3. Approach the mooring buoy slowly from the direction that keeps the bow of your boat into the wind.
4. You may find that at idle speed by shifting alternately from forward to neutral you can coast to the buoy, then shift into reverse for a second to stop the boat as the crew member lifts the pennant on board and attaches it to the bow cleat.
5. Please do not be embarrassed if you miss picking up the pennant for the first time. It happens to all of us at sometime. Just circle around and make another approach. Please do not extend the length of the pennant.
6. To leave the mooring with your dinghy once again on a short line simply let go the pennant and set off for your next destination. Take care not to run over the mooring buoy and pennant as you leave.

These helpful hints are brought to you by Moor-Seacure Ltd.-the premier mooring company in the BVI. And remember, "If it doesn't say MOOR-SEACURE, it probably ISN'T!"

Moor-Seacure moorings are available at these and other fine locations...

• PENN'S LANDING AT FAT HOGS BAY •
• MARINA CAY • LOOSE MONGOOSE AT TRELLIS BAY •
• COOPER ISLAND BEACH CLUB AT COOPER ISLAND •
• LEVERICK BAY AND SABA ROCK IN NORTH SOUND, VIRGIN GORDA •
• ANEGADA REEF HOTEL AT ANEGADA • RHYMERS IN CANE GARDEN BAY •
• TROPICAL KISSES, FOXY'S AND NORTH LATITUDE MARINA
AT GREAT HARBOUR, JOST VAN DYKE •
• ABE'S AND HARRIS' PLACE AT LITTLE HARBOUR, JOST VAN DYKE •
• IVAN'S BAR AT WHITE BAY JOST VAN DYKE •
• SOPERS HOLE MARINA AT WEST END TORTOLA •
• FOXY'S TABOO AT DIAMOND CAY, JOST VAN DYKE •
• THE SANDBOX IN NORTH SOUND •

DON'T BE A DRAG

P.O. Box 3149, Road Town, Tortola, B.V.I. • 284-494-4488 • Fax: 284-494-2513

Navigation

The Buoyage System of the Virgin Islands

In an international effort to standardize buoyage systems, the International Association of Lighthouse Authorities (IALA) has agreed that, in order to meet conflicting requirements, there will be two systems in use throughout the world. These are called systems A and B, respectively. The rules for the two systems were so similar that the IALA Executive Committee felt able to combine the two sets of rules into one, known as the IALA Maritime Buoyage System.

This single set of rules allows lighthouse authorities the choice of using red to port or red to starboard on a regional basis, the two regions being known as region A and region B.

The latter system, system B, is used in North and South America and throughout the waters of the Caribbean. In system B the color red is used to mark the starboard side of the channel when approaching from seaward (red, right, returning). In this respect, it should be noted that the respective buoyage systems for both U.S. and British Virgins are the same.

Navigation

Pilotage through unknown waters is one of the major concerns of the cruising yachtsman. However, in the Virgins, where there is very little tidal rise and fall and only minimal current to worry about, pilotage is extremely simple.

Since the weather is so warm, we don't experience any fog and you can always see the island for which you are heading (unless you are in a rare heavy rain fall).

Reefs and shoals are not a major problem as they are well marked, and providing time is taken to study the pertinent charts on a daily basis, your cruise around the island will be most enjoyable.

The islands themselves are high and volcanic, rising steeply from the crystal clear water. In some cases, it is possible to position your bow almost on the beach, providing you have a stern anchor set.

Since the islands in the chain are close together, you will have no difficulty in

distinguishing them. Using the contour marks on the charts you will usually be able to pinpoint your location.

EQUIPMENT

Every cruising yacht should be equipped with the basic tools of navigation – compass, parallel rules, triangles, dividers, plotters, etc. However, it should be noted that in order to navigate throughout the islands, the only equipment needed besides a detailed chart is a compass, chart, pencil and fathometer. Those wishing to brush up on navigational skills will find ample opportunity, although celestial observations are often difficult because of the proximity of the islands.

READING THE WATER

There is no dark secret attached to the ability to read the depth of the water. It is merely the ability to distinguish water color. Experience is, of course, the best teacher; however, with a few practical hints, even the novice will be able to feel his or her way in to an anchorage within a few days.

It is important to have the sun overhead in order to distinguish reef areas. That is why most charter companies insist that the boats be at anchor by 1600 hours. Do not attempt to negotiate a reef-fringed entrance with the sun in your eyes, and always have someone on the bow keeping an eye on the water in front of the boat.

Deep water of 50 feet and over will be "inky" blue. This can be lighter if the bottom is white sand.

A light green or turquoise would indicate a depth of 15-25 feet. If the bottom has rocks or coral, these will change the color to a brownish shade.

Water of 10 feet and under will show as a very pale shade of green if there is a sandy bottom, or a light brown if rocks and coral are present.

CAUTION: There have been several incidents of people diving off of their vessels not realizing how shallow the water was and sustaining serious damage to their head, back or neck. Be sure you check the water depth prior to performing the graceful dive.

NAVIGATION

THE RIGHT OF WAY AND SAILING AT NIGHT

A general rule of thumb is to stay out of everyone's way. There are times, however, when this is impossible and, in such instances, power boats should give way to boats under sail and all pleasure vessels should give way to commercial shipping. This being the case, it is important in close quarters to hold your course so that the other skipper can take appropriate action to avoid you, without having to double-guess your actions.

If you are crossing ferry traffic, it is prudent to keep a weather eye on approaching vessels and make every effort to stay well clear. Use your VHF channel 16 if you are in doubt and if you do alter course, make sure that the other skipper is aware that you have done so.

Freighters trading between the islands are often underway at night and at times are known not to use their running lights. Don't sail at night!

NAVY VESSELS AND CRUISE SHIPS

When approaching a U.S. Navy vessel or cruise ship, Coast Guard regulations state that you must slow your vessel to 5 knots within 500 yards and maintain a 200 yard distance at all times. Needless to say this is difficult in a harbor like Charlotte Amalie or Road Town where one has to pass large vessels at close quarters!

CRUISING ETIQUETTE

During your cruise through the Virgins, please remember that there are a limited number of places on the smaller islands capable of dealing with garbage.

Check first before carrying it ashore – don't throw it over the side, even if it means keeping it a couple of days in a plastic bag. Always carry any refuse back to your boat, rather than leaving it on the beach.

Many of the beaches throughout the Virgins are private property and the cruising yachtsman must exercise care to respect any notice indicating such restrictions.

MOORING USAGE

Throughout the BVI in various anchorages you will find moorings available for you to use for a nightly fee. Most moorings will have the name of the restaurant or establishment where you should pay your fee, or in some anchorages someone will come in a small boat in the late afternoon – early evening to collect the fee. This fee usually must be paid in cash and the person collecting the fees can give you a receipt if you ask for one. You should confirm that the mooring you are using is either a Moor-Seacure mooring or is professionally maintained.

In the BVI, National Parks Trust moorings are available for daytime use with a permit that may be purchased at the same time as your cruising permit. The buoys within the park limits are designated by different colors. Yellow buoys are for commercial (dive) vessels, red buoys are daytime only and no diving is allowed while white buoys are limited to 90 minutes.

In the USVI National Park area, use of the mooring system is limited to vessels 60 feet and under. Please see details in the Diving, Snorkeling and Marine Parks section.

VIRGIN WEATHER

GENERAL CLIMATE

Located in the northeast trade wind belt, the Virgin Islands are blessed with excellent sailing conditions almost year round. During the winter months when the wind conditions are at their highest, the geographical make up of the islands tends to shelter the sailing area, making for much easier sea conditions than one might logically expect in the vicinity of both the Leeward and Windward islands further to the south. That being said, it is important to understand the seasons of the Caribbean weather patterns which can be viewed as follows:

- **Winter (December–March)** This period can be characterized by heavy sailing conditions with winds and seas reflecting the strong blustery trade winds prevailing at this time. The winds at this time are also referred to as Christmas winds largely referring to the entire season versus late December and early January. The winds during this period can blow from 18-30 knots, more often than not in 3-4 day cycles created by passing high pressure systems.

- **Spring (April–June)** This is perhaps the most settled time of the year and certainly my personal favorite sailing time. The winter trade winds have diminished to a steady 10-15 knots from the northeast to south of east when not modified by tropical waves. Rainfall during this period is light.

- **Summer (July–October)** Although hurricane season officially starts on June 1 and continues through November 30, according to weather expert David

Jones (see note below), statistically, early (June) tropical cyclone activity tends to occur in the western Caribbean. By mid-season, (July to early August) it is more likely to occur within a few hundred miles of the island chain. At the peak of the season (late August to September) it occurs mainly in the south of the north Atlantic, thousands of miles from the Virgins before reverting back in October to the eastern and then western Caribbean.

- **Fall (November–mid December)** A transitional season from the typical summer weather patterns with passing tropical wave activity, to the clearer, heavier trade wind conditions associated with non tropical weather. This period is an extremely short window of opportunity for cruisers to reposition themselves prior to the onset of the heavy trade wind conditions that prevail during the winter months.

Note: An excellent reference source for cruisers wishing to understand Caribbean weather patterns, is *The Concise Guide to Caribbean Weather* by David Jones, available at www.CruisingGuides.com.

WEATHER FORECASTS

Unlike that of most other parts of the world, the weather in the Virgin Islands is extremely stable. Forecasts are broadcast daily on most of the local stations:

St. Thomas: WIVI 99.5 FM (Forecasts at 07:30, 08:30, 15:30, 16:30 with hourly updates); WVWI 10:00 (Forecasts hourly); WSTA 1340 AM; Radio Antilles 830 AM

St. Croix: WSTX 970 AM

Tortola: ZBVI 780 AM, updates hourly on the half-hour 07:30 to 21:30

Puerto Rico: WOJO 1030 AM (English speaking all day at 6 minutes past the hour)

NOAA Weather is broadcast throughout the day on WX 3 or 4 or 6 on your VHF radio.

TIDES AND CURRENTS

The tidal range throughout the Virgin Islands is about 12 inches, depending upon the time of year. You will probably be unaware of any fluctuation. However, you cannot rely upon the rising tide to float you off the odd sandbar. Currents in certain areas can reach 1-2 knots, namely through Pillsbury Sound between St. Thomas and St. John, the Durloe Cays in St. John, and in the narrows between St. John and Tortola.

GROUND SWELLS

During the winter months of November through April, any significant weather in the North Atlantic will produce heavy swells along the entire north coast of the Virgins several days later. These ground swells have little effect on vessels under sail, but can turn a normally tranquil anchorage into pounding surf. Most anchorages exposed to the north are prone to this phenomenon – choose your anchorage accordingly.

WIND CONDITIONS

Owing to the northeast trade winds, the movements of the Bermuda High dominate the wind direction throughout the Virgins. During the winter months of December through March the typical prevailing wind is from the northeast at 18-25 knots. The

The Beaufort Scale (in knots)			
FORCE	WIND	WMO CLASSIFICATION	ON THE WATER
0	Less than 1	Calm	Sea surface smooth and mirror-like
1	1-3	Light Air	Scaly ripples, no foam crests
2	4-6	Light Breeze	Small wavelets, crests glassy, no breaking
3	7-10	Gentle Breeze	Large wavelets, crests begin to break, scattered whitecaps
4	11-16	Moderate Breeze	Small waves 1-4 ft. becoming longer, numerous whitecaps
5	17-21	Fresh Breeze	Moderate waves 4-8 ft taking longer form, many whitecaps, some spray
6	22-27	Strong Breeze	Larger waves 8-13 ft, whitecaps common, more spray
7	28-33	Near Gale	Sea heaps up, waves 13-20 ft, white foam streaks off breakers
8	34-40	Gale	Moderately high (13-20 ft) waves of greater length, edges of crests begin to break into spindrift, foam blown in streaks
9	41-47	Strong Gale	High waves (20 ft), sea begins to roll, dense streaks of foam, spray may reduce visibility
10	48-55	Storm	Very high waves (20-30 ft) with overhanging crests, sea white with densely blown foam, heavy rolling, lowered visibility
11	56-63	Violent Storm	Exceptionally high (30-45 ft) waves, foam patches cover sea, visibility more reduced
12	64+	Hurricane	Air filled with foam, waves over 45 ft, sea completely white with driving spray, visibility greatly reduced

occasional stronger cold fronts, associated with low pressure systems, make their way southeast to reach the Virgin Islands. The initial effect will be lighter winds for several hundred miles ahead of the front. As a strong front approaches, the wind will start to move south and then southeast immediately ahead of the cold front.

As the front passes the wind will shift to the northwest and increase to 20-30 knots with blustery conditions. It should be noted that trade winds conditions are not always stable and can vary in direction by up to 45° during a single day. By March, the winds start to move around to the east, and by June, they are blowing out of the southeast at 10-15 knots. During September to October, the trade winds are weakest, and the weather can be less settled due to developing low pressure systems. By November, the high-pressure system around Bermuda starts to stabilize and 15-20 knot breezes become the norm.

RAIN

While June through October is often characterized as the rainy season, heavy rain squalls can come at any time of year. The prudent skipper should be aware of an approaching squall by watching the sky and clouds to windward.

If a dark squall is approaching, it probably has considerable wind velocity on the squall line, and immediate action should be taken to shorten sail beforehand.

STORMS AND HURRICANES

Despite recent hurricanes, the Virgin Islands have fewer storms than does the Long Island Sound in New York. When the islands do experience a tropical storm or depression, it is usually in the early development of the storm center, and the storms usually do not reach full intensity until they are north of the area. Should a storm approach the islands, remember that they travel very slowly; consequently, with the communication systems used today, sailors can be assured of at least 48 hours warning.

In the event of a severe tropical storm or hurricane, approaching the Virgin Islands, you will be kept well notified by both the local radio stations, VHF marine advisory channels, SSB and, in the case of charter vessels, your local charter company. All major charter companies have well prepared hurricane plans and they will advise you how to proceed.

All vessels in the Caribbean during the hurricane season should carefully monitor the progress of each tropical system and act accordingly.

There are a number of hurricane holes throughout the Virgin Islands and should it be necessary to react to a storm warning, we recommend early action since the designated hurricane anchorages fill quickly:

Tortola: Paraquita Bay, Nanny Cay, Manuel Reef
Virgin Gorda: Biras Creek (under certain conditions)
St. John: Coral Bay, Hurricane Hole
St. Thomas: The Lagoon, Benner Bay

COMMUNICATIONS

AREA CODES

British Virgin Islands	284
U.S. Virgin Islands	340
Puerto Rico	787

Connectivity has become such a major factor in our lives that staying in touch with friends and family while traveling is now more a necessity than a luxury. For cruisers, being in touch is essential, whether it be for safety, weather information or just communicating with other cruisers.

CELLULAR TELEPHONES

For Virgin Island yachtsmen who need to keep in touch, cellular telephone service is generally available throughout the Virgin Islands. Cellular phones can be used for everything from checking in with the office, the family, or for local applications like ordering more provisions and making dinner reservations.

A word of caution: using a U.S. or European cell phone (if they will work) means that you will be roaming in an international area and are therefore very likely to end up with a large bill in the post upon your return home. Check with your service provider regarding roaming charges or consider renting a local phone or SIM card for your personal smart phone. Remember to turn cellular data off on smart phones to avoid hefty fees for a text message that reads, "Hey" from someone back home who forgot you're on vacation.

To obtain a local BVI cell phone, you can go to Cable & Wireless (Lime), CCT Global, or Digicel to rent either a cell phone that will work in the BVI, or a SIM card for your own telephone. Renport, at Wickham's Cay II, rents cell phones, along with DVDs, CDs, etc.

If you rent a local BVI cell phone and call the U.S., you may be paying a lot for that, however, the telephone usage within the BVI will be more reasonable. Many people rent cell phones for emergencies, or if the office simply MUST call you.

COMMUNICATIONS

VHF

Almost every boat sailing the Virgins will be equipped with a VHF radio. Apart from single side band for offshore communications, VHF is used for all local traffic.

The channels vary from boat to boat, but the most commonly used frequencies are listed below.

Channel 16: Initial calling, standby and international distress frequency. Switch to a working channel after contact is established

Channel 12: Portside operations (Charter company to yacht)

Channel 6: Ship-to-ship, safety

Channel 24, 85, and 87: W.A.H. Virgin Islands Radio

Channel 67: VISAR working frequency

Channel 68, 69, 71, 78, 79, 80: Non-commercial working channels

Channel 22A: Coast Guard ("A" is U.S. mode), make initial contact on channel 16

Channel Wx-1 (162.55, Wx-2(162.4), Wx-3(162.475): NOAA Weather broadcasts

Do not allow children or crew members to use the VHF without adequate instruction.

MAKING DINNER RESERVATIONS

Where telephone service is non-existent, many restaurants stand by the radio on VHF Channel 16 and will then have you switch to another working channel to complete your request. It is frowned upon by the local licensing authority to use the VHF Channel 12 for reservations.

RADIO PROCEDURE

Before attempting to make a VHF radio call, think it through. Understand the procedure and the limitations of the equipment you are using.

The call should begin with two repetitions of the station or vessel being called, followed by the name of your yacht, followed by the word "over". It is important to terminate with the "over" as the other party will then key his/her mike and reply.

Example: "...Moorings, Moorings: this is the vessel Bodacious; over..."

If you get no response, repeat the call. If there is still no response, try again in five minutes. When contact is to be terminated, the party will sign off: "...This is Bodacious, clear with Moorings..."

EMERGENCY
U.S. COAST GUARD: 787-729-6770
VISAR: 999 or 911 or 767 (SOS)

COMMUNICATIONS

DISTRESS CALLS

In case of a real, life threatening emergency, you use VHF Channel 16, key your mike and repeat the following: "…Mayday, Mayday, Mayday. This is the vessel Bodacious; over…"

Repeat three times until contact is made. Then give your location and the nature of your problem. It is important to state only the pertinent information and not to cloud the situation with emotion.

When stating your location it is critical to give, in addition to lat/long, both the name of the harbor, if applicable, and the island to avoid confusion. There is a Great Harbour in both Peter Island and Jost Van Dyke, and a Little Harbour in both Peter Island and Jost Van Dyke!

- Stay calm; don't panic.
- Don't allow anyone to use the radio unless they are familiar with the procedure and the problem.

VISAR and the US Coast Guard monitor VHF 16 radio 24 hours a day in case of emergencies.

INTERNET AND E-MAIL

Generally speaking, cruisers should experience little difficulty in locating a WiFi hotspot or cyber café on most of the larger islands throughout both the BVI and USVI. Available bandwidth varies. Most marinas offer WiFi to customers with a security code access. From time to time a reasonable signal can be received at anchor but unless you have a high gain antenna, do not count on it.

In the BVI you may consider renting a portable modem (USB) that allows you to connect wirelessly via the phone lines. This saves a considerable amount of frustration.

There is also a service based WiFi being implemented in conjunction with the BVI Tourist Board (www.bvimarinewifi.com). They advertise available WiFi throughout the BVI but we have not used the service to-date.

VOIP (Voice over Internet protocol): When reasonable bandwidth is available, phone calls can be made utilizing a VOIP service such as SKYPE, which enables you to use your computer to place a call to another computer, assuming they are on line. You will want to turn off the video in order to preserve bandwidth. SKYPE also has a more interesting feature which is called SKYPE out. This allows you to call a telephone number from your computer. You will need to establish an account but the charges are minimal. The software can be downloaded to your computer for free or you can utilize the SKYPE app on your smartphone providing it has a WiFi function.

SSB (SINGLE SIDE BAND):

The primary Caribbean hailing frequency is 8104.0 USB. Once contact is established you will need to switch to a working frequency. This frequency is also used at 8.15am each morning to broadcast the Safety & Security Net.

CUSTOMS, IMMIGRATION & FORMALITIES

PORTS OF ENTRY

Since the Virgin Islands are divided between the U.S. and Britain, you may be crossing international boundaries during your cruise. Therefore it is necessary to clear customs when entering and leaving each respective territory. Failure to observe this formality could result in substantial fines or even the loss of your vessel.

U.S. Customs and Immigration at the waterfront in Charlotte Amalie (tel: 340-774-6755) are open from 8am-noon and 1pm-4:30pm Monday through Saturday. Sunday they are open from 10am to 6pm.

In Cruz Bay, St. John, Customs and Immigration (tel: 340-776-6397) are open from 7am to 5:30pm seven days a week. In Christiansted, St. Croix at Gallows Bay, Customs and Immigration are open from 8:00am to 4:30pm Monday through Friday. Vessels arriving on Saturdays and Sundays must contact the customs at the airport 340-778-0216. All crew members are to present themselves for clearance in the USVI.

To clear in to the BVI, proceed to the nearest BVI port of entry for inbound clearance. Often, if your stay is short and of a known duration, you will be permitted to clear in and out at the same time.

When clearing in it is necessary to have in your possession the ship's papers and passports for all passengers and crew members as well as your clearance from the last port. In the BVI, only the skipper needs to present himself at customs and immigration. It is also recommended that you wear proper attire when making your clearance. In the BVI as of January 1, 2007, passports are required of all U.S. and Canadian citizens to enter the British Virgin Islands. Passports will also be required to enter back into the U.S. Virgin Islands from the British Virgin Islands or other foreign countries.

All other nationalities must have a current passport. If you have questions regarding the need for visas contact your nearest British Embassy or telephone the BVI Immigration Department at 284-494-3471.

- All crew members are to present themselves for clearance in the USVI.
- In the BVI, only the skipper, with all the passports and ship's papers, needs to clear the vessel into BVI waters.

- Yachts dropping passengers off must first clear customs and immigration.
- All private yachts will be given no more than 30 days entry. Extensions will incur a fee.
- Late fees, in addition to customs charges are as much as $8 per vessel and higher on Sundays and public holidays.

PORT CLEARANCE

For vessels in the United States Virgin Islands over 300 tons gross weight, and any vessel carrying paying passengers or paid crew in and out of U.S. waters are now required to submit an advance Notice of Arrival/Departure (NOA/D) to the U.S. Coast Guard before calling at or departing from U.S. ports.

This notice must be filed electronically to the (NVMC) National Vessel Movement

Center website at www.nvmc.uscg.gov, who can answer questions and provide downloadable forms.

For more information call:

U.S. Coast Guard regulation and related questions: 202-372-1244.

Late fees may be charged for after hour arrivals or for arrivals on holidays.

Marinas catering to megayachts often offer clearance services to assist in the clearance procedures. Check with the marina offices in advance.

LOCATIONS OF CUSTOMS

St. Thomas:
Wharfside at the ferry dock, Charlotte Amalie, Yacht Haven Grande

St. John:
Waterfront at Cruz Bay

St. Croix:
Gallows Bay at Christiansted

Tortola:
Road Town at the Government Dock
West End ferry dock

Virgin Gorda:
Government Dock, Spanish Town, Gun Creek, Yacht Club Costa Smeralda

Jost Van Dyke:
Government Dock, Great Harbour

BVI CRUISING PERMITS

For yachts cruising and chartering in BVI waters there is a daily tax payable at the time of clearance or at the commencement of charter. Cruising vessels, dive boats, day charter, and sport fishing boats should contact customs for the required fees at 284-494-3701.

The rates are as follows:
December 1 – April 30:
A. Non recorded boats: $4 per person per day
   Recorded boats: $2 per person per day

May 1 – November 30:
B. Non-recorded boats: $4 per person per day
   Recorded boats: 75¢ per person per day

Cruising permits are issued at Customs and valid for a specific timeframe. Failure to comply with the law can result in a $5,000 fine.

BVI NATIONAL PARKS TRUST PERMIT

In order to use the moorings provided in the marine parks in the BVI, it is necessary to purchase a National Parks Trust permit. Charterers may purchase these permits through their charter company, and visiting private yachts may purchase permits through customs when clearing. The fees are nominal and go directly to the Parks Trust for the installation and maintenance of the buoys.

FISHING PERMITS IN THE BVI

It is illegal for a non-resident to remove any marine organism from the waters of the British Virgin Islands without first obtaining a recreational fishing permit. Call the Fisheries Department at 494-5681.

THE ANCHORAGES OF THE
BRITISH
VIRGIN ISLANDS

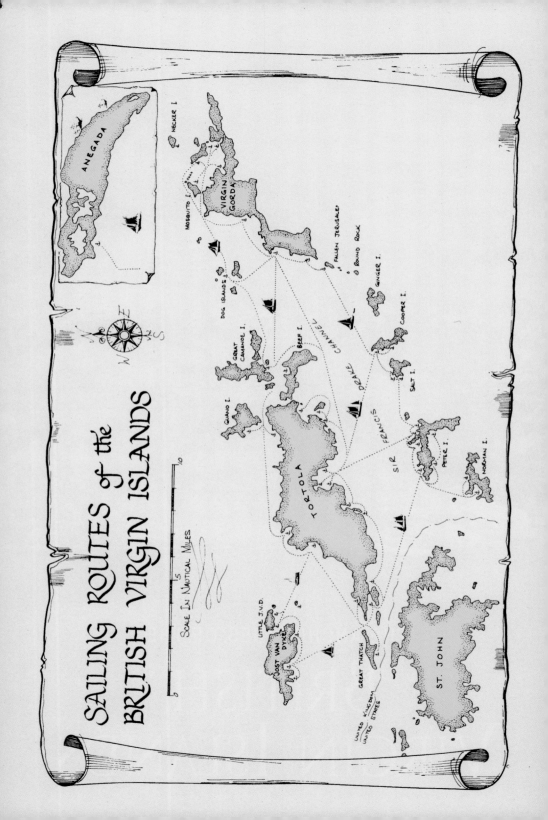

SAILING ROUTES of the BRITISH VIRGIN ISLANDS

ANEGADA

N E S W

Scale In Nautical Miles
0   5   10

HECKER I.

MOSQUITO I.

VIRGIN GORDA

FALLEN JERUSALEM

ROUND ROCK

GINGER I.

COOPER I.

DOG ISLANDS

SALT I.

GREAT CAMANOE I.

BEEF I.

DRAKE CHANNEL

GUANO I.

SIR FRANCIS

PETER I.

NORMAN I.

TORTOLA

LITTLE J.V.D.

JOST VAN DYKE

GREAT THATCH

UNITED KINGDOM
UNITED STATES

ST. JOHN

Message from Premier Honourable
Dr. Orlando Smith, OBE

Dear Yachtsmen:

I am pleased to welcome you to the British Virgin Islands. Our enchanted islands are indeed Nature's Little Secrets and you have made the perfect destination choice.

Discover for yourself why we are the 'Sailing Capital of the World.' Explore our seas and visit our sister islands of Virgin Gorda, Anegada, Peter Island, Jost Van Dyke, Cooper Island, Salt Island, Marina Cay and many more. Sailing through the archipelago will take you to unique islands and hidden coves and anchorages each offering a variety of experiences. Enjoy sports fishing at our wide range of fishing grounds, from the depths of the world renowned North Drop to the bone fishing shallows of Anegada. Or, you can get closer to nature and explore life under the sea at one of our historic shipwrecks or breathtaking coral reefs.

Hike to the top of Sage Mountain to see spectacular vistas of land and sea. Visit one of our many National Parks, Fallen Jerusalem, Little dogs, or Prickly Pear. Discover and experience our rich culture as our Heritage Dancers perform in traditional costume. Discover the sweet sounds of our many fungi bands. Sample our cuisine at one of our local restaurants for a taste of our island specialties created by our award winning "gold-medalists" chefs.

While here, make yourself at home in one of the luxury resorts, the family like villas, charming inns and quaint hotels. Most of all enjoy the company of some of the most warm-hearted, friendly and helpful people in the Caribbean.

I am blessed to be the leader of such a sailor's paradise and will continue to ensure that the BVI remains a highly competitive, safe and diverse sailing destination. As Minister responsible for Tourism, I will ensure that the necessary legislation, policies and procedures are carried out in a manner that will further advance our reputation as a "Yachtsman Friendly Destination."

Once again, welcome to our shores and thank you for choosing the BVI. We are looking forward to introducing you to Nature's Little Secrets and to making your stay so special that you will want to return again and again.

Sincerely,

Dr. Orlando Smith, OBE
Premier and Minister for Tourism

ROAD TOWN TORTOLA, BVI

Road Town, the capital of the British Virgin Islands, is the center of commerce, shipping and social activity. Centrally located on Tortola's south coast, Road Town is situated on the west side of Road Harbour, the longest natural harbor on the island.

Road Town has a rich history. On August 1st, 1834 the Emancipation Proclamation was read at the Sunday Morning Well. This gave slaves their freedom, even though slavery had been officially abolished in 1807. In 1853 a town-wide fire destroyed nearly every building in Road Town. The fire spread because of angry rioters protesting an increase on the cattle tax. Rioters eventually set fire to most of the plantations across the island.

The past two decades have been witness to tremendous growth and development throughout the BVI and Road Town has emerged as a haven for yacht chartering and a center for tourism. The town is a unique blend of past and present. The more recent developments have become a hub for the commercial and administrative buildings of the BVI, while the quiet charms of years gone by remain, like treasures, to be discovered by visitors arriving by air or sea. The oldest building in Road Town, Her Majesty's Prison on Main Street, dates from the 1840s and is undergoing transformation into a museum.

Charts

NV.Charts: St.Thomas to Anegada: Kit: C-13A & 14
NIMA: 25641, Imray-Iolaire: A-231
Admiralty Leisure: 5640-6 & 08B

Waypoints	North	West
BV101	18°24.80'	64°36.20'
BV102	18°24.50'	64°35.00'

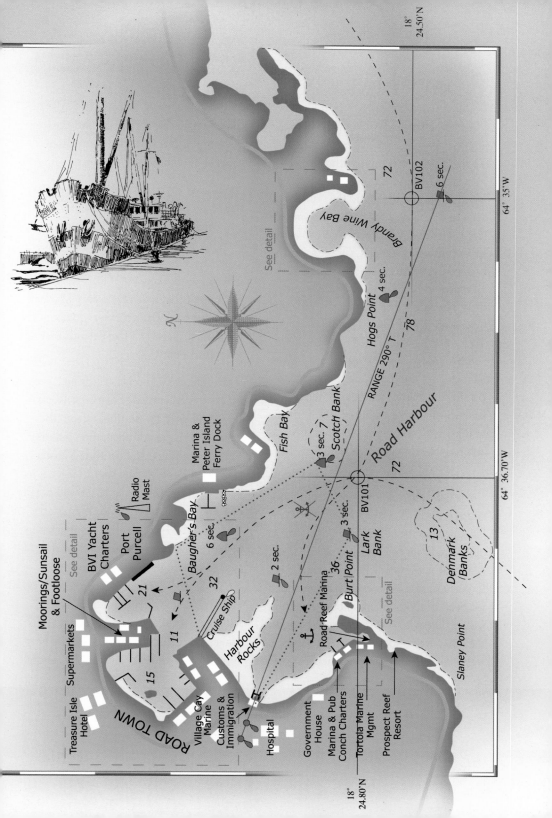

ROAD HARBOUR

Waypoint: BV101- 18°24.80'N 64°36.20'W
Navigation: 6nm east of Soper's Hole at the west end of Tortola
Services: Port of Entry to the BVI

There are ten marinas within Road Harbour and they can be broken down by area. To the west upon entering the harbor is Fort Burt Marina and the Road Reef Marina. Tucked in behind the cruise ship dock at the head of the harbor are the two large marina developments known as Wickham's Cay I and II. Once inside the breakwater on the starboard side is the extensive facilities of the Moorings and on the other side of the entrance is Village Cay Marina and Inner Harbour Marina. To the north beyond the Port Purcell area and behind the seawall to starboard of the Moorings is the Joma Marina, home to BVI Yacht Charters and to port, the service facilities of Tortola Yacht Services. Further to the southeast and to starboard upon entering Road Harbour is Baugher's Bay.

Navigation & Piloting

Road Harbour is approached from the south or west via the Sir Francis Drake Channel and the entrance is largely free of obstruction for the cruising sailor. There is no reason to use the buoyed channel on the eastern side of the bay as it is intended for deep draft commercial or cruise ship traffic. There is however, a range between the outer green buoy (flashing 6 sec) near waypoint BV102 (Brandy Wine Bay) on the eastern side of the bay and the government/ferry dock in the center of town. This course is 290° true.

Make your approach at the center of the bay (waypoint BV101). This will place you between the red buoy (flashing 8 sec) marking Scotch Bank (7.8 feet/2.37m of water) and the green (flashing 3 sec) marking Lark Bank (14.4 feet/4.38m of water). Although there is plenty of water inside the Lark Bank marker, do not get too close to shore as a reef extends east from Burt Point.

The inner green marker (flashing 2 sec) marks the extremity of Harbour Rock that extends to the southeast from the new government administration building. Vessels heading into Fort Burt Marina and Road Reef Marina should leave it to starboard. No anchoring is allowed north of a line between the government ferry dock and the Lark Bank green marker in order to keep the ferry route clear. For vessels clearing into the BVI from the USVI or other foreign ports, do not tie up alongside the government dock, as the surge can be excessive and the ferry traffic makes this difficult. Anchor off the Fort Burt Marina and take the dinghy ashore.

Road Harbour at night

Scotch Bank

Fl.R.8s

BV101

Fl.R.6s

Fl.G.3s

Lark Bank

Fl.G.2s

Burt
Point

N

Fort Burt & Road Reef Marinas

Tortola

Waypoint: BV101- 18°24.80'N 64°36.20'W
Services: Ice, Fuel, Marina, Taxi, Restaurant,
Chandlery, Garbage Disposal, Provisioning

Navigation & Piloting

Once inside the buoys at the mouth of Road Harbour,
head for the government dock (approximately 292°m)
until the Fort Burt Marina is abeam. Make sure that you leave the inner green buoy
(marking the SE end of Harbour Rocks) to starboard. This approach will bring you
clear of the reef that extends to the north from the mangroves at Burt Point. Approach
the docks and anchorage from the northeast in order to avoid the sandbar that extends
to the north from Road Reef. Anchor to the northeast of the docks about 300 feet out
on a sandy bottom.

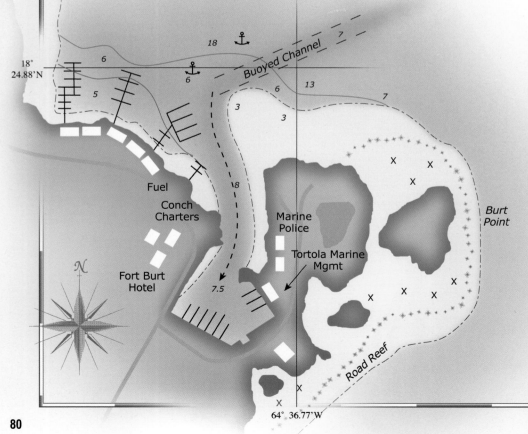

If you are proceeding to Road Reef Marina, there is a buoyed channel (7ft / 2.2m) northeast from Fort Burt Marina. Unless you have prior clearance from the marina (VHF12) or are returning a vessel to the TMM charter base, we do not recommend committing to this channel owing to limited maneuvering room once inside. Make your turn to port when you are close to the Fort Burt Marina docks, leaving Conch Charters and Smiths Ferry dock to starboard. There are a couple of shallow spots close to the roadside beneath Fort Burt Hotel, so favor the port side of the channel as you enter the pool of Road Reef Marina.

Ashore
FORT BURT MARINA

Fort Burt Marina accepts transient boats and offers gas, diesel, water and ice as well as telephone, TV cable hook-ups and of course, electricity. Pull alongside and check for slip availability with the dockmaster. Next to the Fort Burt Marina near the Pub is Tradewind Yachting Services, retailers of marine batteries, outboards, and they sell, repair, and certify life rafts. Fort Burt Marina is the home of Conch Charters, established in the BVI over twenty years ago. Steeped in history, Drake's Point Restaurant at Fort Burt (up the hill from the marina) has an amazing view of the harbor, Drake's Channel and the islands to the south.

ROAD REEF MARINA
Road Reef Marina is managed by Tortola Marine Management, a charter boat company in business for thirty years! Electricity, ice and water are available as well as WiFi from the TMM office. The marina can accommodate vessels 60 feet in length, with a maximum draft of 7.5 feet. The beam size is unrestricted. The marina is open daily from 8am-5pm and they monitor VHF channel 12.

In the same complex that houses the marina office is the marine division of the British Virgin Island Police, the Royal BVI Yacht Club, VISAR Base Station, Doyle Sailmakers and Island Care Electronics. Road Reef Plaza, next door to the marina has a variety of shops including a Riteway market that sells provisioning to the yachting community. Crandall's, a West Indian bakery, is across the road from Road Reef Marina.

The Government Dock

As the main port of entry to the British Virgin Islands, all vessels arriving from the U.S. Virgin Islands or other foreign ports must clear with customs and immigration before proceeding to a marina.

To clear customs and immigration in Road Town anchor off the Fort Burt Marina and the skipper can dinghy in to clear customs. You may only bring your dinghy to the dock since it is for the use of the ferries only. You must clear in before you or your crew can go ashore or to a marina. The captain can bring the necessary papers without his crew. Please see the section on Customs and Immigration in the Planning the Cruise section. If you arrive after customs is closed, put your yellow quarantine flag up and remain on the vessel, anchored out until customs opens. You can call Customs and Immigration to announce your arrival and to tell them you will be in when they open: 284-494-3475.

ROAD TOWN INNER HARBOUR
WICKHAM'S CAY I & II

Tortola

Navigation: 1nm from harbour entrance
Services: Full service marina, Fuel, Ice, Water, Laundry, Garbage Disposal, Restaurants, Marine support services. No moorings available, anchorage outside of breakwater

Navigation & Piloting

From waypoint BV101 between the red and green buoys at the entrance to Road Harbour, head NW at approximately 311°m. This will take you clear of the green buoy (fl2sec) marking the extremity of Harbour Rock (leave to port) and inside the cruise ship dock (note a quick flashing 3 sec light marking the dolphin at the end of the dock) and position you at the green marker outside of the breakwater and entrance to the Inner Harbour Complex. You can take this marker either side as there is 25 feet of available water. Although often an uncomfortable anchorage, just south of the breakwater is fine for a lunch stop or a quick run ashore for provisions.

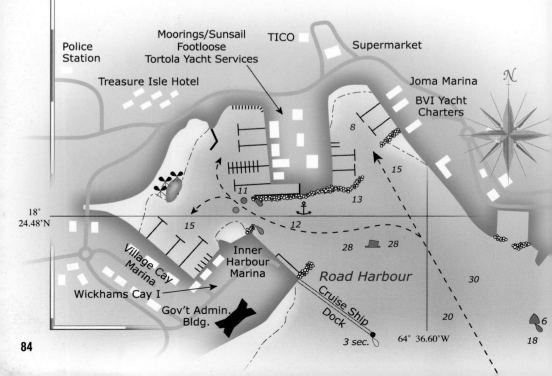

Police Station

Moorings/Sunsail
Footloose
Tortola Yacht Services

TICO

Supermarket

Treasure Isle Hotel

Joma Marina

BVI Yacht
Charters

8

15

11

13

18°
24.48'N

15

12

28   28

Village Cay
Marina

Inner
Harbour
Marina

Wickhams Cay I

Gov't Admin.
Bldg.

Road Harbour

Cruise Ship Dock

30

20

3 sec.

64° 36.60'W

6

18

BV101

Proceed through the double breakwater (80 feet wide) and on through a final set of port, starboard markers just inside of the breakwater where you will have 15 feet of water depth since the entrance was changed and dredged. To starboard is the Moorings / Sunsail marina complex where fuel, water and transient slips are available (VHF12). To port is Village Cay Marina and Inner Harbour Marina with a controlling depth of 11 feet. Call the dockmaster for instructions, both marinas monitor VHF 16. There are no mooring buoys within the basin.

VILLAGE CAY MARINA

Village Cay Marina, in the center of Road Town, boasts over 100 slips for yachts up to 190 feet long, and as much as 11 foot draft. Amenities include fuel, water, cable TV, a swimming pool, showers, garbage disposal, and free WiFi. Send the chef off the boat for provisions at the Dockmaster's Deli, visit the dive shop, boutique and the Oasis Salon and Spa. One of the best features is the waterside restaurant and bar. It's a relaxing place to have a drink and watch all the yachts and dinghies coming and going at the marina. If you want to have a night ashore, there is a nice (small) hotel with views of the marina and beyond. You are within walking distance of the shops in downtown Road Town. For water or fuel contact the dockmaster on Channel 16 or call 284-494-2771.

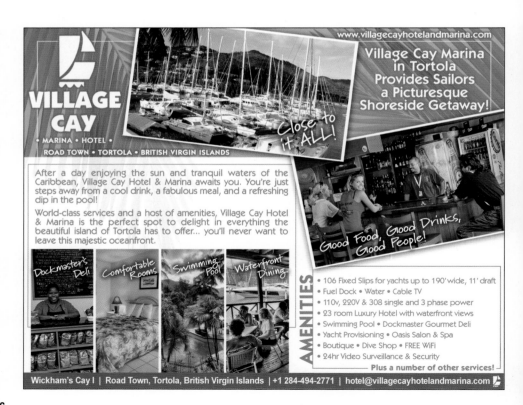

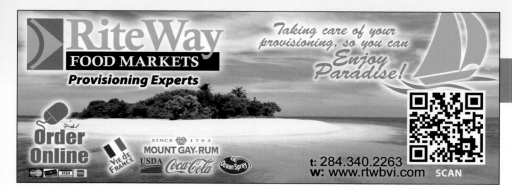
INNER HARBOUR MARINA

This marina is adjacent to Village Cay Marina to the south. At present they have 22 slips, but will be adding an additional 50 slips. The dredging to a 14 foot depth has been completed. Security cameras have been installed. VPM Yacht charters are operating on the dock. They will have fuel available for the high season (November through June). You may call the dock-master on VHF channel 16 or call him on the marina number 284-494-3010, or on his cell phone at 284-499-1144.

Adjacent to the marina is the Marine Depot ships chandlery for all of the boater's needs. The Ample Hamper provisioning store is also situated nearby offering gourmet items to purchase or to eat on the spot. Numerous banking facilities are also close at hand including First Caribbean Bank, Banco Popular, and Scotia Bank.

The large multi-story building to the south of Village Cay is the Government of the Virgin Islands Administration Complex, adjacent to the cruise ship dock and the local village shopping market.

A short walk puts you onto Main Street with access to all of the Road Town shops and restaurants.

The Moorings Sunsail Marina Complex (Wickham's Cay II)

One of the Caribbean's most comprehensive marina facilities, Wickham's Cay II Marina is the base for several charter companies. The marina is home to the Moorings, Moorings Power, Moorings Luxury Crewed Yachts, Sunsail and Footloose Charters. Dockage is also available for visiting yachts when there are free slips.

The Mariner Inn Hotel with 32 recently renovated rooms overlooks the activity in the marina. The hotel offers all the amenities including wireless internet. There are now seven, five star luxury rooms with a view of Road Harbour and the Sir Francis Drake Channel. The Mariner Inn Restaurant and Bar is open seven days a week serving breakfast, lunch and dinner. Guests staying in the hotel or in the marina are welcome to the restaurant and to use the swimming pool.

At the southern end of the complex you will find the Moorings, Moorings Power and Moorings Crewed Yachts on docks A and B at the inner harbor. The Moorings Village is home to Charlie's Restaurant and Bar (named for Charlie Cary, the founder of the Moorings). It is perched over the water at the base of "B" dock. Charlie's is open for lunch and dinner (until late) with an in-house pizza oven and an upscale menu. It is casual, with no reservations required.

At the Moorings Village you will also find a boutique, a sales office for the Moorings yachts, concierge services and a spa. If you need to cool down, try the café for an ice cream or a thirst quenching beverage from the coffee bar.

Transient yachts may go to "C" dock for overnight dockage, and you may want to call the marina on VHF Channel 12 for availability of dock space and docking instructions. Dockage is on finger piers and can accommodate vessels with a draft of 9 feet. Vessels up to 120 feet may tie up at the T dock when it is available. Amenities include water, ice, and electricity. Fuel (gasoline and diesel) and ice are sold at the bulkhead between docks "B" and "C".

The reception area at the Moorings Marina

SAILING, CREWED & POWER YACHTING VACATIONS

The Moorings will bring your dream to reality by providing the newest yachts along with unparalleled customer service to ensure you have the most exceptional boating vacation possible. Our 40-year reputation for integrity, quality and reliability has satisfied the most discriminating boaters. Experience your most unforgettable vacation ever with The Moorings.

www.moorings.com   888.952.6014   The Moorings®

NORTH AMERICA I CARIBBEAN I MEDITERRANEAN I SOUTH PACIFIC I INDIAN OCEAN I FAR EAST

Sunsail, chartering both bareboats and flotillas, is located on the "D" dock. The Sunsail office is at the base of the dock. Behind the office are showers and an ATM. Last Stop Sports rent water toys and dive equipment. HIHO's shop sells casual fun surf clothing. There is also a gift shop with t-shirts, books, and gifts to bring home with you. Renport rents mobile phones to blenders to iPods and more for the length of your charter. You can also rent DVDs for the trip in case you get a rainy day. If you are interested in purchasing a Sunsail boat, the brokerage office is nearby.

Footloose Charters is located at the opposite end of the marina from the Moorings. Across from the Wickham's Cay II Marina is Tortola Yacht Services, one of the foremost yacht care centers in the Caribbean operating since 1965. This full service boatyard has a 70 ton Travelift, dry storage, Caribbean Refinishing (concentrating in Awlgrip application), yacht brokerage, and the well-stocked Golden Hind Chandlery.

Also associated with the boatyard is Caribbean Technology, Wickham's Cay II Rigging, Marine Power Service for both engines and outboards, Cay Electronics, and Island Yacht Management.

PORT PURCELL

JOMA MARINA/
TORTOLA YACHT SERVICES

Navigation

From the green buoy just outside of the breakwater to the Inner Harbour complex, proceed to the north and enter the small basin leaving the stone breakwater that connects with the Moorings, to the west, to port. A second, shorter breakwater to starboard extends from the northeast adjacent to Port Purcell.

Once inside the breakwater, there is a new marina facility immediately on your port hand (this marina will not be available until a breakwater is built to protect from swells), further north is the dock associated with Tortola Yacht Services.

On the starboard side is the Joma Marina complex. The water depth is 8-10 feet and 15 feet on the T-dock.

JOMA MARINA

Across the water from Tortola Yacht Services near Port Purcell is the Joma Marina, the base for BVI Yacht Charters. It is located in a breezy area within walking distance of two big markets and restaurants, as well as Parts and Power. BVI Yacht Charters uses most of the marina for their charter boats, but as the season gets busy and the boats are on charter, check with them to see if there are any available slips. They monitor VHF Channel 16. The marina is open from 8am to 5pm daily. It is a very convenient location.

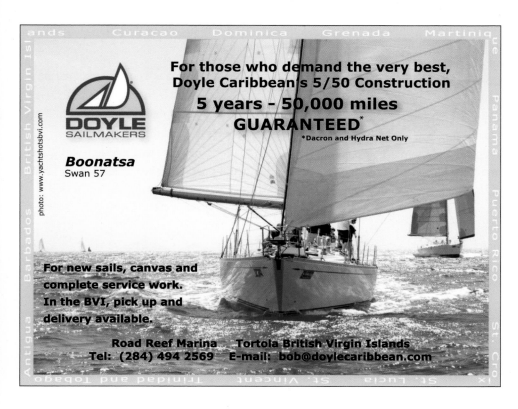

Baugher's Bay

Waypoint: BV101- 18°24.80'N 64°36.20'W
Navigation: 0.5nm NE from the buoyed harbor entrance
Services: Restaurant, Ferry, Commercial Marina

Navigation & Piloting

From waypoint BV101 at the entrance to Road Harbour, Baugher's Bay is a little over a half mile ahead to the northeast on your starboard side. The anchorage is straight forward with no obstructions. As you approach the marina, there is a large mooring buoy due west of the breakwater, this is for the fuel tanker, so keep clear. If you are anchoring, the preferred location would be to the south of the small breakwater, in order to keep out of the way of the Peter Island ferry that uses this location. The marina monitors VHF16.

Ashore

For those going to Peter Island Resort, this is where the Peter Island ferry picks up and drops off passengers. The pick up spot is to the left of the old CSY marina looking from the sea.

The old marina is a commercial marina and not available for transient boats. Upstairs at the marina is the Chillin' Café, a sports bar and restaurant serving Caribbean flavors on the waterfront. Lunch and dinner are served from 11am to 10pm. Sunday they serve brunch from 10-3pm.

Ashore in Road Town

When going ashore in Road Town, it is important to observe the local dress code, which prohibits swimwear, brief attire and shirtless males. In order to avoid embarrassment, please cover up!!

Road Town has some beautiful old West Indian buildings, complete with red tin roofs and Victorian dado work around the porches. A walk down Main Street, towards the east, from Fort Burt Hotel, which guards the western end of the harbor, will reveal all sorts of delights tucked away behind newer buildings or squeezed shoulder to shoulder

along Main Street. Most of the shops are clustered along Main Street and Waterfront Drive from Peebles Hospital to the bottom of Joe's Hill.

The Philatelic Bureau of the post office, across the street from the Sir Olva Georges Square, is a must stop for anyone who would like to take home a collection of the exotic and colorful stamps of this tropical territory. You may wish to get caught up on the news at home with a New York Times or a

magazine from Esme's Shoppe on the Square. Also located across from the Square is the BVI Registry Office for those thinking about getting married in this amazing, tropical paradise.

The Virgin Islands Folk Museum, giving you a window to days gone by, is situated in a quaint West Indian building past the post office. On the waterfront Capriccio di Mare offers breakfast, lunch and dinner from 8am. They also serve a great cappuccino while you wait for the ferry arrival across the street and gaze at the boating activity in the harbor.

The ferry dock at the center of town, on the waterfront, houses customs and immigration, as well as the adjacent office of the BVI Tourist Department. A taxi stand is right there making it convenient for the ferry passengers or anyone to get where they want to go.

Straddling the waterfront and Main Street you will find Pusser's Company Store and Pub. This is a delightful, air-conditioned pub where you can cool down with a beer or lemonade and a deli sandwich or pizza. If you haven't tried a Pusser's Painkiller, this may be just the right time! Friday nights the Pub is jamming at happy hour. The Pusser's Company Store, with tropical and nautical clothing for ladies and men, watches, luggage and nautical accessories attached to the Pub, leads to Main Street. Next door, Le Grand Café serves breakfast, lunch and dinner from 8am to 11pm. Le Grand Café tends to draw the late night crowd in their bar for a drink and a chat!

Further along the waterfront to the east is the Seaview Hotel and Maria's By the Sea, a restaurant which features local Caribbean cuisine and seafood overlooking Road Harbour.

The brightly colored Crafts Alive Market, right on the waterfront features local souvenirs of all kinds, including t-shirts hats, baskets, shell work and more

Back on Main Street, handcrafted silver and gold jewelry is a specialty of Samarkand. Shirt Shack on Chalwell Street has all kinds of t-shirts and casual cotton clothing.

Sunny Caribbee Spice Company and Art Gallery are located in a delightful old West Indian house. The shop carries specially packaged herbs and spices from the islands that make wonderful gifts for friends or yourself. The air-conditioned art gallery is next door with art treasures displayed for sale. They have a large selection of paintings and prints from all over the Caribbean.

Little Denmark has the best selection of Cuban cigars on the island, safely kept in a humidor. If cigars aren't your thing, they also have jewelry, watches and fishing

equipment to name a few of the diverse items they sell. Serendipity sells books and cards. Latitude 18° carries tropical clothing, quality sunglasses, bags and other assorted goodies.

Smith's Gore Real Estate is perched on a huge boulder across from Little Denmark. Further down Main Street is Her Majesty's Prison, an old and interesting edifice, and one we hope you will never have to see from the inside! St. George's Anglican Church is another lovely landmark worth a visit.

Arriving in Road Harbour from the sea, you will see an old, purple Victorian building just above Road Town. The Bougainvillea Clinic, affectionately known as the "purple palace" and a Road Town landmark, is world-renowned for its aesthetic and reconstructive surgery as well as operating as a clinic offering emergency and general care for visitors.

Continuing past the church on your left is Joe's Hill, which leads up to Mount Sage or over to Cane Garden Bay. The panoramic view is breath-taking at the top of the hill and the temperature is usually cool and breezy.

If you are up for an adventure and don't mind a light hike, a visit to the Sage

Mountain National Park is highly recommended. This 92-acre reserve, managed by the National Park Trust, includes the 1,780-foot Mt. Sage and a forest with 15-to 20-foot tall fern trees, Bulletwood trees, West Indian and Broadleaf Mahogany and White Cedars (the BVI national tree). Hikers on the park's trails will pass the scattered remains of old houses and a variety of orchids, and might spot several species of birds, including the Antillean crested hummingbird and the pearly-eyed thrasher.

Back in Road Town; if you are still feeling energetic, continue on Main Street past Sunday Morning Well, past the courthouse and high school to the Botanical Gardens across the street from the police station.

The J.R. O'Neal Botanic Gardens, is a four-acre park maintained by the National Parks Trust and the BVI Botanical Society. The gardens, which include a lush array of indigenous and tropical plants also encompass the ruins of the century old agricultural station.

Established in 1979 and named after the BVI's first conservationist, Joseph Reynold O'Neal who was also a leading figure in the formation of the National Parks Trust and the establishment of the BVI's first national park at Mount Sage National Park.

As you enter the gardens you will walk through the avenue of royal palms leading to the fountain, which makes a captivating entrance for visitors.

Paths disappear into corners of the garden lined with colorful blossoms draped over shady pergolas.

The botanic collections represent the different habitats of the BVI such as the rainforest, coastal environments and dry forests, in addition to displays of exotic species and an extensive collection of palms. A gazebo of orchids both, native and exotic can be discovered by the pond, where lilies float and tortoises swim. The nursery at the garden is an important repository for endangered species of flora found within the BVI, ensuring their survival from habitat loss.

The gardens are a refreshing place to stop away from the hustle and bustle of Road Town, there is a small entrance fee and donations are always welcome.

Many other shops and services, too numerous to mention, are waiting for you to discover in Road Town. Check with the Tourist Department, the Welcome Magazine, or even the yellow pages of the telephone book to find what you are looking for.

ISLAND CONNECTIONS

EMERGENCIES
VISAR (Virgin Island Search and Rescue)
VHF Channel 16
Tel: 767 (SOS), or 999,
or 911 or 284-494-4357
(494-help)
www.visar.org

ROAD REEF

MARINAS
Road Reef/Tortola Marine Management
VHF channel 12
Tel: 284-494-2751
http://sailtmm.com

Fort Burt Marina
Fuel, water, ice, telephone,
electricity, cable TV,
showers available
VHF channel 12
Tel: 284-494-4200

Penn's Marina
VHF channel 12
Tel: 284-494-7959
Dockage, moorings
Penns Landing Marina,
Tortola, BVI on FB

CHARTER COMPANIES
Conch Charters
VHF channel 12
Tel: 284-494-4868
www.conchcharters.com

Tortola Marine Management (TMM)
Road Reef Marina
VHF channel 12
284-494-2751
http://sailtmm.com

ELECTRONICS
Road Reef Marina
Island Care Electronics
Tel: 284-494-3998
http://icebvi.com

SAILMAKERS
Doyle Sailmakers
Tel: 284-494-2569
www.doylesails.com

MARINE REPAIRS & SALES
Tradewinds Yachting Services
Tel: 284-494-3154
www.tradewindsbvi.com

RESTAURANTS NEAR ROAD REEF MARINA
Royal BVI Yacht Club
Tel: 284-494-8140
Open to the public for
dining, offering interna-
tional fare
Lunch 12-3pm, dinner
from 6pm
www.royalbviyc.org/
restaurantandbar.html

Crandall's Bakery
Tel: 284-494-5156
Across the street from
Road Reef Marina
Featuring lobster and
conch patties, fried fish
chicken and roti as well
as bakery items.
Open from 5am-5pm
http://crandallspastry.com

Drake's Point Restaurant
At Fort Burt Hotel
Tel: 284-443-3385
Family style menu with a
fantastic view of the harbor
and channel
Open 7am until...
Drakes Point at Fort Burt
Hotel on FB

The Pub
Tel: 284-494-2608
On the harbor serving
breakfast, lunch and dinner
For lunch: burgers and West
Indian fare, dinner includes
seafood, steaks, ribs
Open Monday-Saturday
7am-10pm, Sunday
from 5pm

*Town Dock is for ferries
only. Please refer to the
section on Customs and
Immigration procedures
under Planning the Cruise.*

ROAD TOWN WATERFRONT RESTAURANTS
Capriccio di Mare
Tel: 284-494-5369
International and Italian
sidewalk café
Across from the ferry dock
For lunch and dinner
Open 8am-9pm
Monday-Saturday

Pusser's Road Town
Tel: 284-494-3897
Located on Waterfront
Road near the ferry dock.
English style pub for lunch
& dinner open 11am-10pm
daily. Be comfortable in
an air-conditioned pub
with a waterfront view of
Road Harbour
www.pussers.com/
t-road-town-pub.aspx

Le Grand Café
Located in a charming
garden setting across from
the waterfront in the heart
of Road Town. With an
open-air lounge and bar,
the café serves lunch and
dinner and features late
night live music and DJs
on the weekends.
Lunch M-F 11:30am
to 3pm
Dinner 6:30-9:30pm, 10
on weekends
Reservations requested

Maria's by the Sea
Tel: 284-494-2595
West Indian fare with
specialties in seafood and
a harbor view
Open daily for breakfast,
lunch and dinner
7am until late
www.mariasbythesea.com

Government House

WICKHAM'S CAY I
RESTAURANTS

**Dockside Bar & Grille
at Village Cay**
Open daily from 7:30am
serving breakfast, lunch
and dinner.Live music
every Wed, Sat night
Tel: 284-494-2771

**Bat Cave
Baugher's Bay**
Road Town night life, call
to find out what's going on.
Tel: 284-494-4686

Spaghetti Junction
Serves North American
and Indian cuisine
Lunch 11:30am-2:30pm
Dinner 6-10pm
Tuesday-Saturday
Tel: 284-494-4880

PROVISIONS
Dockmaster's Deli
Tel:284-494-5188
www.villagecayhotel
andmarina.com/amenities
/Restaurants/Dockmasters
Menu.aspx

DIVE SHOP
Aquaventure
Tel:284-494-4826
www.aquaventurebvi.com

WICKHAM'S CAY II

MARINAS
**Wickham's Cay II
Marina**
Moorings
VHF channel 16
Tel: 284-494-2333

**Joma Marina
BVI Yacht Charters**
VHF channel 16
Tel: 284-494-4289

CHARTER COMPANIES
BVI Yacht Charters
VHF channel 16
Tel: 284-494-4289
www.bviyachtcharters.com

The Moorings
VHF channel 16
Tel: 284-494-2333
www.moorings.com

Sunsail
VHF channel 16
Tel: 284-495-4740
www.sunsail.com

Footloose
VHF channel 16
Tel: 284-494-0528
www.footloosecharters.com

BOATYARD
Tortola Yacht Services
284-494-2124

CHANDLERY
Golden Hind
Wickham's Cay II
284-494-2756

MARINE REPAIRS
Caribbean Technology
Wickham's Cay II
Tel: 284-494-3150

**Wickham's Cay II
Rigging**
Tel: 284-494-3979

Marine Power Service
Wickham's Cay II
Tel: 284-494-2738

Cay Electronics
Wickham's Cay II
Tel: 284-494-2400
http://cayelectronics.com/about/bvi

**Island Yacht
Management**
Wickham's Cay II
Tel: 284-494-6781
www.islandyacht.com

Caribbean Refinishing
Wickham's Cay II
Tel: 284-494-3979

RESTAURANTS
Moorings Mariner Inn
Wickham's Cay II
Overlooks the marina
International, lunch from
12pm to 3pm, candlelit
dinner 1:30-9:30pm
Tel: 284-494-2333
www.bvimarinerinnhotel.com/RestaurantBar.aspx

Charlie's
Wickham's Cay II
Perched on the water's edge
serving an upscale menu
Open late
Tel: 284-494-2333
www.bvimarinerinnhotel.com/RestaurantBar.aspx

Deli France
Wickham's Cay II
International take out or
eat in. Sandwiches, salads,
cheeses from Europe
Open M-F 8am-6pm
Saturday until 2pm

Verandah Restaurant
At Treasure Isle Hotel Intl
Air conditioned restaurant
serving continental and
Caribbean style cuisine
Open daily, breakfast,
lunch and dinner
Tel: 284-494-2501
www.treasureislehotelbvi.com/dining.php

GROCERY STORES
Riteway
This comprehensive store
carries just about everything
you need or want. It is
walking distance from
Wickham's Cay II. You
will find English and
American brands as well
as Spanish and Indian.
They will provision your
boat for you.
Tel: 284-494-2263
www.rtwbvi.com/store-locations

One Mart
This market is close to
Port Purcell, they seem
to be well stocked with fresh
and frozen foods. It is
probably not close enough
to walk from Wickham's
Cay II, but it is a very
short trip in a car.
Tel: 284-494-6999
www.onemartfoods.com/location.html

TICO
Located on Wickham's
Cay II close to the Moorings.
They have an extensive
inventory of beer, wine,
spirits, and mixers. TICO
has been in business for
nearly 40 years.
Tel: 284-494-2211
www.ticobvi.com/cgi-local/ws400.cgi

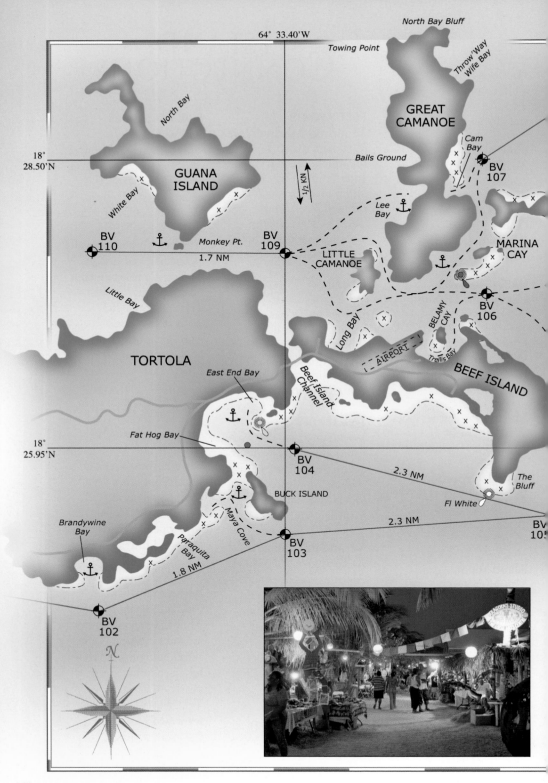

North Bay Bluff

Towing Point

Throw'Way
Wife Bay

64° 33.40'W

GREAT
CAMANOE

North Bay

Cam
Bay

18°
28.50'N

Bails Ground

x
x x
x

BV
107

GUANA
ISLAND

1/2 KN

Lee
Bay

⚓

White Bay

x

x

MARINA
CAY

x

BV
110

⚓

Monkey Pt.

BV
109

LITTLE
CAMANOE

⚓

1.7 NM

x

Little Bay

BELAMY
CAY

BV
106

x

Long Bay

x
x

TORTOLA

East End Bay

AIRPORT

Trellis Bay

BEEF ISLAND

⚓

Beef Island Channel

x

x

Fat Hog Bay

x

x x

18°
25.95'N

BV
104

2.3 NM

The
Bluff

x

x

⚓

BUCK ISLAND

Fl White

Brandywine
Bay

x

Maya Cove

2.3 NM

BV
105

Paraquita Bay

⚓

BV
103

1.8 NM

BV
102

N

100

EASTERN TORTOLA

SCRUB ISLAND

Waypoints	North	West
BV101	18°24.80'	64°36.20'
BV102	18°24.50'	64°35.00'
BV103	18°25.10'	64°33.20'
BV104	18°25.95'	64°33.20'
BV105	18°25.30'	64°30.90'
BV106	18°27.30'	64°31.50'
BV107	18°28.55'	64°31.50'
BV108	18°30.00'	64°32.40'
BV109	18°27.70'	64°33.20'
BV110	18°27.70'	64°35.00'
BV111	18°30.00'	64°35.00'

Charts

NV.Charts: St.Thomas to Anegada: Kit : C-13 & 14

NIMA: 25641, Imray-Iolaire: A-231

Admiralty Leisure: 5640-6,7,3B

BRANDYWINE BAY

Waypoint: BV102-18°24.50'N 64°35.00W
Navigation: 1nm NE of Road Harbour: 4nm W of Beef Island Bluff
Services: Restaurant, Garbage (at head of beach)

This lovely curve of a bay with a stunning white sand beach is just east of Road Town on the southern side of the island. It provides a comfortable overnight anchorage in the usual east/southeast tradewinds, but can develop an uncomfortable surge if the wind moves to the south.

Close to Road Town and East End, Brandywine is a great last night dinner ashore anchorage.

Navigation & Piloting

Brandywine Bay is tucked in behind a reef that extends out from both sides of the headlands. The opening between the two sections of the reef is wide and safe for entry in the center with a depth of 10 feet. The entrance is straightforward and easy to see in reasonable light. It should be noted that the bay shoals off on all sides.

Anchoring & Mooring

Although the Brandywine Estate Restaurant, situated on the headland to the east of the bay and overlooking the Sir Francis Drake channel, has in the past maintained several moorings in the center of the bay exclusively for dinner guests, the new owners indicate that they are not yet maintained and therefore recommend that you use your own ground tackle. Please do not pick up any of the moorings in front of the white waterfront apartments as they are private.

If you choose to anchor, select a spot to the east or west of the mooring field and beware of the shoal water that extends from all shores. If there is a southerly surge, you may want to consider a stern anchor in order to keep the bow of your vessel facing the entrance to the bay.

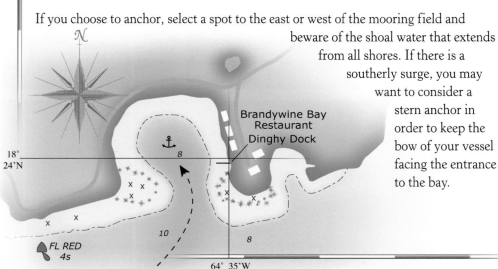

Brandywine Estate
Restaurant

Ashore

As you face the row of condominiums on the water's edge on the eastern side of the bay, you will see the Brandywine Estate dinghy dock located about 50 yards to their right. Once ashore, follow the pathway to the left of the dock to where it meets the concrete road on the Brandywine Estate, and then it is just a short walk up the hill to the restaurant.

Brandywine Estate monitors VHF channel 16 after 2pm and is available by telephone all day for reservations and instructions for mooring (if they should install some in the future).

Brandywine Estate, with views of the boats in Sir Francis Drake, serves delicious French meals – the cuisine is as spectacular as the view. There is an outside lounge that is breezy with a front row view of the channel.

The white sand beach at the head of the b ay is a good spot for a walk, a swim, or just lazing the day away. Garbage can be deposited in the green dumpster by the roadside.

Maya Cove
Hodges Creek

Waypoint: BV103 18°25.10'N 64°33.20'W
Navigation: 2.5nm NE of Road Harbour
Services: Restaurants, dockage, moorings, water, fuel, ice, garbage disposal, scuba shop

Tortola

Maya Cove or Hodges Creek as it is shown on the charts is approximately a half mile west of Buck Island on the southeastern shore of Tortola. Sheltered by the reef, it is always cool and relatively free of bugs. The small marina on the eastern side of the bay by the entrance and the marina at the head of the bay to the north are both private marinas and do not take transient yachts. The large three story building with the red roof is the Hodges Creek Marina, a full service facility. Moorings are available via the marina on VHF 16. There is limited room to anchor due to the mooring field but a good alternative is to anchor in the lee of Buck Island in 7-10 feet of water (see below). Hodges Creek is home to Marine Max Yacht Charters, in addition to a number of other charter companies.

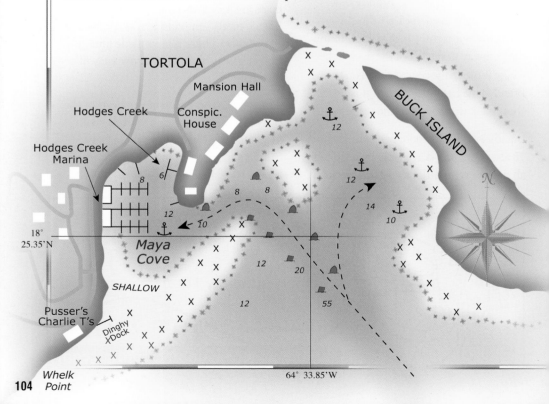

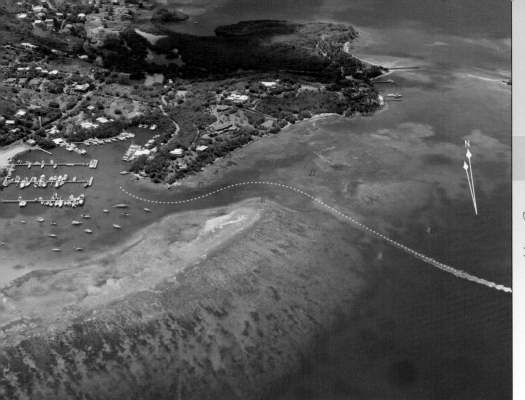

Navigation & Piloting

When approaching Maya Cove from the west, it is well to remember that the reef extends from Whelk Point all the way to the buoyed entrance at the northeastern end of the reef. Entry should be made under power.

From the Buck Island waypoint (BV103) the channel markers are easy to see and are located under a promontory of land approximately 75-100 feet high. The channel is well marked with four sets of red and green buoys but be aware that the channel takes a sharp turn to port at the inner green buoy. Proceed into the anchorage past the inner red marker, but do not head too far into the southwest corner of the cove as it shoals off rapidly.

BUCK ISLAND

From the waypoint (BV103) work your way up into the northeastern corner where you can anchor in 7-10 feet of water on a sand bottom off the western shore. Very few yachts anchor here which makes it even more attractive. In certain sea conditions the anchorage can be rolly, but generally it provides a safe anchorage. Do not go too far up toward the northwest tip of the island since it shoals off rapidly. There is no passage between Buck Island and Tortola and no landing is permitted on the island itself.

Ashore

Hodges Creek Marina is a full service marina which provides water, ice, and showers; and they monitor VHF channel 16.

Calamaya, the marina restaurant, serves a variety of Caribbean and Mediterranean cuisine for breakfast, lunch and dinner. The restaurant has a ring side view of the activity in the marina while you are dining.

Sail Caribbean Divers (a PADI Gold Palm Five Star Resort) maintain their headquarters at the Hodges Creek Marina and offer dive tours and instruction. Nestled into the corner of the reef on the southern end of the Cove is Charlie 'T's Lobster House – an excellent restaurant and bar. Go carefully in the dinghy as it is very shallow (or walk). Charlie 'T's has fabulous views of the Sir Francis Drake Channel and the reef that protects it. This is a favorite place to have a Pusser's Pain Killer, a delicious meal and enjoy the view of the surrounding reef and the boats sailing by in Sir Francis Drake Channel.

There are two other marinas you will see in this anchorage, but they are private.

There is a small anchorage in 7 to 10 feet of water on the western shore of Buck Island. Very few yachts anchor here. In certain sea conditions, it can be very rolly, but usually is quite comfortable.

Take care not to go too far toward the northwest tip of the island, as the bottom shoals rapidly. There is no passage between Buck Island and Tortola except by dinghy with the engine tilted up. As this is a privately owned island, going ashore is strictly prohibited.

All Sailors Are Created Equal
Clearly All Charter Vessels Are Not

Nothing says a bareboat has to be bare. Our charter fleet is the newest and best-equipped in the British Virgin Islands, with standard water makers, electric heads, touch-screen Raymarine electronics and more, for unbeatable ease on the seas. Only MarineMax Vacations offers the easy-to-use Max Furler, a down-wind sail that enables fast passages between the islands. A new base in Tortola's Hodges Creek Marina, backed by the most experienced and helpful staff in the industry, further delivers on our promise to provide you with the very best vessels, equipment and service.

CALL OR VISIT US ONLINE
YACHT CHARTER VACATIONS: 888-461-5497 • 813-644-8071
YACHT OWNERSHIP PROGRAM: 866-934-7232 • 813-644-8070
www.MarineMaxVacations.com

Fat Hog's Bay & East End Bay

Waypoint: BV104-18°25.95'N, 64°33.20W
Navigation: 4.2nm NE of Road Harbour;
Services: Restaurants, Fuel, Ice, Water, Provisions, Dive shop, Showers, Garbage disposal

Fat Hog's Bay and East End Bay are located just north of Buck Island and west of the Bluff on the point of Beef Island. These beautiful, well-protected bays are conveniently located in the middle of the BVI cruising grounds and very close to the airport. Surrounded by the area known locally as East End, the bays are well populated by local fishermen and cruisers.

Navigation & Piloting

Both anchorages are easily accessible from Sir Francis Drake Channel by leaving Buck Island to port and transiting between the green can and Red Rock, a 20-foot high rock formation marking the southwestern end of Red Rock reef. Inside of the entrance be aware that Fat Hog's Bay shoals off to the west so head due north to Harbourview Marina or turn to the east toward the moorings field or the buoyed channel into Penn's Landing Marina. Do not attempt to cross directly from Harbourview Marina to Penn's as there is a shallow area to the west of the marked channel.

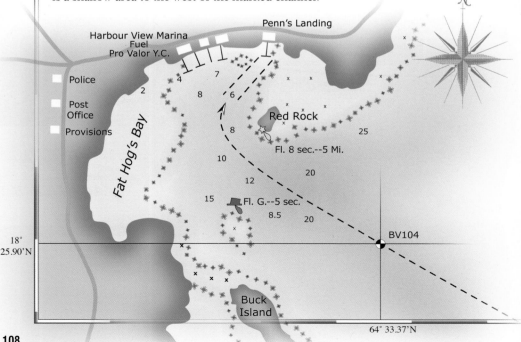

RED ROCK

Fl.G.5s

N

Anchoring & Mooring

The average depth from Red Rock into East End Bay is about 9 feet (2.7m) with good holding ground and excellent protection behind the reef. You may pick up one of the white mooring balls on the eastern side of the channel. Please do not anchor within the mooring field or obstruct the channel by anchoring inside of it. You may call ahead to Harbourview or Penn's Landing on VHF channel 16.

Ashore

Three marinas operate within Fat Hogs Bay: Harbourview Marina, James Young Marina and Penn's Landing. These marinas are conveniently very close to the airport.

The modern, well-maintained Harbourview Marina has dockage for vessels from 50 – 80 feet in length. They are open from 8am to 5pm daily and monitor VHF channel 16.

Amenities include ice, water, diesel fuel (through Pro Valor Charters), laundry facilities (make sure to bring some quarters), showers and a few charming rooms for those wishing to get a break from the boat for a night or two. An outside bar is available pool-side for marina guests and others to gather for an afternoon drink.

Harbourview Marina includes the following businesses: Harbourview Marine Supply Chandlery and UBS Dive Center. Kong Ming Asian Restaurant is located across the street along with Emile's, and the Cantina serving Mexican fare. UBS Dive Center offers individualized dive trips from a wide selection of sites, as well as rendezvous diving.

Pro Valor Charters operates from the Harbourview Marina. It is the location of their offices and is where the charterers start and end their charter.

The Harbourview Marina is getting a face lift! New owners have updated the docks and installed lights both above the docks and below so you have a good view of the fish. A new poolside restaurant is planned in the very near future.

Pro Valor sell diesel and use the James Young Marina for maintenance and slip rentals. They have also had moorings installed by Moor Seacure.for rent at $25.00 per night. Moorings can be paid for at the Pro Valor office or to a staff member at the James Young Marina.

Rite Breeze Food Market has a fairly new store right next door to the Harbourview Marina offering a deli counter, fresh meats and great produce. Gone are the days of heading to Road Town by taxi to pick up provisions. Parham General Store is also just a walk away between Penn's Landing and Harbourview Marina where you'll find household items and many fix-it tools and parts – they are closed on Sundays. There is an ATM at Thelma's just east one block from the James Young Marina dock.

Penn's Landing offers water, ice, showers and overnight dockage. Moorings maintained by Moor Seacure can be paid at Penn's. The Red Rock Restaurant & Bar at Penn's is open for dinner and offers great casual seaside dining. The Sailors Ketch Seafood Market supplies a wide variety of freshly-caught local fish in addition to imported seafood and chicken. Alphonso's Gas Station is located just east of Penn's where you can purchase dinghy fuel and ice.

Looking Northwest across Beef Island toward Guana Sound

TRELLIS BAY (BEEF ISLAND)

Waypoint: BV106 - 18°27.30'N 64°31.50W
Navigation: 5nm due west of Virgin Gorda Yacht Harbour; .75nm S Marina Cay
Services: Moorings, Provisions, Restaurants, Internet, Ice, Water Sports rentals, Ferry Service, Art Studio and Gift Shops

Tortola

Located on the north shore of Beef Island, Trellis Bay was once a major anchorage in the BVI with a hotel, large marine railway and jetty. The railway and hotel have since been abandoned and the ferries servicing the surrounding islands and Virgin Gorda now use the jetty. The anchorage is well protected even in adverse weather conditions and its proximity to the airport makes it convenient for embarking and disembarking passengers, as it is a short 5 minute walk from the terminal to the beach bars lining the inner bay. Bellamy Cay, home to The Last Resort is centrally located in the bay. Over the years, the activity of the local residents within the bay has developed into a community that provides a variety of services and entertainment to the visiting yachtsmen.

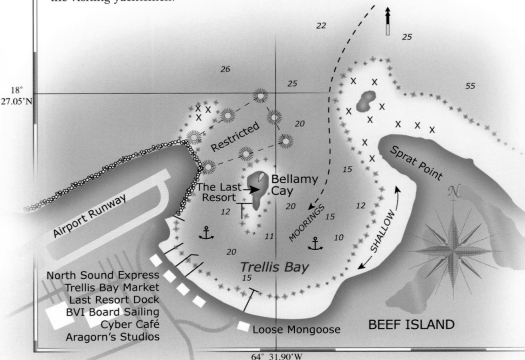

North Sound Express
Trellis Bay Market
Last Resort Dock
BVI Board Sailing
Cyber Café
Aragorn's Studios

Loose Mongoose

BEEF ISLAND

64° 31.90'W

Navigation & Piloting

Since the extension of the airport, the navigation into and out of the bay has continued to evolve. Approaching Trellis Bay from the east, you will see a yellow north marker due north of the rocks at the tip of Sprat Point (locally known as bird-shit rock), leave it to port and enter the bay via the channel between Bellamy Cay and Sprat Point.

The yellow buoys (to starboard) mark the extremities of the airport runway "restricted" area and vessels entering the bay should leave them and Bellamy Cay to starboard.

Approaching

Vessels transiting from the west across the end of the runway, must stay outside of the yellow buoys marking the designated restricted area and are requested to contact the airport on VHF 16 to report course and mast height. Staging an approach further to the north is a better plan.

Yachtsmen should also be aware that no vessel may enter or exit the bay from the west side of Bellamy Cay.

Anchoring & Mooring

Although the bay may often appear crowded, there is usually enough room to accommodate the fleet. Numerous moorings are available at the going rate and payment is usually collected by dinghy or can be paid for at the Loose Mongoose ashore. Although anchoring is tight, because of the mooring balls there is usually some room at the southeastern end of the bay.

THE FIRE BALL
FULL MOON PARTY

2013				2014			
Jan	26	Jul	22	Jan	15	Jul	12
Feb	25	Aug	20	Feb	14	Aug	10
Mar	27	Sep	19	Mar	16	Sep	8
Apr	25	Oct	18	Apr	15	Oct	8
May	24	Nov	17	May	14	Nov	6
Jun	23	Dec	17	Jun	12	Dec	6

The B.V.I.'s top cultural event of the month.
A family-friendly beach party with a West Indian buffet,
local music, Moko Jumbi dancers and Aragorn's fire sculptures.
PLAN YOUR VACATION AROUND THE MOON!
TRELLIS BAY VILLAGE

At the southwestern end of the bay there is ongoing ferry traffic so allow room for them to maneuver. When entering the bay and transiting from the southeast side of Bellamy Cay to the southwest do not turn too quickly as a reef extends from Bellamy Cay south into the Bay, the end of which is occasionally marked with a buoy. The area to the south of Sprat Point is very shallow so avoid it. There are usually some shallow draft cruising vessels tucked in there giving the impression that the anchorage extends further than it does.

On the eve of a full moon party, it is recommended that you make plans to arrive early afternoon in order to secure a mooring or anchorage.

Ashore

The community of Trellis Bay offers an interesting and fun combination of restaurants, water sports, entertainment, local artists and local crafts. And now organic fruits and vegetables are cultivated by Aragorn from his Good Moon Farm on the fertile north side of Tortola. He sells them to the anchored boats in the bay or they can be purchased at Aragorn's Studio. It is a short trip from Marina Cay or Scrub Island if you want to visit this interesting enclave on your way to or from a day of sailing.

Check for the date of the Trellis Bay monthly full moon party in their ad above complete with dancing mocko jumbies (stilt dancers) and amazing fire

TRELLIS BAY

115

balls (created by artist Aragorn) at the water's edge with dancing and live music. The moon is bright and lights up the bay; the breeze is cool and the activity on the beach is lively and not to be missed!

The Last Resort on Bellamy Cay, a tiny tropical island, is an absolute must on a cruise around the Virgins. The Last Resort has had several donkeys, the most recent of which is said to be Mary. A little long in the tooth, it sounds as though Mary is still spirited, happily accepting carrots to munch on.

The meals here are excellent as is the atmosphere. Happy hour is from 5-6pm daily with half priced drinks and bar snacks. Dinner is from 6:30 – 9:30 daily. Lunch is available during the season and on weekends. Call before heading out to confirm they are serving. Live music is provided nightly by the singing chef and/or the "house" band, with Tony Snell himself making the occasional guest appearances.

Located on the beach on the south shore of Trellis Bay is the Beef Island Guest House with a bar and restaurant called De Loose Mongoose. Happy hour is daily from 5-7pm and on Sunday they provide a barbecue with live entertainment. The Beef Island Guest House also has a few rooms available.

Trellis Bay is a haven for artists and local craftsmen. Aragorn's Studio is the creation of Aragorn Dick-Read, who works in

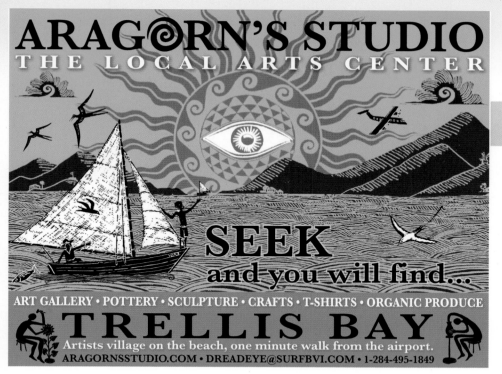

copper, ceramics and silkscreen. The studio is identified as the building with the thatched roof on the beach. Aragorn is famous for his copper sculptures and one of a kind wood-cut and hand-painted fish print t-shirts. Courses in pottery and crafts are taught in Aragorn's Studio. It is fascinating to go ashore and watch the artists and artisans at work. Keep an eye out for his boat laden with t-shirts, crafts, fresh bread and organic fruits as he stops at the boats in the anchorage.

Trellis Bay is home of Gli Gli, the largest Carib Indian dugout sailing canoe in the Caribbean. Gli Gli is available for day charters, providing a unique and historical sailing experience. More of the traditional West Indian vessels will be built in Trellis Bay, affording a unique opportunity for visitors to see the boats from earlier days.

For those who wish to learn to windsurf, the BVI Boardsailing School is located on the beach next to Aragorn's. Windsurfing is an increasingly popular sport in the Virgin Islands due to the steady winds combined with the consistently good weather. Trellis Bay provides an excellent learning environment.

The Cyber Café has a row of computers with high speed internet access. When you are finished catching up with your email, the Trellis Bay Kitchen makes excellent sandwiches and smoothies. As with all of the Trellis Bay establishments, it is close to the airport and makes a great place to wait for your flight.

Stop in at the HIHO shop ("hook in hold on") for all kinds of tropical clothing and surf wear. HIHO is also the sponsor of the

annual Highland Spring windsurfing races in Tortola, which draws contestants from all over the world.

D'Best Cup features a variety of espresso drinks, ice cream, smoothies, pastries, beer, wine and mixed drinks. This is a great place to grab a coffee or a smoothie and a snack after checking in at the airport and also a last chance to purchase a gift for the folks back home, or a souvenir for yourself.

The brightly colored Trellis Bay Market provides all the necessary items when you are running low on provisions, including cigars, beer, wine, liquor, bread, fresh and frozen meats and vegetables. Even ice cream can be purchased and rushed back to the boat's freezer. Trellis Bay Market is easily found at the base of the ferry dock.

Don't miss the Many Splendid 'Tings gift shop. Jan Dart has some very special items to bring back with you. The shop will be open daily starting November 1. She carries local artists' jewelry, books, prints, hand painted maps of the Virgin Islands, and hand painted t-shirts along with other splendid 'tings.

Aragorn at work

Trellis Bay Art Community

MARINA CAY
SCRUB ISLAND & CAM BAY

Waypoint: BV106 18°27.30'N, 64°31.50'W

Navigation: 8nm NE Road Harbour, 4.5nm west of VGYH

Services: Restaurant, hotel, fuel, ice, water, garbage disposal, WiFi, Pussers Store, Ferry to Trellis Bay

Tortola

Marina Cay, nestled behind a reef and lying between the islands of Camanoe and Scrub, is easy to enter and provides visiting yachtsmen with good holding in an all-weather anchorage. There are numerous mooring balls available, therefore limiting anchoring to the northeast or northwest behind the mooring field.

Navigation & Piloting

Approaching Marina Cay from the east, you have three choices. The recommended route is to go around the north end of the island. There is good water up to the large,

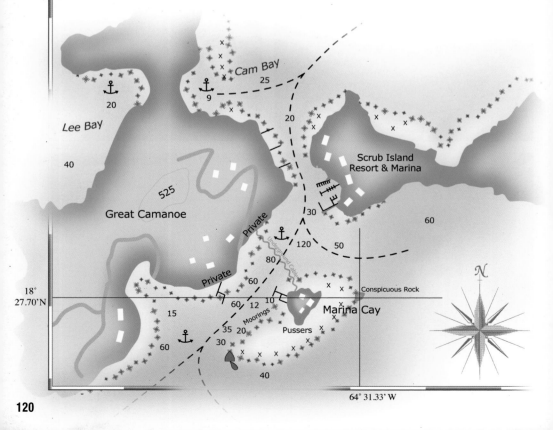

SCRUB IS.

MARINA CAY

GREAT CAMANOE

Rocks
Awash

N

conspicuous rock that marks the northeast end of the reef. Leave it to port and pass between Marina Cay and Scrub Island into the anchorage.

Alternatively, approaching from the south or west, you should favor the southern tip of Great Camanoe. A red buoy marks the southwest extremity of the reef, leave it to starboard as you enter the anchorage.

If the light is good and you are approaching from the north or northeast, it is possible to approach Marina Cay between Scrub Island and Great Camanoe. This transit should be made under power and only in good light. From waypoint BV107 proceed through the channel which although narrow carries 25 feet. On your port hand will be the Scrub Island Resort and Marina and ahead will be Marina Cay.

Anchoring & Mooring

Numerous fully maintained moorings are available on a first come basis. These moorings are maintained by Moor-Seacure and payment can be made at the marina. If you are anchoring, keep clear of the mooring field by anchoring further to the northeast between Marina Cay and Scrub Island. Also be aware of the underwater cable between Great Camanoe and Marina Cay, just to the north of the dock. There are signs indicating the location but they are not always evident.

Additional anchoring space is available behind the mooring field to the west and southwest.

Camanoe Island is private and off limits to visiting yachtsmen. Please be considerate with respect to the proximity of the private homes on Camanoe, keeping noise levels down and respecting the residents' privacy.

Ashore

Marina Cay has a full service fuel dock offering ice, water, garbage disposal, laundry facilities and showers for yachtsmen. They monitor channel 16. Pusser's Marina Cay provides free ferry service from the main dock in Trellis Bay – check with them for departure times.

Marina Cay is an amazing islet almost surrounded by a reef. It is an idyllic spot, the quintessential tropical island. Ashore you will find a Pusser's Company Store stocked with their tropical and nautical clothing, unique accessories, gifts and a small mini-mart.

The hilltop bar at the Robb White House on the highest point of Marina Cay is a great place for a drink with a spectacular view and a happy hour with entertainment. There is an internet café in the house, and much of the island, including the anchorage, has free WiFi access.

The beach restaurant offers casual dining at the grill with live entertainment often. Don't forget to order a Pusser's Painkiller to put you in the party mood. The island even boasts four charming rooms and two villas for those wanting some time ashore. There is excellent snorkeling on the reef around the island. Dive BVI offers dive trips and instruction daily. An air station is in operation and Ocean Kayaks and Hobie Cat rentals are available.

SCRUB ISLAND MARINA

Navigation: Approach from the north via Waypoint BV107
(Cam Bay) between Scrub and Camanoe or follow directions to Marina Cay
Services: Ice, Water, Showers, Restaurants, Hotel, Provisions, Ferry to Trellis Bay

Just to the north of Marina Cay is the BVI's luxury development: Scrub Island Resort, Spa & Marina. The marina is tucked into the western end of Scrub Island and protected by a natural reef and breakwater. This 55-slip, full-service marina was opened in mid-2010 and is equipped to accommodate vessels up to 160 feet. In addition to the marina, the resort offers two restaurants, a gourmet market and café and world-class hotel rooms overlooking the marina. The restaurants are open to visiting yachtsmen and a dinghy dock is located at the foot of the middle dock.

The marina has a maximum depth of 14 feet, but vessels over 7 feet should contact the marina prior to arrival. The approach depth is 25 feet. The marina monitors VHF channel 16.

Ashore

The Scrub Island Marina offers 55 deep water slips available for lease or transient docking, and is equipped to accommodate vessels up to 160 feet. Available at the marina is ice, water, electricity (110v/220v with 30 amp, 50 amp and 100 amp), garbage disposal, and wireless internet. You can also purchase provisions at the gourmet market near the marina.

Facilities include restrooms, showers and changing facilities. Laundry valet is also available. Scrub Island is an amazing resort close enough to Tortola for easy access with ferries and water taxis.

Tierra! Tierra! is the name of the restaurant overlooking the pool and down the channel. At night the lights from Beef Island and Trellis Bay sparkle. It is casual, open air dining, serving lunch and dinner. The menu features American and Caribbean cuisine.

For more elegant dining you will want to try the Caravela restaurant. Named for the wooden caravel ships from the 1500s, of which Columbus' Pinta was one. The Caravela Restaurant serves breakfast and dinner in a contemporary room with sweeping views of Camanoe Pass and surrounding waters.

You can get to Scrub Island from Tortola by water taxi if you aren't on a boat. The water taxi leaves from Trellis Bay at the North Sound water taxi dock (in Trellis Bay). It is a short trip over to Scrub Island. The water taxi is free for resort and marina guests and runs hourly from 6:30am to 10:30pm.

Entrance to Cam Bay

CAM BAY

Waypoint: BV107 18°28.55'N 64°31.50'W
Navigation: 0.6nm N Marina Cay; 6.4nm from Mountain Point VG
Services: None

Cam Bay is a small delightful anchorage located on the eastern shore of Great Camanoe. Many of the charter companies have placed it off limits but the crewed charter captains have used it extensively when the charter party needed a little solitude. Cam Bay is not hard to enter but there is limited room once inside so if you see more than four to five boats at anchor you may want to re-group and anchor at Marina Cay or tie up at Scrub Island Marina for the evening.

Tucked in behind the reef you get the cooling effect of the trade winds but retain the calm and protection of the reef.

Navigation

Approaching from the north from waypoint BV107 proceed south toward the Scrub Island Cut, Cam Bay will be to starboard.

The entrance to the bay is protected by a reef that starts at the northern end and continues south for some distance. The entrance is about 200 feet wide and carries 10 feet of depth. The reef from the southern end of the bay extends approximately 200 feet to the north before the opening. Enter under power with good light and someone on the bow. Head for the beach before turning to starboard for a short distance and then rounding up within 150 feet of the reef. Drop the anchor in about 10 feet of water, take a quick dive to check the anchor is well set and enjoy the solitude. Do not proceed too far to the north since the water shoals off quickly.

Approaching from the south, via Scrub Island Cut, Cam Bay will open up to port. Make sure you have identified the location of the reef before making your entrance. Do not anchor in the entrance since you will not benefit from the protection of the reef and will probably have to endure a rolly uncomfortable evening.

CAMANOE PASSAGE

GUANA SOUND

Waypoint: BV109 - 18°27.70'N 64°33.20'W
BV110 - 18°27.70'N 64°35.00'W

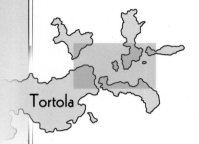

Tortola

Traveling west to Guana Sound from Marina Cay or Trellis Bay, two routes are available and both need to be fully understood prior to starting the transit. The first is the narrow passage between Great and Little Camanoe and the second is between Little Camanoe and Beef Island (Tortola).

CAMANOE PASSAGE

Many of the charter operators insist that only the narrow passage between Great Camanoe and Little Camanoe be used. The channel, although narrow, carries nearly 20 feet of depth and it is recommended that it be negotiated under power, since the wind will become erratic due to the land formation. Stay to the center of the channel and identify the rocks on the northeast corner of Little Camanoe before turning to port and into the Guana Channel. When a ground swell is present during the winter months the water can break heavily on this small reef.

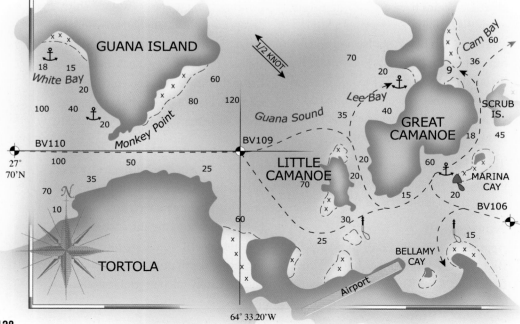

The Camanoe Passage

BEEF ISLAND PASSAGE

There are two notable obstructions to navigation to be aware of when using this passage to pass into Guana Sound, the reef that extends from the southwest end of Little Camanoe and the shoal that lies to the south of the yellow cardinal marker due south of the Camanoe passage. Due to airport restrictions (see Trellis Bay) it is suggested that your approach from the east is toward the southern tip of Little Camanoe until you identify the yellow cardinal marker which must be left to port. Once past the marker do not turn west, but head southwest until you are clear of the reef. The reef to starboard extends southwest from Little Camanoe, after which you are in deep water and the approach to Guana Sound is clear of obstruction.

THE GUANA CHANNEL

Heading due west from the north end of Little Camanoe, toward Monkey Point, you will enter Guana Sound and the Guana channel that divide Tortola and Guana Island. Although the channel looks narrow from a distance, there is a minimum of 1/4 mile at the narrowest point and 25 feet of water under your keel. Sailing to the west with the wind on your quarter you should be able to sail through. Keep to the center of the channel leaving Guana and Monkey Point to starboard. As you pass the point you will see yachts at anchor across the sandy area that joins Monkey Point to the rest of Guana Island.

LEE BAY (GREAT CAMANOE)

Waypoint: BV109 (Guana Sound) 18°27.65'N 64°33.70'W

Navigation: 2.1nm due E from Monkey Point; 2.7nm NW Trellis Bay

Services: None

Although often ignored in favor of the more popular anchorages in this region, Lee Bay on the west coast of Great Camanoe, provides a quite respite for those wishing more seclusion. Lee Bay is well protected in most weather conditions and cooled by the breeze that flows over the saddle of land that provides a backdrop for Cam Bay on the other side of the hill. The approach to Lee Bay from the east is via the passage between Great and Little Camanoe. The passage can carry 20 feet and although narrow, is straightforward. There is a rock on the northeast end of Little Camanoe, be sure to identify it and stay clear toward the center of the channel. Lee Bay will open up to starboard. Approaching from the west from Guana and Monkey Point, head to the northern end of Little Camanoe until you can identify the Bay. The entrance is straightforward with no obstruction.

Anchoring & Mooring

The best spot to anchor is in the northeast corner of the bay in front of the saddle of the hill in 15 feet of water. The holding ground is good and apart from the occasional low coral growth, the bottom is clear. Please take care not to anchor in coral.

When a northerly sea condition is present during the winter months and surf is breaking on the northern tip of Camanoe, the resulting ground swell can work its way into this anchorage. Depending upon the condition, a second anchor should be deployed or an alternative anchorage identified until sea conditions return to normal.

White Bay, Guana Island

WHITE
BAY

GUANA
IS.

N

MONKEY
PT.

Monkey Point, Guana Island, with White Bay in background

MONKEY POINT/GUANA ISLAND

Waypoint: BV110 - 18°27.30'N 64°35.00'W

Navigation: 1.7nm due west from Little Camanoe; 4.5nm E of Rough Point (BV112)

Services: National Park Moorings

At the southern tip of Guana Island is a delightful anchorage known as Monkey Point. An excellent day anchorage, Monkey Point is situated on the western side of the rocky outcrop that marks the southern extremity of the island. There are several National Park moorings in place for those with a permit. (Yellow balls are for commercial use only).

The small beach area and excellent snorkeling make this a great lunch stop. When there is a northerly swell running, the anchorage can be rolly.

Monkey Point, Guana Island

WHITE BAY/GUANA ISLAND

Waypoint: BV110 - 18°27.30'N 64°35.00'W
Navigation: 4.5 nm W of Rough Point Waypoint (BV112)
Services: None (This is a private Island)

Easily identified by the long stretch of beautiful white beach, White Bay is located on the southwest side of Guana less than a mile from Monkey Point. The anchorage, located at the northern end, is relatively deep (15–25 feet) and when anchoring be careful not to swing into the coral heads closer to the shore as the wind will tend to back in this area.

To the north of the anchorage you will notice the rock formation that looks like the head of a large Iguana for which the island was named. This is a private island and trespassing is prohibited. Beach access is available to the high water mark throughout the BVI.

LITTLE BAY/TORTOLA

Navigation: .75nm SW of Monkey Point
Services: None

Sailing west from Monkey Point or east from Jost Van Dyke, there are numerous white sandy beaches apparent to the south. They are all exposed, but when the weather is calm, we recommend Little Bay as a lunch stop only. If there is any surf activity apparent on the beach, do not anchor here. Use the anchorage at Monkey Point or continue further east through the cut. The bottom is sandy and holding is good in 15 feet of water.

EMERGENCIES
VISAR (Virgin Island Search and Rescue)
VHF channel 16
Tel: 767 (SOS), or 999, or 911, or 284-494-2512 (494-help)
www.visar.org

BRANDYWINE BAY

RESTAURANTS
Brandywine Estate Restaurant
Open lunch and dinner
Closed Tuesdays
Reservations requested
Tel: 284-495-2301

MAYA COVE/ HODGES CREEK

MARINAS
Hodges Creek Marina
VHF channel 16
Tel: 284-494-5000

DIVE SHOPS
Sail Caribbean Divers
VHF channel 16
Tel: 284-495-1675
www.sailcaribbeandivers.com

RESTAURANTS
Calamaya
Tel: 284-495-2126
Breakfast 7am-10:30,
Lunch 11:30-3, Dinner 6:30-11pm
Calamaya-Restaurant on Facebook

Pusser's East - Charlie T's Lobster House
Tel: 284-495-1010
Open daily 11am-10pm
Serving burgers, pizza, rotis for lunch and an array of seafood and steak in the evening
www.pussers.com

FAT HOGS BAY

MARINAS
Harbourview Marina
VHF channel 16
Tel: 284-495-0165
www.provalorcharters.com

Penn's Landing Marina
VHF Channel 16
Tel: 284-495-1134
Penns-Landing-Marina-Tortola-BVI on F

CHARTER COMPANY
Pro Valor Charters
VHF channel 16
Tel: 284-495-1931
www.provalorcharters.com

CHANDLERY
Harbourview Marine Supply Chandlery
Tel: 284-495-2586
www.bviharbourview.com

PROVISIONING
Rite Breeze Food Market
Tel: 284-495-1682
www.rtwbvi.com/store-locations

Sailors Ketch Seafood Market
Tel: 284-495-1100
www.sailorsketch.com

RESTAURANTS
Kong Ming Asian Terrace Restaurant
Tel: 284-495-1174

Emile's Restaurant & Cantina
Tel: 284-495-1775

Red Rock Restaurant & Bar
Tel: 284-495-1646
www.redrockbvi.net

DIVING
UBS Dive Center
Tel: 284-494-0024
www.scubabvi.com

TRELLIS BAY

RESTAURANTS
Last Resort
Tel: 284-495-2520
Serving dinner and
drinks 6:30-9:30pm
Reservations requested
Great entertainment
Use their hotline
telephone located in
Trellis Bay for water taxi
service
Dinghies may tie up at
their dock

De Loose Mongoose
VHF channel 16
Tel: 284-495-2303
Open Tuesday through
Saturday
8am-10pm
www.beefislandguest
house.com

D'Best Cup
On the beach at
Trellis Bay Monday
through Saturday

Serves breakfast,
espresso, lunches 6:30
am to 6pm, Sundays
from 9am to 6pm

Trellis Kitchen
Tel: 284-495-2447
International food serving
local juices, smoothies,
sandwiches and pizza
Open daily 7am-11pm
www.trelliskitchen.
posterous.com

SHOPS
Aragorn's Studio
Selling art, pottery, t-
shirts and gift items
Tel: 284-495-1849
www.aragornsstudio.com

Many Splendid 'Tings
Open daily
Gift items, hand painted
T-shirts, hand painted
maps and charts, local
jewelry and more

HIHO
Caribbean clothing
Tel: 284-494-7694
http://shop.go-hiho.com

PROVISIONING
Trellis Bay Market
Tel: 284-495-1421
Trellisbaymarket on FB

Good Moon Farm
Locally grown organic
fruits and vegetables
Available at Aragorn's
Studio
Tel: 284-495-1849
www.goodmoonfarm.com

Cyber Café
Next to Trellis Kitchen
Provides computer use
and Internet connections
www.windsurfing.vi/
cyber.html

FERRY SERVICE
North Sound Express
From Beef Island to
North Sound
Tel: 284-495-2138

Marina Cay Ferry
From Trellis Bay to
Marina Cay
Tel: 284-494-2174
www.pussers.com/
t-marina-cay-
reservations.aspx

Scrub Island Ferry
To Scrub Island from
Trellis Bay
Leaves Trellis Bay
6:30am-10:30pm
Leaves Scrub Island 15
minutes before the hour
www.scrubisland.com/
maps-directions-
transportation.html

MARINA CAY

MARINAS
Pusser's Marina Cay
VHF Channel 16
Tel: 284-494-2174
Fuel dock, ice, water
www.pussers.com/
t-marina-cay.aspx

RESTAURANTS
Pusser's Marina Cay
VHF Channel 16
Tel: 284-494-2174
Serving international and
local fare
Lunch and dinner
Reservations requested
Free ferry service;
call for schedule
www.pussers.com/t-
marina-cay.aspx

HOTELS
Pusser's Marina Cay
Featuring 4 single rooms
and 2 villas
Tel: 284-494-2174
www.pussers.com/
t-marina-cay.aspx

SHOPS
Pusser's Company Store
Full line of Pusser's
apparel with
Limited grocery items
www.pussers.com

DIVE TRIPS
Dive BVI
Tel: 284-440-3440
Air fills, equipment, tours

SCRUB ISLAND

MARINAS
Scrub Island Marina
VHF channel 16
284-440-3440
www.scrubisland.com/
scrub-island-marina.html

RESTAURANTS
Tierra! Tierra!
Open daily for lunch and
dinner

Open air, poolside
Reservations requested
Tel: 284-440-3440
www.scrubisland.com/
dining-on-scrub-
island.html

Caravela
Modern elegance
Open daily for breakfast
and dinner
Reservations requested
(check for dress code)
Tel:284-440-3440
www.scrubisland.com/
dining-on-scrub-
island.html

DIVE TRIPS
Dive BVI
Tel: 284-440-3440
Air fills, equipment,
tours

WESTERN TORTOLA

Charts

NV.Charts: St.Thomas to Anegada: Kit: C-13 &14
NIMA: 25641, Imray-Iolaire: A-231
Admiralty Leisure: 5640-5&6

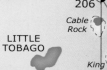

Mercurius
Rock

BV
206

Cable
Rock

GREAT TOBAGO

4.2 NM

LITTLE
TOBAGO

BV
205

King
Rock

5 NM

4.3 NM

N

THATCH CAY

UV
613

Middle Passage

GRASS CAY

MINGO CAY

CONGO CAY

UV
502

Leeward Passage

SAINT THOMAS

64° 50'W

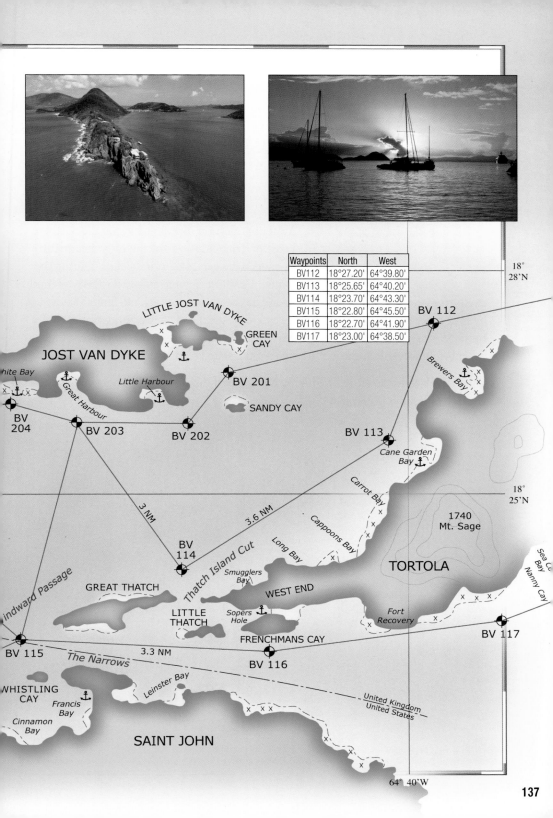

Waypoints	North	West
BV112	18°27.20'	64°39.80'
BV113	18°25.65'	64°40.20'
BV114	18°23.70'	64°43.30'
BV115	18°22.80'	64°45.50'
BV116	18°22.70'	64°41.90'
BV117	18°23.00'	64°38.50'

18° 28'N

BV 112

LITTLE JOST VAN DYKE

GREEN CAY

JOST VAN DYKE

hite Bay

Little Harbour

BV 201

SANDY CAY

Brewers Bay

Great Harbour

BV 204

BV 203

BV 202

BV 113

Cane Garden Bay

18° 25'N

Carrot Bay

3 NM

3.6 NM

Cappoons Bay

BV 114

Thatch Island Cut

Long Bay

1740 Mt. Sage

TORTOLA

Sea Co Bay

Nanny Cay

Smugglers Bay

GREAT THATCH

indward Passage

LITTLE THATCH

Sopers Hole

WEST END

Fort Recovery

BV 115

BV 117

The Narrows

3.3 NM

FRENCHMANS CAY

BV 116

WHISTLING CAY

Francis Bay

Leinster Bay

United Kingdom
United States

Cinnamon Bay

SAINT JOHN

64° 40'W

137

BREWER'S BAY

Waypoint: BV112 – 18°27.20'N 64°39.80'W
Navigation: 2nm North of Cane Garden Bay;
5nm West of Guana Is.
Services: Beach Bar

Tortola

Without question, Brewer's Bay, on the northern coast of Tortola, is one of the most beautiful unspoiled bays in the Virgin Islands. During the winter months it is vulnerable to northerly ground swells owing to the northerly exposure and has been posted as an "off-limits" anchorage by many charter companies due to the extensive coral and charted underwater cables. In the 25 years we have been writing this cruising guide we are unaware of anyone fouling the cable, however it is our job to point out the stated obstructions.

When the weather is settled we highly recommend this anchorage where you will find yourselves in limited company.

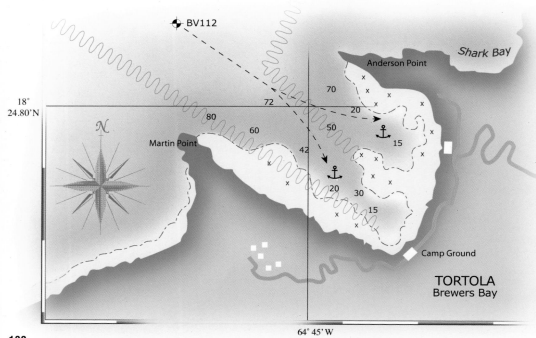

Navigation & Piloting

Brewer's Bay is divided by a reef that extends from the shore out toward the northwest. There are two anchorages; the northern one which is more protected from the swell that works its way round the point, and the southern anchorage which is easier to negotiate, but a little more exposed. Both anchorages require good light overhead and someone posted on the bow to spot for coral heads. Do not enter this anchorage in times of northerly ground swells!

From the waypoint (BV112) west of Anderson Point head into Brewer's Bay on a course of 120°m. This will take you toward the lower (right) anchorage. It is suggested that you visually locate the center or middle reef before working your way into the anchorage where you can drop the hook in 15-20 feet of water. Do not anchor in coral and do not pick up any moorings.

Ashore

While the snorkeling is excellent, time should also be taken to explore ashore. For those interested in a shore side walk, it would be worthwhile walking up the road to the east, toward Mount Healthy to see the ruins of Tortola's only remaining windmill. Only the base of the original mill has survived the passing years, along with the broken remains of the old distillery building. There is also a very casual beach bar called Nicole's.

Brewer's Bay Campground is located on the beach at Brewer's Bay.

Mount Healthy Windmill.

139

Cane Garden Bay

Tortola

Waypoint: BV113 – 18°25.65'N; 64°40.20'W
Navigation: 4nm NE Soper's Hole;
5nm East Great Harbour, JVD
Services: Moorings, Ice, Water, Fuel, ATM,
Restaurants, Entertainment, Provisioning, Garbage
Disposal, Taxi

Regarded by some as one of the more beautiful anchorages in the BVI, Cane Garden Bay is picture postcard material, with a white palm fringed beach stretching the entire length of the bay and a backdrop of green hills climbing 1500 feet to Sage Mountain and the rain forest. There are times when you will see beach chairs along the beach. These are for cruise ship passengers visiting from their ship.

When the weather is settled Cane Garden is a delightful anchorage with good holding, however, during the winter months, when the northerly ground swells build and the surf is breaking on the reef, it is advisable to seek another anchorage.

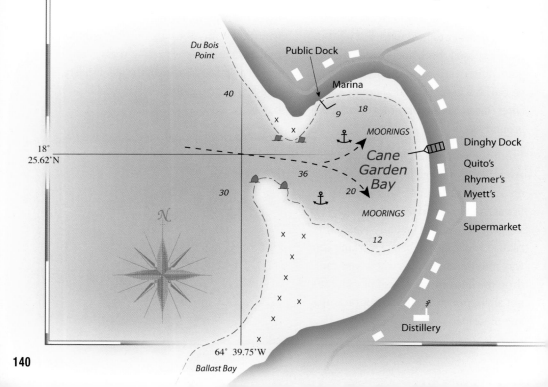

Navigation & Piloting

Approaching from the west, you will sail past Smuggler's Cove, Belmont, Long Bay and Carrot Bay before reaching Cane Garden Bay. If you have any doubt, or your GPS is not working, line up the south side of Jost Van Dyke directly under the peak of Tobago and this range will bring you to the entrance.

The entrance to Cane Garden is toward the northern end of the bay; the reef extends both north and south and is marked with two sets of red and green buoys, one of which is invariably off station. Enter between the buoys and once well inside the reef you will have plenty of room to anchor on a sand bottom or pick up one of the numerous mooring balls. The various establishments usually send an emissary out in a dinghy to collect mooring fees just about the time you are settling into the first gin and tonic.

Anchoring & Mooring

When anchoring, keep clear of the marker buoys designating the swimming area. The bottom affords excellent holding in 15-20 feet of water. The moorings usually identify the establishment responsible for collecting the fees.

Owing to the mountainous backdrop to the bay, the wind tends to change direction, so check your swinging room in relation to other vessels, particularly if you are on an anchor and close to the mooring field. Please exercise caution maneuvering through the bay as there are often swimmers making their way across the bay by way of the great circle route. If there is a northerly ground swell developing, the prudent skipper will seek another anchorage.

Ashore

To experience a sunset at Cane Garden Bay is nothing less than a special magic that creates an unforgettable memory. It is a quintessential Caribbean beach with the sounds of reggae in the background, the palm leaves rustling in the trade winds and the long white beach framing the clear turquoise waters of the bay.

The dinghy dock in Cane Garden Bay is located in the middle of the bay by the rocks and it is lighted at night. On the far eastern side of the bay is the Cane Garden Bay public dock where you can tie up to fill your water and fuel tanks and buy ice at Hodges Gas Station. However, there are no overnight facilities at this dock. The dock head has approximately 9 feet of water, be sure to check the depth at the dock before moving your boat there. Make sure not to cross into the swimming area (marked with white buoys) in your boat.

Cane Garden Bay is lined by several terrific beach bars for the choosing. You can usually hear the live music from the anchorage – jump in your dinghy and head for shore to rock the night away!

There is almost always live entertainment nightly at one establishment or another, or at several! Check ashore to find where the music will be on any given night.

Next to the dinghy dock is Quito's Gazebo serving lunch and dinner. Quito performs alone and with his band, The Edge, several nights a week. Quito's is a favorite amongst both visitors and locals. The place is jamming when the band is playing!

Just west of Quito's on the beach is Al Henley's Big Banana Paradise Club open from 7am serving delicious breakfasts, lunch, dinner and drinks at the bar inside, or on the deck outside.

Rhymer's Beach Bar and Restaurant further west along the beach is the pink building. Rhymer's serves breakfast, lunch and dinner daily with live entertainment on special occasions. Ice, telephones, showers, and a small market, stocking most necessities, are available on the premises.

Still going west along the beach is Stanley's Welcome Bar, one of the original beach bars in the bay, famous for the palm tree with the tire swing. A storm took the tree and swing down many years ago, but it was always Stanley's landmark. Stanley's serves lunch and dinner from 10am.

Pleasure Boats handles small boat rentals from the beach, with kayaks, pedal boats, motorboats and wind-surfers.

Next down the beach, nestled in the trees, is Myett's Garden & Grille Restaurant. The restaurant is open for breakfast, lunch and dinner daily with reservations. There is live music most nights featuring calypso, fungi or reggae. Check out Olivia's new

expanded gift shop. An ATM is available if you need some cash. For a really relaxing vacation, try their new spa for a massage. The communications center is complete with telephones, fax and computers with high speed internet connections.

The Elm Bar and Gift Shop are open daily until 7pm, 5pm on Sundays. Occasionally they have live music on Sunday afternoons.

Supplies can be purchased from a well-stocked branch of Bobby's Market on the road behind the beach, or at Callwood's Grocery Store, and Rhymer's Beach Bar has a small shop for incidentals.

There is a police station located near Bobby's Market. There is also a dumpster across from Bobby's.

Mr. Callwood's rum distillery affords visiting yachts a glimpse back into history. White and gold rum are still produced from the cane grown on the hillsides and bears the label Arundel from the name of the estate purchased by the Callwood family in the late 1800's. It is recommended that you ask permission prior to wandering through the distillery, and the purchase of a bottle or two is expected.

Soper's Hole/West End

Tortola

Waypoints: BV115(N) 18°22.80'N, 64°45.50'W;
BV116(S) 18°22.70'N, 64°41.90'W
Navigation: 7nm SW Road Harbour;
4.5nm SE Jost Van Dyke
Services: BVI Port of Entry, Provisions, Dockage,
Moorings, Ice, Water, Fuel, Slipway, Restaurants

West End is shown on the charts as Soper's Hole, a very deep well-protected harbor, about a mile long, lying between Frenchman's Cay to the south and Tortola. It is a port of entry for vessels arriving and departing British waters, and a ferry stop between the British Virgin Islands and the U.S. Virgin Islands. Ferries also depart from this bay to Jost Van Dyke.

Navigation & Piloting

Approaching from the north the favored passage would be to enter Soper's Hole between Steele Point at the west end of Tortola and Great Thatch. There is plenty of water but be prepared for some pretty fickle wind changes and occasional heavy gusts off the surrounding hills. If you are entering from Drake's Channel, slip in between Little Thatch and Frenchman's

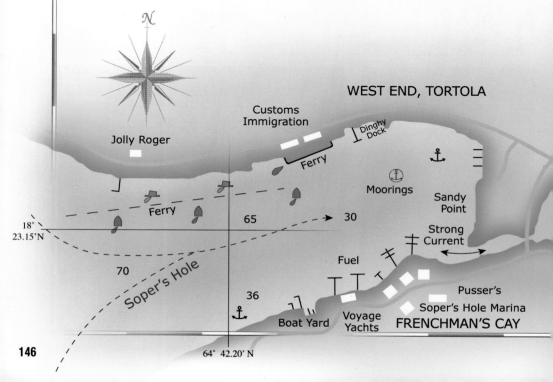

WEST END, TORTOLA

Cay. Once again there is deep water fairly close to shore but be prepared for a strong current.

As you enter the anchorage, there is a buoyed channel on the northern side of the bay. This is largely for commercial craft and leads to the customs and immigration services located at the public/ferry dock; private vessels should proceed east down the center of the anchorage.

Vessels wishing to clear in and out of the BVI are permitted to anchor or pick up a mooring, rather than come up alongside the public dock, and then dinghy over to the customs/immigration office behind the ferry dock leaving the dinghy at the small dock located just east of the ferry dock. This ensures that private yachts clearing in and out do not interrupt the ferry traffic. Please note that only the skipper is required to go ashore (make sure you have a complete crew list, passports, clearance papers, etc) and should a vessel, wishing to enter the BVI, arrive after hours, it is required that the vessel fly a yellow "Q" flag and the crew remain aboard until the vessel is properly cleared.

Anchoring & Mooring

The harbor is so deep in places that yachts will find themselves in 60-70 feet of water. There are numerous mooring balls available at the normal rate for overnight, (no charge for a short lunchtime stop) but should you decide to anchor and assuming the vessel is under 50' the best place is up in the northeast corner near V.I. Shipwrights where the water depth is 20-35 feet.

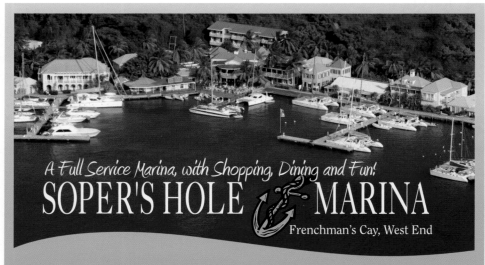

There are moorings available from Soper's Hole Wharf & Marina, which are maintained by Moor-Seacure and can be paid for at the marina. Further to the west there are balls available from Soper's Hole Yacht Services. Be sure not to obstruct the slipway. Most of the marinas monitor VHF 16.

Ashore

The West End customs office is located in the building on the ferry dock and is open Monday through Friday from 8:30am to 4:30pm. For clearance outside of those hours overtime fees will apply. Taxis are available in abundance when the ferries arrive. Some supplies are available from Zelma's Courtesy Grocery & Snack Bar, and ice from the Rocky Willow Bar & Restaurant across from the ferry building. Further west on the road by the ferry dock is the Jolly Roger Inn. Perched next to the sea, with a dinghy dock, it provides views of all the activity in the harbor. The Inn serves breakfast, lunch and dinner, as well as a late night menu including pizza.

On the southeast side of the harbor Soper's Hole Marina will accommodate dockage for vessels up to 180 feet with a 20-foot draft. Both slips and moorings are available along with several charming air-conditioned rooms. This is the location for the Voyage Yacht Charters fleet who manage the marina.

Soper's Hole Yacht Services has a KMI SeaLift that can haul almost any kind of vessel up to a 14 foot draft including monohulls and catamarans. The yard offers fuel, water, showers, provisioning and WiFi. Security is provided around the clock. They are open Monday through Friday from 8am to 4pm.

At the marina you can fill up on fuel, water and ice and dispose of your garbage. Free WiFi is provided for marina guests. There is a First Caribbean Bank ATM located on the premises. The marina monitors VHF 16.

The two story Pusser's Landing features waterfront dining with two restaurants and bars, an outdoor terrace and the Pusser's Company Store. Downstairs, the restaurant offers a more casual ambiance, with an open air bar, on the deck dining and the Company Store which carries Pusser's special line of nautical and tropical clothing, watches, luggage, nautical accessories and even cigars. Upstairs the Crow's Nest Restaurant offers more elegant dining. Friday, Saturday, and Sunday nights you can dance to the sounds of live music! Pusser's is open seven days a week and monitors VHF channel 16.

Sunny Caribbee has a wonderful gift shop here with a full array of fragrant spices, seasonings, sauces, cosmetics, and art gallery. You won't walk out of their shop empty handed.

For provisioning the Harbour Market is located at the base of Sheppard's Marina. Normal opening hours are 8am to 6:30pm. Harbour Market offers a large variety of provisions, gourmet foods, liquor, beer and wine. Credit cards are accepted.

Culture Classic Boutique sell casual clothes and swimwear. Billabong sells surfwear. Bon Marche rents DVDs and can fill up your empty propane tank. BVI Apparel

Factory Outlet sells souvenirs and t-shirts. Zenaida has fascinating jewelry sarongs, and other treasures. Island Surf and Sail offer rentals for surf boards for those who are looking for waves. Latitude 18 is on the waterfront next to Voyage Yacht Charters with clothing, sunglasses and BVI Yacht Club gear for the whole family.

If you've decided to move to the islands, check with Smith Arneborg Architects if you want to build a home from scratch.

A popular destination after a long day of sailing and sunning is the Ice Cream Parlor followed by a visit to Serenity Spa for a massage, or facials, manicures and pedicures.

Bluewater Divers is located on the waterfront with tank rentals, dive trips, and a shop with clothing and gift items.

D'Best Cup features a variety of coffee drinks, ice cream, smoothies, pastries, beer, wine, sandwiches and snacks. They also have a variety of gift items.

At the western end of Soper's Hole is the Frenchman's Cay Marina. They have 30 boat slips with a controlling depth of 30 feet. According to the owner/manager, they will also have room for two or three mega yachts. Dockage is available at $1 to $2 per foot and the facilities are scheduled to include 220/110v electricity, WiFi, showers and plans are being developed for a nearby restaurant. Contact the dockmaster on VHF 16. At the head of the dock, The Ample Hamper shop is scheduled to be opened for the 2012/13 season. As with the sister store in Road Town, they will carry food and other provisioning items along with gourmet items.

Walking back to the east, past the Harbour Market about half a mile, situated on twelve private acres at the very eastern tip of Frenchman's Cay and looking out over Sir Francis Drake Channel, is the delightful Frenchman's, a boutique hotel with nine cottages, tennis courts, hiking trail and The Club House Restaurant. Reservations are suggested. Telephone: 284-494-8811.

Nanny Cay
(Hannah Bay)

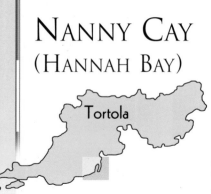

Tortola

Waypoint: BV117 (18°23.00N, 64°38.50W)
Navigation: 2.2nm SW of Road Harbour / 4.2nm East of Soper's Hole
Services: Full service 200 berth marina, Chandlery, Hotel, Ice, Garbage disposal, Provisions, Restaurants & bars, Wifi

Approaching Hannah Bay or Nanny Cay from Road Town to the east, or Soper's Hole to the west, the first landmark will be the masts of the boats hauled out in the boatyard and at the dock. Nanny Cay forms a peninsula, jutting out from the south coast of Tortola and was originally developed by dredging an entrance through the reef at the south end of the bay. Fully protected from the northeast trade winds, Nanny Cay Marine Centre and Hannah Bay Marina offer a full service marine environment. There is no room for anchoring once inside the breakwater and no moorings are available.

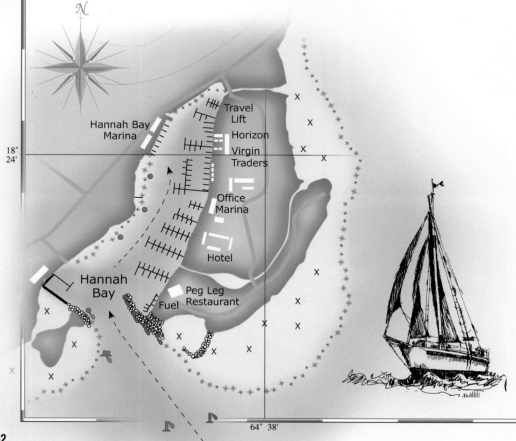

Navigation & Piloting

Whether making your approach from the east or west it is advisable to stay a quarter mile off the shoreline in order to avoid the coral and shoal water extending from the south shoreline of Tortola and to the east and north into Sea Cow Bay. The Peg-Leg Landing restaurant, set on stilts, has always served as a reliable marker, although the roof, once a bright red has recently been painted pink. Head for the southern most point of Nanny Cay until the lighted red and green channel markers are visible. The first set of markers are stakes and the channel will carry 10 feet. Yachts with a draft over ten feet (but with a maximum of 11.5 feet) should call the marina first for instructions on channel 16 as access is dependent on the state of the tide.

Stay in the middle of the channel and follow the red and green buoys NNW between the breakwaters and into the bay. The inner starboard markers are located on the breakwater.

There are invariably several yachts anchored to the west just inside the entrance. The water is very shallow and designated as a no anchoring zone.

A new marina development is still under construction just inside the port side breakwater at the entrance. This 20 berth facility, Hannah Bay Marina, is managed by Nanny Cay Marine Centre.

Since the port side of the channel is shallow, stay to starboard and keep an eye open for the privately maintained green buoys to port.

Garden Marina is to your port and the Nanny Cay Marine Centre sprawls to the right.

Since the Nanny Cay marina runs at high occupancy, it is advisable to contact the marina on VHF 16 prior to arrival should a berth be required. The fuel dock is on your starboard hand just beyond the breakwater.

Ashore

Nanny Cay describes itself as "more than a marina – it's a living, breathing, bustling nautical community" – and they just might be right! The marine center offers a wide range of services including the boatyard, marina, hotel, restaurants and everything else a yachtie could need or want. The 200 slip marina can accommodate yachts up to 140 feet long, 10-foot draft, and 33 feet wide. Amenities available within the marina include showers, water, laundry, ice and fuel. Provisions may be purchased from Bobby's Supermarket; CYM Management stocks a selection of South African wines,

soft drinks and food products. Storage lockers may be rented through the marina. There is also a First Bank ATM on-site at the Nanny Cay taxi stand by the marina office.

There is a wide variety of services based at Nanny Cay. BVI Marine Management, Marine Maintenance Services and Aquadoc can, between them, provide mechanical, refrigeration, air conditioning, welding, water-maker, generator and electrical repairs, and 24-hour chase boat service. Johnny's Maritime Services, Antilles Yachts and CYM Yachts (official Oyster repair center) can provide yacht management, maintenance and delivery services.

BVI Painters, Tony's Marine Refinishing Service, and V.I. Marine Refinishing provide fiberglass and gelcoat repairs and finishing

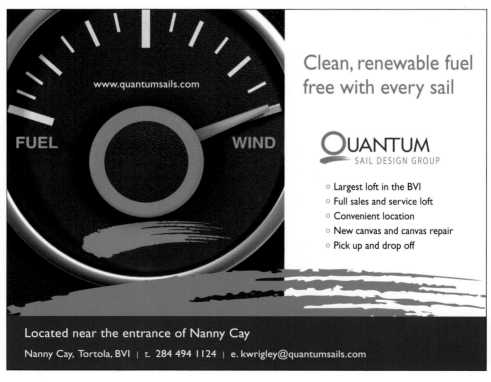

including Awlgrip. E&S Yacht Maintenance and Yacht Shop offer shipwright services including full interior refits. BVI Yacht Sales will sell you a yacht while Caribbean Marine Surveyors or West Indies Marine Surveyors will survey it. Richardson's Rigging will go aloft to check and repair your rigging and Quantum Sails loft can build and repair your sails.

The 2,800-foot Budget Marine Chandlery (operated by Nanny Cay) carries over 6,000 marine related products and offers a fast special order service. It is open from 8am to 5pm daily except on Sunday when it closes at 3pm.

Nanny Cay's full-service boatyard has storage for 260 yachts and two boat lifts. One is a conventional Acme Marine Hoist capable of lifting monohulls up to 68 feet long, 10 feet draft and weighing up to 50 tons. The other is a wide-body Marine Travelift, capable of lifting and moving catamarans up to 32 foot beam and 70 tons in weight making it the widest lift capacity in the BVI and the largest capacity lift of its type north of Trinidad.

Nanny Cay also offers a highly secure cradle storage system that earned its status as an approved hurricane storage facility

by Pantaenius, one of the world's leading insurers of luxury yachts.

The hotel, nestled in a tropical garden, offers standard and deluxe hotel rooms as well as the recently completed waterfront two and three-bedroom townhouses. The townhouses can accommodate up to six guests and offer a view of the channel. They also have private decks with dock space for a small powerboat.

For the shopper, Arawak Boutique and Island Roots sell clothing, souvenirs and interesting gifts to bring home. Bamboushay creates pottery in every shape and size. There's also the Nutty Banana ice cream shop and Island Roots specialty coffee bar for an espresso hit.

Two restaurants and a beach bar complement the marina. Genaker Café is open all day for breakfast and lunch in the heart of the marina. Peg Legs Landing, an al fresco restaurant on the point, is open for dinner with the bar opening at 5pm, and overlooks the Sir Francis Drake Channel. The Beach Bar, on the beach near the pool, is open from midday and offers a lunch menu. All three are open seven days a week.

Blue Water Divers, a well established dive company, has been based in Nanny Cay

for over twenty years. They operate a dive shop, conduct dive tours and perform in-water bottom cleaning. Nanny Cay is their main base of operations.

Horizon Yacht Charters, a highly regarded charter company, makes Nanny Cay Marina their base of operations, along with Virgin Traders who specialize in motor yachts for charter. Island Time and King Charters

rent powerboats by the day, or longer. To learn to sail, there's the Rob Swain Sailing School and Sistership.

For those who must stay in touch, there is property-wide free wifi access for guests.

There is currently no Customs and Immigration at Nanny Cay. You must clear in at one of the ports of entry.

Bomba's Shack

Rafiki
Madison, WI

CLASSIC STYLE

Designed in the Caribbean

Hiho

Authentic · BVI · Registered

WWW.GO-HIHO.COM

Sea Cow Bay/Manuel Reef Marina

Waypoint: BV117 18°23.00'N; 64°38.50'W
Navigation: 5.5 nm NW West End,
2nm SW Road Harbour
Services: Dockage, Water, Ice, Garbage Disposal,
Showers, Electricity, Restaurant

Tucked up into the coastline north of Nanny Cay is Sea Cow Bay and Manuel Reef Marina. Totally protected from the prevailing trades, this 40 slip marina has matured substantially since our last visit and provides an excellent spot for owners to leave their vessels under management service while away from the island. The maximum water depth is 9 feet.

Navigation & Piloting

Approaching from the southwest (BV117) and the Sir Francis Drake Channel, continue past Nanny Cay until you are able to see all the way up into Sea Cow Bay and the end of the dock at the marina (about 329°m). The shoreline is dotted with reef so make sure you

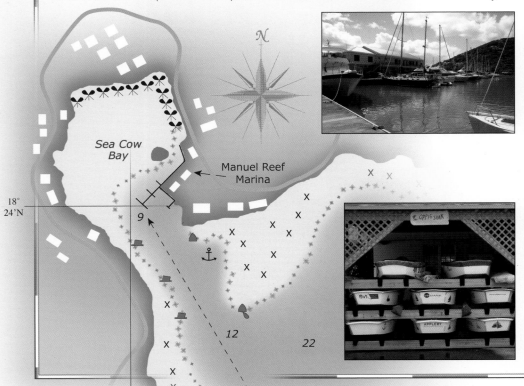

are in the center of the channel. The main buoy to identify is the red nun marking the southwestern tip of the reef on your starboard hand. At the time of our last survey the channel was well marked with both red and green buoys but the first red is the critical one to identify.

Anchoring & Mooring

Owing to the very shallow nature of Sea Cow Bay, the only option other than docking at the marina would be to anchor in 10-12 feet of water just out of the channel on the starboard side before the bulkhead. There are usually two or three yachts anchored here so make sure that you do not swing into the channel.

Call the marina on VHF 16 for docking instruction.

Ashore

Manuel Reef Marina is conveniently situated between Nanny Cay and Road Town. The marina offers electricity, water, and showers as well as yacht management services. The marina office is located at the west end of the building on the second floor. The marina is the base for Bare Cat Charters, Husky Salvage and a car rental service. Check out the Boat House Restaurant, open Monday through Saturday serving lunch and dinner. Bobby's Market will soon be coming to Manuel Reef Marina to help you with any provisioning you require.

The Watersports Centre is the base for Sailon BVI, a Royal Yachting Association teaching center teaching both young sailors and adults wishing to learn how to sail in the beautiful waters of the British Virgin Islands.

ISLAND CONNECTIONS

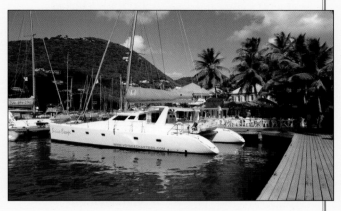

EMERGENCIES

VISAR (Virgin Island Search and Rescue)
VHF channel 16
Tel: 767 (SOS), or 999, or 911 or 284-494-4357 (494-help)
www.visar.org

BREWER'S BAY

RESTAURANTS
Nicole's Restaurant & Bar
Very casual beach bar

CANE GARDEN BAY

EMERGENCIES
Cane Garden Bay Police Dept.
VHF channel 16
284-495-9828

RESTAURANTS
Quito's Gazebo
Tel. 284-495-4837
Open Tuesday-Sunday
Serving lunch and dinner
http://www.quitorymer.com/Page446.htm

Big Banana Paradise Club
Tel: 284-495-4606
Serving breakfast, lunch and dinner

Elm Beach Bar
Tel: 284-494-2888
Serves lunch and dinner from 11am
www.elmbeachsuites.com/bar.html

Rhymer's Beach Bar & Restaurant
Tel: 284-495-4639
Serving breakfast, lunch and dinner

Stanley's
Tel: 284-495-9424
Serving lunch and dinner
http://canegardenbay-beachhotel.com/restaurant.htm

Myett's Garden & Grille
Tel: 284-495-9649
On the waterfront
Serving breakfast, lunch and dinner
www.myettent.com/restaurant.htm

SPA
Myett's Sea Spa
Tel: 284-495-9649

PROVISIONS
Bobby's Market
284-495-9971
www.bobbysmarketplace.com

Rhymer's Beach Bar & Shop
284-495-4639
http://canegardenbay-beachhotel.com/store.htm

NANNY CAY

MARINAS
Nanny Cay Marina
VHF channel 16
Tel: 284-494-2512
www.nannycay.com/marina-services

Hannah Bay Marina
Contact this marina through Nanny Cay Marina

Garden Marina
Does not take transient boats

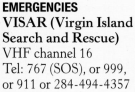

RESTAURANTS

Genaker Café
Open daily for breakfast and lunch. Happy hour 4:30-7pm. Candlelit dinners in high season
Tel: 284-494-2512
www.nannycay.com/genaker-cafe

Peg Legs Landing Restaurant & Bar
Serves dinner and drinks from 5pm-midnight daily
284-494-0028
www.nannycay.com/peglegs-restaurant

The Beach Bar & BBQ
Open daily from 10am on the beach serving beer and mixed drinks, lunch. Happy hour 4:30-6:30.
284-494-2512
www.nannycay.com/nanny-cay-beach-bar

Captain Mulligan's Sports Bar
Open daily from noon to midnight serves burgers, fries and drinks
Tel: 284-494-0602
Captain Mulligan's on FB

PROVISIONS

Bobby's Market
Tel: 284-494-2894
www.bobbysmarketplace.com

HOTELS

Nanny Cay Hotel
Tel: 284-494-2512
www.nannycay.com/about-nanny-cay-hotel

BOAT YARD SERVICES

BVI Marine Management
Tel: 494-3382

Johnny's Maritime Services
Tel: 284-494-3661

BVI Painters
Tel: 284-494-4365

Tony's Marine Refinishing Services
Tel: 284-494-0140

E & S Yacht Maintenance
Tel: 284-495-7500

BVI Yacht Sales
Tel: 284-494-3260
www.bviyachtsales.com

Caribbean Marine Surveyors
Tel: 284-494-2091

Richardson Rigging
Tel: 284-494-2739
www.richardsonsrigging.com

Budget Marine
Tel: 284-444-6588
www.budgetmarine.com/Store.aspx?id=Tortola

VI Marine Finishing
284-494-0361

DIVE

Bluewater Divers
Tel: 284-494-2847

SAIL LOFT

Quantum Sails
Tel: 284-494-1124
www.quantumsails.com

YACHT CHARTER

Horizon Yacht Charters
284-494-8787
www.horizonyachtcharters.com/bvi/bvi.html

Virgin Traders
284-495-2526
virgintraders.com

BOAT RENTALS
Island Time
Tel: 284-495-9993
www.islandtimeltd.com

King Yacht Charters
Tel: 284-494-5820
http://sailingcharters.com
/tours/british-virgin-
islands

SAILING SCHOOLS
Rob Swain
284-494-0432
www.swainsailing.com

SEA COW BAY/ MANUEL REEF MARINA

MARINAS
Manuel Reef and Woods Marine Services
VHF channel 16
Tel: 284-494-0445
www.manuel-reef-
marina.com

YACHT CHARTER
Bare Cat Charters
Tel: 284-495-2202
www.barecat.com

RESTAURANT
Boat House Restaurant
284-495-0007

PROVISIONING
Bobby's Market
coming soon

Bomba's Shack

WEST END

WEST END CUSTOMS
284-495-4221

WEST END IMMIGRATION
284-495-4443

MARINAS
Soper's Hole Wharf and Marina
VHF channel 16
Tel: 284-495-4589
www.sopersholemarina.
com

Soper's Hole Yacht Services
VHF 16
Tel: 284-495-3349
www.sopersholeyacht-
services.com

Sheppard's Marina
284-495-4099

RESTAURANTS
Pusser's Landing Restaurant & Bar
Tel: 284-495-4603
www.pussers.com/
t-pussers-landing.aspx

Jolly Roger Inn
Tel: 284-495-4559
www.jollyrogerbvi.com

PROVISIONING
Harbour Market
Tel: 284-495-4423
www.rtwbvi.com/harbour

Ample Hamper Too
284-495-4684
www.amplehamper.com

Sunny Caribbee
Tel: 284-495-0081
www.sunnycaribbee.com

Zelma's Courtesy Grocery and Snack Bar
Tel: 284-495-4211

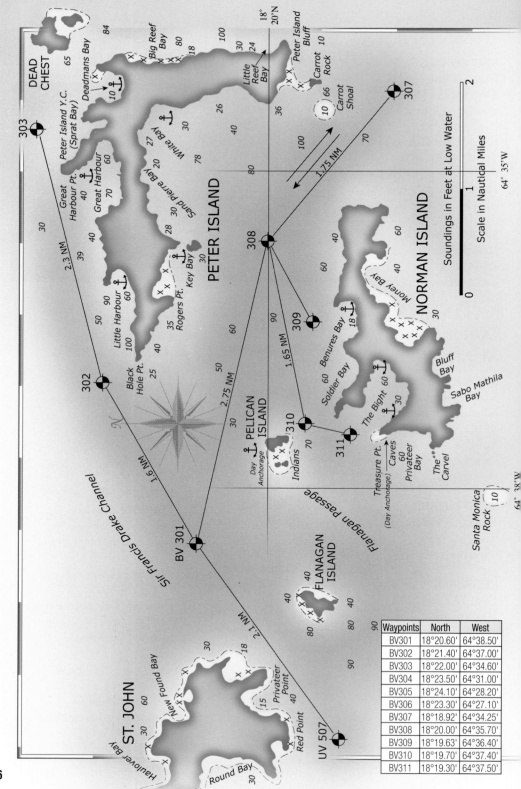

Waypoints	North	West
BV301	18°20.60'	64°38.50'
BV302	18°21.40'	64°37.00'
BV303	18°22.00'	64°34.60'
BV304	18°23.50'	64°31.00'
BV305	18°24.10'	64°28.20'
BV306	18°23.30'	64°27.10'
BV307	18°18.92'	64°34.25'
BV308	18°20.00'	64°35.70'
BV309	18°19.63'	64°36.40'
BV310	18°19.70'	64°37.40'
BV311	18°19.30'	64°37.50'

DEAD CHEST

Deadmans Bay

Big Reef Bay

Little Reef Bay

Peter Island Bluff

Carrot Rock

Carrot Shoal

Peter Island Y.C. (Sprat Bay)

Great Harbour Pt.

Great Harbour

White Bay

Sand Pierre Bay

PETER ISLAND

Key Bay

Rogers Pt.

Little Harbour

Black Hole Pt.

2.3 NM

1.75 NM

1.65 NM

2.75 NM

Soundings in Feet at Low Water

Scale in Nautical Miles

303

307

308

309

310

311

302

BV 301

UV 507

NORMAN ISLAND

Money Bay

Benures Bay

Soldier Bay

The Bight

Bluff Bay

Sabo Mathila Bay

Caves

Privateer Bay

The Carvel

Treasure Pt.

(Day Anchorage)

Santa Monica Rock

PELICAN ISLAND

Day Anchorage

Indians

Sir Francis Drake Channel

Flanagan Passage

FLANAGAN ISLAND

ST. JOHN

New Found Bay

Privateer Point

Red Point

Haulover Bay

Round Bay

1.6 NM

2.1 NM

18° 20'N

18° 18'

64° 35'W

64° 38'W

166

THE CHANNEL ISLANDS
NORMAN & PETER

When you imagine the days of piracy, you might not know that these islands play a large part in your imaginings. Known as *Freebooters Gangway*, the gentle waters of the Sir Francis Drake Channel, named for the famed and successful circumnavigating privateer commissioned by the Royal Navy, have played host to many pirates, some carrying a Letter of Marque, and others with their own agendas.

Norman Island has caves in Privateer Bay to explore by sea, and a "pirate ship" restaurant and bar anchored in the Bight. Peter Island is equally replete with beautiful bays in which to anchor, turquoise waters to snorkel, and shipwrecks beneath on which to dive.

Pirates – The Bight

Charts
NV.Charts: St. Thomas to Anegada: Kit C-13 & 14
NIMA: 2561, Imray Iolaire; A-231
Admiralty Leisure: 5640-5,6,7

THE BIGHT
NORMAN ISLAND

Waypoint: BV311 – 18°19.30'N; 64°37.50'W
Navigation: 5.7nm SSW Road Harbour
Services: Restaurants, Bars, Moorings

Norman is the first island of any size that, together with the islands of Peter, Salt, Cooper and Ginger, form the southern perimeter of the Sir Francis Drake Channel. Often referred to by the locals as "Treasure Island", legends of Norman Island are replete with stories of buried pirate treasure. A letter of 1750 stated, "Recovery of the treasure from Nuestra Senora buried at Norman Island, comprise 450,000 dollars, plate, cochineal, indigo, tobacco, much dug up by Tortolians."

The main anchorage on Norman Island is the Bight, an exceptionally well-sheltered anchorage.

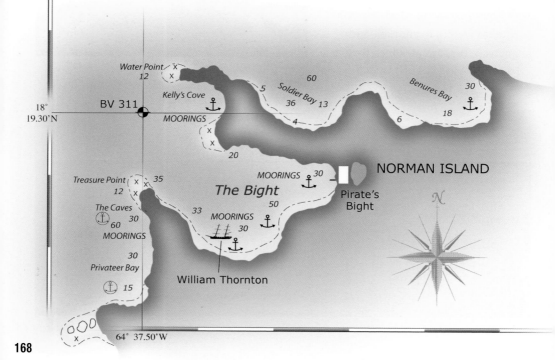

KELLYS COVE

THE BIGHT

TREASURE POINT

PRIVATEER BAY

Carvel
Rocks

Navigation & Piloting

Approaching Norman Island from the south, Santa Monica Rock located 0.7nm SW of Carvel Rocks, covers a small area that is covered by 11-12 feet (3.6m) of water. While this is of no concern to the average yachtsman, during periods of heavy swells it is well to take note. Approaching from the northeast, leaving Pelican Island to starboard, Ringdove Rock is located approximately 300 yards west of Water Point and has 14 feet (4.3m) of water over it.

If your approach brings you by Pelican Island, remember that you cannot pass between the Indians and Pelican Island.

The entrance to the Bight is straight forward and without hazard. Enter between the headlands, keeping in mind that there is shoal water just off both points. Kelly's Cove, a delightful small anchorage at the northern end of the bay, will be immediately identifiable upon rounding Water Point into the Bight.

Anchoring & Mooring

Considerations when deciding where to pick up a mooring or drop anchor in the Bight are whether to be near the partying or away from it. The William Thornton (Willy T), a converted steel schooner, anchored in the SW section of the Bight can be lively late into the night; the same applies to Pirates Bight Beach Bar & Grill ashore; if you are hanging on a mooring just offshore.

The best anchorage is well up in the northeast corner of the bay or the southeast section. The anchorage is deep, so you will need to get far enough in to anchor on the shelf in 15-30 feet of water. There are many mooring buoys (well maintained by Moor-Seacure) in place that you may pick up on a first come basis at the current rate. Someone will come by dinghy to collect the mooring fee usually in the early evening. If you anchor instead of picking up a mooring be sure that you are well clear of the moorings and have plenty of room to swing without fouling a mooring. Be aware that the wind tends to funnel down through the hills, giving the impression that the weather is much heavier than it is once you are outside of the bay.

Ashore

A dinghy trip to Treasure Point and the caves for snorkeling and exploring is a must. Tie up your dinghy to the line strung between the two small round floats. This avoids dropping an anchor and destroying coral. You may also take your sailboat and pick up a National Parks mooring during the day (with a permit). Good snorkeling also exists on the reef at the eastern end of the harbor just south of the beach.

Located in the Bight of Norman Island is the William Thornton, a floating restaurant named for the architect of the U.S. Capital building. The vessel is a converted 100 foot schooner. Lunch is served from noon to 3pm and the bar is open daily from noon. Nicknamed the "Willy T," stories abound about many wild nights of partying aboard. The ambiance is casual and often riotously fun! The "Willy T" monitors VHF 16.

Pirates Bight Beach Bar & Grill commands a view of the Bight from the head of the bay. This is a great place to watch the sunset and escape the boat for awhile, or have a couple of rum punches and dance the night away. Happy hour is from 4-6pm. Lunch is served from 11:30-4pm, and dinner from 6pm. They feature West Indian and international cuisine.

KELLY'S COVE

A fine alternate anchorage to the Bight is Kelly's Cove, a small, secluded anchorage set against a rugged hillside backdrop. Close enough in proximity to the main anchorage and Treasure Point to allow access by dinghy, Kelly's Cove is a delightful anchorage that provides excellent snorkeling from the boat.

As you approach the Bight, Kelly's Cove is situated under Water Point to the east. The entrance is straight forward, but anchoring needs careful consideration owing to the limited amount of swinging room. There are some overnight moorings in this area leaving limited room for anchoring unless a stern line is taken ashore. If you are dropping the hook, make sure that it is not in coral and the water is shallow enough (20'-25') to control the swinging room due to back winding.

Close by under Water Point, the National Parks Trust has installed several daytime moorings for snorkeling and diving. There is no charge assuming one has purchased a permit.

TREASURE POINT

To the south behind Treasure Point are the caves, an excellent spot for a morning or afternoon snorkel. There are numerous National Parks Trust moorings available for permit holders. In order to protect the coral from further destruction, no anchoring is permitted. If all of the mooring balls are taken, move further to the south where you can anchor, or pick up a mooring in Privateer Bay and dinghy back.

The snorkeling is excellent along the mouths of four caves and a dinghy mooring system is in place for those arriving by dinghy to get close enough to the caves without disturbing swimmers and snorkelers in the water. Bring your snorkel gear and a flashlight for some cave exploration. Caution: Do not use your outboard engine between the dinghy mooring line and the shore.

One of the charms of this area is the abundance of small colorful fish. Please do not feed them as it tends to make them aggressive.

Kelly's Cove

PRIVATEER BAY

Further to the south of Treasure Point is Privateer Bay often used as a day anchorage to access both the caves at Treasure Point and Carvel Rock, which provides excellent snorkeling in the appropriate weather conditions. Exposed to the north but usually protected by the headland, Privateer Bay can make a delightful overnight stop in the right conditions and still be close enough to action in the Bight by dinghy.

Although nine mooring balls are now available, anchoring can prove problematic in this area, since the bottom drops off rapidly and patches of dead coral and rock on the seabed should be identified prior to setting the anchor. Anchor in 15-20 feet.

The Caves at Treasure Point

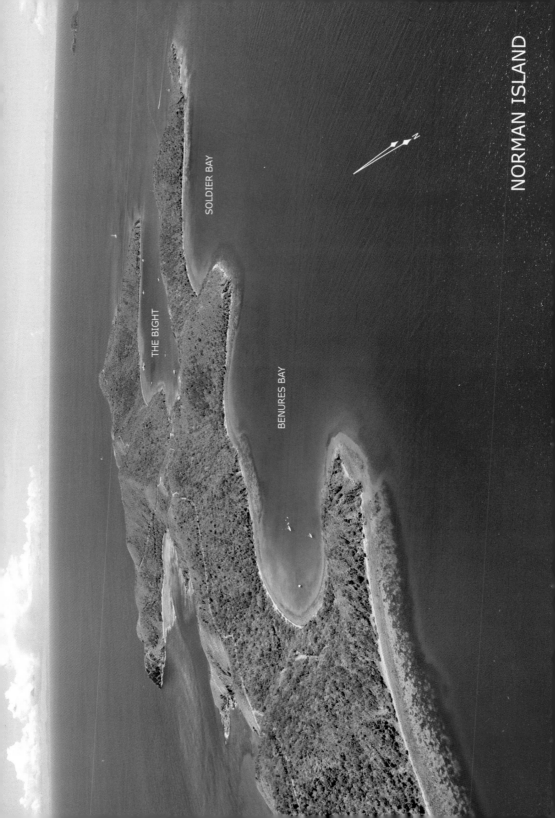

NORMAN ISLAND

THE BIGHT

SOLDIER BAY

BENURES BAY

BENURES BAY (NORTH COAST)

Waypoint: BV309 – 18°19.63'N; 64°36.40'W
Navigation: 6nm SW of Frenchman's Cay; 1nm east of Water Point
Services: Moorings (Soldier Bay)

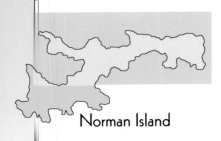

Norman Island

Under normal trade wind conditions, there are two delightful anchorages on the north coast that, while limited in available anchoring room, provide a tranquil setting a little out of the mainstream of cruising and charter traffic. Both of these anchorages should be avoided when the wind moves to the north for short periods during the winter months.

The larger and more protected of the two bays, Benures Bay lies to the east on the northern coast of Norman Island. The approach is straightforward as there is no shoal ground to be concerned about until you are in close proximity to the beach.

Anchor up in the northeast corner of the bay and as close to the pebble beach as possible. At the time of the last survey, no moorings were available. The bottom is sand, so the holding is excellent in 15-20 feet of water and the snorkeling is great. To sit in the cockpit savoring a gin & tonic and watching the sun slowly set down the channel to the west is close to perfect.

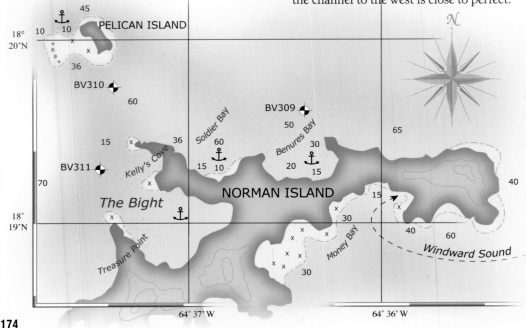

SOLDIER BAY

A little over half a mile east of Water Point is Soldier Bay, a small anchorage capable of accommodating a limited number of vessels and ideal during the summer months when the wind is light and the trade

Benures Bay

winds are blowing from the southeast. The entrance to Soldier Bay is free of any foul ground until the shoreline. If anchoring you will need to identify a sandy stretch to lay down the anchor in 25 feet of water or pick up one of the five mooring balls managed from Pirates Bight Beach Bar. Holding is good and the snorkeling is excellent.

SOUTH COAST / MONEY BAY

Location: 18°19.00'N ; 64°36.00'W
Waypoint: BV307 (Carrot Rock) 18°18.92'N; 64°34.25'W
Navigation: 3.2 nm east and south of Benures Bay
Services: None

Tucked away on the south coast of Norman is an idyllic anchorage that can be used as a daytime stop or overnight. Under certain conditions the swell can work itself into this little bay and therefore a stern anchor would prove prudent.

Approaching from the east, you will pass the rocky headland forming the southeastern tip of Norman Island; stand well clear since you will be on a lee-shore and the sea

conditions will reflect the fact that they have traveled unbroken for 100 miles or so.

Money Bay is located in the eastern end of the second bay to the west of the headland.

Care should be taken to make sure you know exactly where you are. There is plenty of water depth even though the seas are rough in this area. Locate the large rock formation marking the southern end of the bay and proceed into the center of the bay, dropping the anchor in 10' water on a sandy bottom. There is a reef that extends from the rocks at the entrance back toward the beach, so care should be taken to identify its location upon entry.

The most comfortable location is to anchor down toward the reef with a stern line or second anchor run out to the beach. This will keep your bow to the wind and head to the sea. At the time we visited this anchorage significant shore side development was in progress. Be aware that the anchorage could have changed significantly since then.

As this is a privately owned estate, do not go ashore.

Pelican Island & The Indians

Waypoint: BV310 – 18°19.80'N ; 64°37.40'W
Navigation: 5nm SE Frenchman's Cay, 5nm SSW Road Harbour
Services: National Parks Moorings

Pelican Island and the Indians should be considered a day anchorage only. Located one mile NNW from Water Point and highly visible from the channel because of the unique formation of the four red rocks known as the Indians. Do not attempt to sail between Pelican Island and the Indians. Approach them from the north and pick up one of the ten Parks Trust mooring balls. A reef extends between the two and provides excellent snorkeling as does the area immediately around the Indians. As part of the National Parks Trust, this area is protected and no anchoring is permitted. If the moorings are taken you may consider anchoring in Kelly's Cove at the mouth of the Bight (.5nm) and taking the dinghy over assuming you have a capable outboard and the sea conditions are light.

This anchorage is very exposed and can be uncomfortable. The snorkeling is excellent and well worth the trip.

Deliverance

At around 5pm daily, the supply vessel Deliverance makes the rounds to the yachts in the Bight, Cooper Island, and Peter Island selling ice, bottled water, breads, pastries, fruit, veggies, booze and other goodies you may require. Give them a wave or call them on VHF 16 and they will soon be at your side. Special orders may be placed before 10am via VHF or telephone 284-542-2181.

The Indians

THE CHANNEL ISLANDS
PETER ISLAND

LITTLE HARBOUR

Peter Island

Waypoint: BV302 - 18°21.40'N; 64°37.00'W
Navigation: 3.2nm SE Nanny Cay
Services: None

Sailing to the east the next island is Peter. Captain Thomas Southey wrote his impressions of the island in his chronological history of the West Indies over 100 years ago:

"In May (1806) the author with a party visited Peter's Island, one of those which form the bay Tortola, a kind of Robinson Crusoe spot, where a man ought to be farmer, carpenter, doctor, fisherman, planter; everything himself."

Navigation & Piloting

There are several good overnight anchorages on Peter Island, the westernmost of which is Little Harbour. Although it doesn't look it on the chart, Little Harbour is a well-protected overnight stop with good holding ground.

When approaching from the NW the first landmark is a dilapidated white house which can be difficult to see on the north west point forming the eastern side of the harbor. There are no obstructions but do not cut the point too close as the reef extends 100 feet toward the west from the shore.

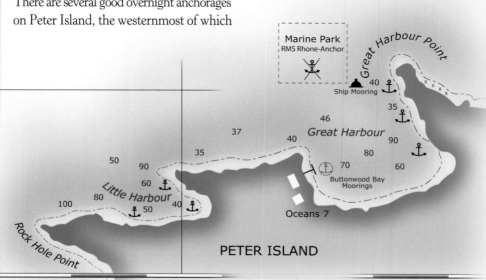

Little Harbour

Anchoring

There are no moorings and therefore the best spot to anchor is well up in the eastern reaches of the bay, in 15-25 feet over a sandy bottom. You will be back-winded, so check your swinging room relative to other vessels and use two anchors if necessary. If the anchorage is crowded, anchor close to shore on the southern coast of the bay in order to stay in 25-35 feet of water. The center of the bay drops off rapidly. Be careful not to anchor in the coral reef on the southwestern side of the anchorage. It is 40-50 feet below the surface, and is not easy to see and therefore, easy to damage. Please help protect the coral reefs.

In recent years it is noted that more yachts are mooring stern to the shore on both the north and south sides of the bay. This tends to restrict the available room to anchor, due to the back-winding effect. A stern line tied to a tree or around a convenient rock will keep you from swinging, but make sure your anchor is well set.

Ashore

Peter Island is a private island. There are no facilities ashore at Little Harbour. It is a quiet, usually, well-protected harbor where you can watch the frigate birds dive for fish, watch the sunset and the stars and moon at night. It is often used by crewed yachts that anchor stern to the shore and tie off to a rock or tree.

The house you see on top of the point is now in ruins. Ashore in the bay are the remains of a dock. It is not recommended that you go ashore here.

GREAT HARBOUR

Waypoint: BV303 - 18°22.00'N; 64°34.60'W
Navigation: 4nm SSE Road Harbour
Services: Moorings, Restaurant, Bar

Great Harbour, situated on the north side of the island is approximately half a mile across and a well protected anchorage that, until recent years, was largely neglected by the charter fleet because of the depth and lack of moorings. There is ample room to anchor along the eastern point although it can be tricky to locate an ideal location to get the anchor set.

Navigation & Piloting

Approaches to Great Harbour are clear and free of any obstruction. There is a large ship-mooring at the north end of the bay. Skippers should familiarize themselves with the location of the National Parks Trust protected area, the site of the lost anchor of the RMS Rhone that was sunk off of Salt Island in 1867, while attempting to gain sea room to the south in a hurricane.

Anchoring & Mooring

Entering Great Harbour, Buttonwood Bay and the Oceans Seven Beach Bar & Restaurant will be on the western side of the bay. There are numerous mooring balls available on a first come basis. Payment can be made ashore if you are staying overnight. To the east, in the inner corner of the bay is a protected fishing area, where local fishermen run their nets out into the bay. Stay clear of this activity and locate a spot in about 20 feet of water along the headland that extends to the northwest. Make sure your anchor is well set by reversing at 1500 rpm's and, if possible, take a snorkel and swim over it for peace of mind.

Ashore

Buttonwood Bay, on the western side of Great Harbour is home to the restaurant and bar called Oceans Seven. You can pick up a mooring and jump in the dinghy, tie up to the dock and pay for your mooring at the restaurant. They request reservations for dinner – check to find out if they are having entertainment or special events. Oceans Seven is open daily from 10am- 9pm with happy hour at 4-6pm. They serve West Indian dishes as well as international. It is a casual breezy location in Great Harbour. There are no garbage facilities ashore or any shops for provisioning.

SPRAT BAY PETER ISLAND RESORT

Peter Island

Waypoint: BV303 - 18°22.00'N; 64°34.60'W
Navigation: 4nm SSW of Road Harbour
Services: Moorings, Restaurant, Bar, Dockage, Fuel, Ice, Water

Sprat Bay is easy to spot from the Sir Francis Drake channel by the row of roofs comprising the hotel section of the Peter Island Resort. The entire bay, Deadman's Bay and several beaches on the south coast of Peter Island are part of the resort.

Navigation and Piloting

Making your entrance to Sprat Bay, it is important to familiarize yourself with the location of the reefs on either side of the channel. The main reef extends north and slightly west of the main bulkhead; so do not get too close to the western shore.

Entering on a heading of 141° magnetic, you can either tie up to the dock, which now sports new finger piers or pick up a mooring. Do not go too far into the southern end of the bay when maneuvering, as it is shallow. There are four moorings available for a fee of $65.00 per night (pay the dock

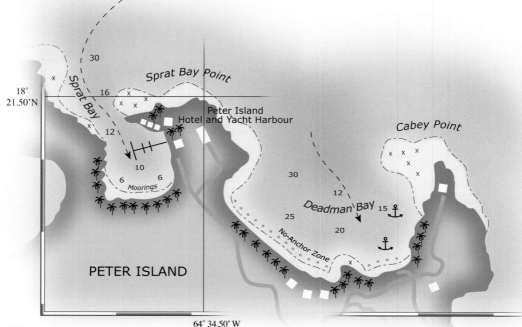

master ashore). The moorings cannot be reserved in advance. The dinghy dock is located at the western part of the marina. You may call the dock master on VHF Channel 16.

Ashore

The Peter Island Resort dock has 15 mid-sized slips and can accommodate up to 3 additional vessels alongside and a 175-foot T-dock for larger vessels. As of June of 2010, the rate for transient vessels is $125 per night up to 50 feet. Check with the dockmaster for the rates for larger vessels and to confirm current rates. For visiting day guests, the dockage is $20 per hour; again confirm these rates by contacting the dockmaster. Pumping marine

heads into the harbor is not permitted. Fuel is available as well as water. Garbage can be left for a fee of $4 and ice may be purchased.

Originally built by Norwegians in the late 1960s, the resort has been completely renovated. The hotel and restaurants extend along the bulkhead. Yachtsmen docking at Peter Island are welcome to use the Tradewinds Restaurant, Drake's Channel Lounge, Deadman's Beach Bar and Grill, Little Deadman's Beach, the Boutique, and the Dive Shop. Reservations are requested at the restaurants. Make sure to ask for the details of the dress code. There is no provisioning available at the resort.

Sprat Bay

Deadman's Bay

Waypoint: BV303 - 18°22.00'N; 64°34.60'W
Navigation: .5nm from Sprat Bay & 2.6nm west of Salt Island
Services: Restaurant, Beach Bar, and Trail

The easternmost anchorage on Peter Island, Deadman's Bay is a spectacular crescent of white sand with palm trees blowing in the trades. The anchorage itself is exposed to the north and therefore can be rolly due to the surge making its way around the northeastern point, making it a better day stop except in very settled southerly conditions. A reef extends 300 feet to the west from Cabey Point.

Anchoring

Move your vessel up into the southeastern corner, outside the swim markers, when anchoring. The bottom is grassy and it is sometimes difficult to get the anchor set, but the snorkeling is excellent. Do not anchor inside the line of markers designating the controlled swimming area on the western end of the beach. If there is any ground swell activity, we recommend that you seek another anchorage.

Ashore

This is a picture perfect beach to visit despite the sometimes rolly water action. The snorkeling along the rocks to the east is excellent. The beach is divided by some rocks; the beach to the west is for the use of hotel guests only, and yachtsmen are requested to respect the line of buoys designating the swimming beach. However, the Deadman's Bay Beach Bar is open to cruising and charter yachts as well as the hotel guests. In season the resort often holds beach barbecues here with steel bands playing on the beach.

The path at the very eastern end of the bay leads over to Little Deadman's Beach, an interesting beach to explore. The huts there are reserved for hotel guests.

Deadman's Bay, looking across to Deadchest Island

The Real Dead Chest

Though there are few that haven't at least heard of the film *Pirates of the Caribbean*, most are unaware of the identity of the real Dead Chest Cay, Dead Man's Bay, and the actual hidden treasure chest full of "Pieces of Eight". The story unfolds in the British Virgin Islands, our very own veritable paradise.

On the south side of the Sir Francis Drake Channel and just to the east of Peter Island is the cay named Dead Chest. In the days of yore a "dead man's chest" was the name for a coffin, the outline of which you can make out when viewing the island from the northwest. Look even longer and the coffin appears to contain a shrouded body with a raised head. As long ago as the late 1700s the cay's moniker was Dead Chest, clearly marked on Jeffrey's 18th century chart of the Virgin Islands. Folklore has it that the infamous pirate Blackbeard marooned fifteen men on the cay with nothing but a bottle of rum. Some apparently tried to swim the half mile to Peter Island's eastern cove but didn't make it, giving this beautiful palm lined bay the ominous name, "Dead Man's Bay".

At a much later date author Robert Louis Stevenson researched events in the area, studying nautical charts (his passion), as well as historical events and Caribbean lore. The well documented piracy of a huge treasure, much of which had been buried on Norman Island, most likely provided him with valuable information the culmination of which resulted in the much loved Treasure Island. Thus, Dead Chest Cay came to be immortalized in the famous refrain:

Fifteen Men on the Dead Man's Chest,
Yo-ho-ho and a bottle of rum!
Drink and the devil had done for the rest.
Yo-ho-ho and a bottle of rum!

Perhaps the most captivating aspect of the many similar themes of the film and the true story of the piracy in the Virgin Islands is that both involve treasure chests. In the BVI a daring act of piracy led to the burying of a cache of treasure on Norman Island in the year 1750. Some 160 years after the event a treasure chest of "Pieces of Eight" was discovered in the southernmost cave on the leeward side of the peninsula that crests at Treasure Point. Mention of the discovery is made in no less than three publications!

"Yo–ho-ho and a bottle of rum!!"

Julian Putley is the author of "The Virgins' Treasure Isle," the story of the daring piracy and subsequent burying of it on Norman Island in the BVI.

Key Point & White Bay
(The South Coast of Peter Island)

Peter Island

Waypoint: BV308 - 18°20.00'N; 64°35.70'W
Navigation: 2nm NE Water Point (Norman Is)
Services: None

There are two anchorages on the south side of Peter Island that are worthy of mention, but some regard to sea and weather conditions should be noted when planning to anchor, since southerly conditions can make Key Point uncomfortable.

Approaches and Anchoring

The ideal approach is from the SW and deep water. When approaching Key Point from the west, give Rodger's Point a good offing since there is a small reef that extends south.

Key Cay is separated from the mainland (Key Point) by a narrow isthmus of land that allows the trade breeze to flow freely across the anchorage.

Tuck yourself up into the northeast corner and anchor on a sandy bottom in 15-18 feet of water. There are some coral heads in the area so make sure that you locate a good sandy spot before dropping the hook.

The snorkeling is excellent and the anchorage is open to the prevailing breeze, keeping it free from bugs. The island is private and no services are available.

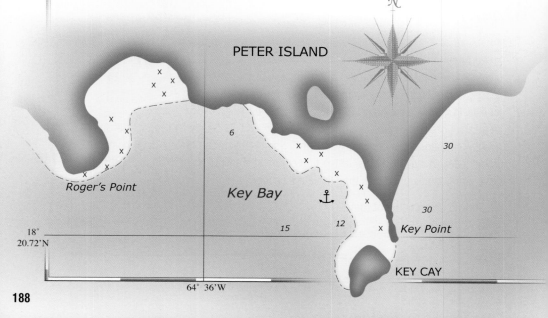

PETER ISLAND

6

30

Roger's Point

Key Bay

30

15

12

Key Point

KEY CAY

18° 20.72'N

64° 36'W

WHITE BAY

Waypoint: BV308 - 18°20.00'N; 64°35.70'W
Navigation: 3nm NE Water Point (Norman Is)
Services: None

Tucked up in the NE corner of the island before the coast turns to the south, White Bay is a reasonable anchorage when the ground swells caused by the normal flow of current are not running. We would recommend it as a day anchorage only in normal conditions. An approach from the southwest is ideal and straightforward.

Making your approach from the south (waypoint BV307 Carrot Shoal), make sure that you give Carrot Rock on the southernmost tip of Peter Island plenty of sea room and are aware of the location of Carrot Shoal (covered by 9'6"/2.9m of water). There is a 1.5 to 1.75 knot current flowing through this area that can run to the NW or to the SE.

Anchor on a sandy bottom in 15 feet of water.

Since White Bay is for the use of guests of the Peter Island Resort, landing is not encouraged although access to beaches throughout the BVI is always available to the high tide mark.

WHITE BAY, PETER ISLAND

Little Harbour, Peter Island

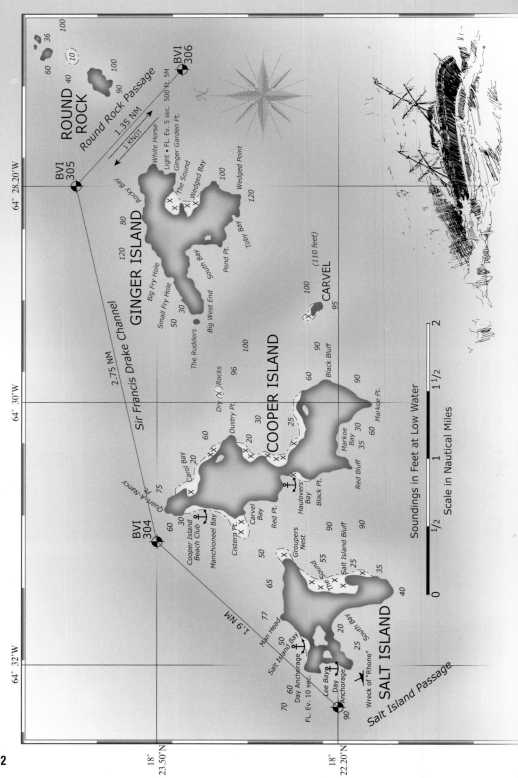

ROUND ROCK

60   36   100
10
40   100
90   100

BVI 306

Round Rock Passage
1.35 NM
1 KNOT

White Horse
Light ● Fl. Ev. 5 sec. 500 Ft. 5M
Ginger Garden Pt.

BVI 305

Rocky Bay
The Sound
Wedged Bay

Wedged Point
Toby Bay
120

Pond Pt.
South Bay

GINGER ISLAND

Big Fry Hole
Small Fry Hole
Big West End
The Rudders

80   120   100   90

50   30

Sir Francis Drake Channel
2.75 NM

100
Dry (X) Rocks
96
CARVEL
(110 feet)
100   95

COOPER ISLAND

Dustry Pt.
60   20   30   25
Carol Bay
20
60   75

Quart-a-Nancy Pt.

BVI 304

Cistern Pt.
Carvel Bay
Red Pt.
Manchioneel Bay
Cooper Island Beach Club
30   60

Haulovers' Bay
Black Pt.
Markoe Bay
Red Bluff
Markoe Pt.
Black Bluff
60   90   90   90   35   30   60

Groupers' Nest
The Sound
55
Salt Island Bluff
90   90   25   35
50   65   77
40

SALT ISLAND

Man Head
South Bay
20   25
Salt Island Bay
Salt Island Anchorage
Lee Bay
Day Anchorage
Wreck of "Rhone"
Fl. Ev. 10 sec.
70   60   50   90

Salt Island Passage

N

Soundings in Feet at Low Water

Scale in Nautical Miles
0   1/2   1   1 1/2   2

64° 28.20'W   64° 30'W   64° 32'W

18° 23.50'N   18° 22.20'N

192

THE CHANNEL ISLANDS
SALT, COOPER & GINGER ISLANDS

The sailing and snorkeling paradise, formed by the chain of small islands designating the southern boundary of the Sir Francis Drake Channel (Freebooters Gangway), Salt, Cooper & Ginger Islands, together with Fallen Jerusalem and the Dogs to the east are home to some of the most spectacular snorkeling and dive sites in the BVI, including the Wreck of the Rhone, Alice in Wonderland (Ginger Island) and Cistern Point off of the point of Cooper Island.

Ginger Island is uninhabited and has no tenable anchorages. Fallen Jerusalem was declared a National Park and bird sanctuary in 1974 and has a small day anchorage, with excellent snorkeling, on the north side also accessible by dinghy from the Baths when the weather is light.

SALT ISLAND BAY

Waypoint: BV303 (Deadchest) - 18°22.00'N; 64°34.60'W

Navigation: 5nm SE Road Harbour ; 2nm east of Peter Island

Services: National Park Moorings at Lee Bay

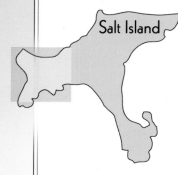

Salt Island, a little over two nautical miles east from Peter Island, is a relatively low island rising to less than 400 feet at the northern end. At the eastern extremity, a rock is awash and restricts the channel between Salt and Cooper Islands. Caution should be exercised in this regard. At the western end lies the famed wreck of the Rhone.

Named for the island's three evaporation ponds, Salt Island was once an important source of salt for the ships of Her Majesty's Navy. The island and its salt ponds, although belonging to the Crown, were operated by the local populace. Each year at the start of the harvest, the Governor, as annual rent, accepted one bag of salt. In 1845, a barrel was quoted at one shilling and, although inflation has taken its toll, salt is still sold to visitors. The residents of the settlement just off Salt Bay have all moved off of Salt Island to the more populated islands with all the modern conveniences.

Anchoring & Mooring

Salt Island Bay, north of The Settlement is clear of hazards, but the prudent skipper is advised to ensure that the anchor is well set before going ashore. You may anchor in 10- 20 feet of water on a sandy bottom.

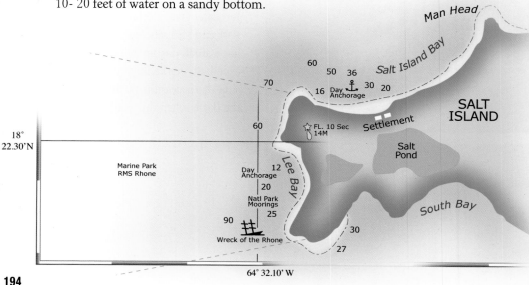

SALT ISLAND BAY

LEE BAY

MARINE PARK
RMS RHONE

N

Evaporation Pond, Salt Island

There is a small jetty and if you are going ashore, make sure that you secure the dinghy on the beach, either by pulling it well up the beach or using the dinghy anchor to prevent the surge from liberating it.

During the high season, the anchorage to the west (Lee Bay) can get crowded with divers and snorkelers anxious to see the wreck of the RMS Rhone. Consider leaving the boat in Salt Island Bay and taking the dinghy around to Lee Bay where you can secure it to the dinghy tether by courtesy of the National Parks Trust.

LEE BAY

Although exposed and recommended as a day anchorage only, Lee Bay, located on the west end of the island, is an alternative to Salt Bay for those wishing to dive or snorkel on the wreck of the Rhone. The National Parks Trust has installed moorings for the use of permit holders only. They are designed for boats under 50 feet to pick up in order to dinghy over to the Rhone. Anchoring over the Rhone is strictly prohibited as the National Parks Trust protects it. Constant anchoring by boats has destroyed some of the coral. Remember that the yellow mooring balls are for commercial vessels only. Watch out for divers!

Ashore

Salt Island has a few fishermen who fish off of the island, but it is no longer settled. There are no services or restaurants ashore.

The Royal Mail Steamer Rhone

On the morning of October 29, 1867, the R.M.S. Rhone was at anchor outside of Great Harbour, Peter Island. The Rhone, under the command of Captain Robert F. Wooley, had left Southampton on October 2, 1867, and was taking on cargo and stores for the return crossing. The R.M.S. Conway, commanded by Captain Hammock, lay alongside.

The stillness of the tropical day was undisturbed as the sun blazed down from a clear sky upon calm seas. As the morning wore on, the barometer began to fall, hinting the weather might deteriorate. The seas, however, remained untroubled. Although the captains alerted themselves, work was allowed to continue. Captain Wooley hailed Captain Hammock that he did not like the look of the weather and, as the hurricane season was over, it must be a northerly brewing. Wooley felt they should shift to the northern anchorage of Road Harbour, Tortola.

About 11am., the barometer suddenly fell to 27.95 degrees. The sky darkened, and with a mighty roar a fearful hurricane blew from the north/northwest. The howling wind whistled through the shrouds and tore at the rigging. With engines going at full speed, the ships rode the storm.

At noon there came a lull in the storm. The Conway weighed anchor and headed toward the northern anchorage of Road Harbour. As she steamed across the Sir Francis Drake Channel, she was hit by the second blast of the hurricane. Her funnel and masts were blown away, and she was driven onto the island of Tortola.

The Rhone tried to weigh anchor during the lull, but the shackle of the cable caught in the hawse pipe and parted, dropping the 3,000-pound anchor and some 300 feet of chain. With engines running at full speed, she steamed seaward in order to seek sea room to weather the second onslaught. She had negotiated most of the rocky channel and was rounding the last point when the hurricane, blowing from the south-southeast, struck, forcing her onto the rocks at Salt Island where she heeled over, broke in two, and sank instantly, taking most of her company with her.

— Courtesy of R.M.S. Rhone
  by George and Luana Marler

The Wreck of the Rhone

COOPER ISLAND
MANCHIONEEL BAY

Waypoint: BV304 - 18°23.50'N; 64°31.00'W
Navigation: 6nm SE Road Harbour
Services: Moorings, Ice, Restaurant, Hotel, Gift Shop and Dive Center.

Cooper Island

Cooper Island, located northeast of Salt Island is less than two miles in length and about 500 feet high. On the east side of the island about 300 yards off of Dustry Point on the northeast side there is a patch of rocks aptly named Dry Rocks. Further to the south and less than a mile east-northeast of the southern extremity is the 110 foot high Carvel Rock.

BV304

Quart-A-Nancy Pt.

60

55   30

Manchioneel Bay

40   36

30

Cooper Island Beach Bar

50

Moorings

27

20

COOPER ISLAND

Dinghy Moorings
Cistern Pt.

Grouper's Nest

55

6

Carvel Bay

36

Red Point

25

SALT ISLAND

Hallovers Bay

25

18° 22.80'N

64° 31.10' W

HALLOVERS BAY

CISTERN PT.

Navigation & Piloting

The principal anchorage on Cooper Island is Manchioneel Bay located on the northwest shore. When approaching the bay from the north, around Quart-O-Nancy Point, you will be on your ear one minute and becalmed the next. The point shelters the wind entirely, and we would recommend lowering sail and powering up to the anchorage.

Traveling from Manchioneel Bay south to Haulovers Bay or approaching from Salt Island to the west, be aware of a rock barely awash just north of the eastern point (Grouper's Nest) of Salt Island. With Cistern Point on the Cooper Island side and the rocks off the end of Salt, the passage between the islands is restricted. We do not advise sailing through.

Anchoring & Mooring

There are thirty moorings off of Cooper Island owned and operated by Moor-Seacure. They can be identified by the pick-up pennant beneath the buoy and a pay-at-the-bar sticker. The fee is $30 per overnight stay. The other 10 most southerly moorings near Cistern Point are privately owned, and a dinghy will come to collect the fee. Anchoring is not permitted in the mooring field or in the seagrass. Manchioneel Bay is one of the Department of Environment and Fisheries seven permanent seagrass monitoring sites that provide food and shelter for sea turtles and many species of fish.

If you are anchoring, make sure to back down on your anchor and check it visually by snorkeling over it. The south end of the bay would be the preferred spot to anchor, as the mooring balls are less dense. Since this anchorage is popular, both as a first and last night stop, because of its proximity to Road Town, the mooring balls fill quickly and we have witnessed on many occasions two or three vessels racing through the anchorage toward the last mooring ball. With swimmers in the water, we urge restraint.

199

Ashore

There is a good sandy beach fringed with palm trees and offering views of many of the islands to the west including spectacular sunsets. Please exercise caution in your dinghy and look out for snorkelers and swimmers. The snorkeling is excellent at each end of the beach, and there is a dinghy line at Cistern Point if you wish to explore the deeper water. Dinghies may tie up at either of the two jetties to visit Cooper Island Beach Club, the Sea Grape Boutique, or Sail Caribbean Divers.

Under new ownership since 2009, Cooper Island Beach Club has undergone substantial renovations. The Harris family has also invested in many green initiatives behind the scenes, such as a state-of-the-art solar-powered system that provides over 75% of the resort's power. The restaurant serves a varied international menu and dinner reservations are essential in the busy season. Go ashore during the day, phone 284-495-9084 or call on VHF-16 before noon to avoid disappointment. Happy hour starts at 4pm and the bar deck features comfortable outdoor sofas and parasols for shade. Ice is usually available at the bar and from the boat Deliverance that visits the mooring field each afternoon.

Cooper Island Beach Club has guest cottages available each with a private bathroom and beachfront balcony; perfect for before- or post-charter, or just a night off of the boat.

Next to the Beach Club to the north the Sea Grape Boutique has resort clothing, island souvenirs, local art, books, and essential sundries you may need.

Although there is no regular schedule, the Beach Club boat goes to Tortola several days a week, to transfer guests or to pick up supplies, so check at the office if you need transportation.

Sail Caribbean Divers, a PADI Five Star IDC facility offers a full range of scuba diving experiences catering to all levels. They will meet you at the Cooper Island jetty and within 15 minutes you can be diving on colorful coral reefs and some of the best wreck diving in the Caribbean, including the world-renowned wreck of the RMS Rhone. Their staff is on-site daily offering air-fills, PADI dive courses, and equipment rentals including kayaks and snorkel gear.

HAULOVERS BAY

A little over half a mile south of Manchioneel Bay is the small anchorage known as Haulovers Bay (shown on UK Admiralty Charts as Hallovers). Transiting between Salt and Cooper you will leave Cistern Point, the western extremity of Cooper, to port and do not venture too far west toward Salt Island. Directly north of the Grouper's Nest (eastern most point of Salt Island) is a rock awash.

Haulovers is a reasonable overnight anchorage except during southerly conditions when it can be rolly. There is a reef at the south end of the bay so anchor in 20 feet of water.

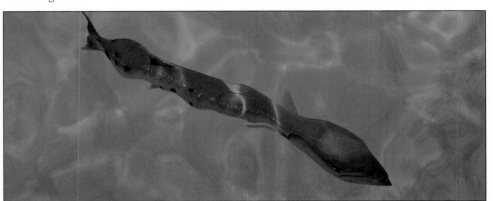

The resident Cooper Island barracuda

THE DOGS (WEST DOG, GREAT DOG, GEORGE DOG & SEAL DOG)

Virgin Gorda

Waypoint: BV403 (Gt.Dog) - 18°28.42'N; 64°26.80'W
Navigation: 6.2nm NW Cooper Island, 2.5nm NW St.Thomas Bay, Virgin Gorda
Services: National Parks Trust Moorings, Snorkeling, Dive Sites

Great, George, West and Seal Dogs lay a couple of miles to the west of Virgin Gorda, and generally speaking, have good water all around them. They are all in a protected area of the National Parks Trust. They make a delightful lunch stop on the way up from the islands to the south but when the northerly ground swells are running in the winter months they can be uncomfortable even as day anchorages.

It is not possible to sail or power between West and East Seal Dogs. If there is not a sea running there are three good daytime anchorages in the lee of Great Dog and George Dog.

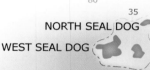

80
35
NORTH SEAL DOG
WEST SEAL DOG
EAST SEAL DOG
70
85

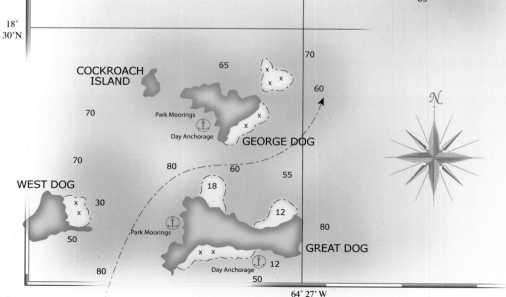

18° 30'N

70

COCKROACH ISLAND

65

70
Park Moorings
Day Anchorage

70

80

WEST DOG

x
x
30

50

80

18
Park Moorings

x x
Day Anchorage

60
55

12

GEORGE DOG

80

GREAT DOG

12

50

64° 27' W

GEORGE DOG

On George Dog, the best anchorage is in the bay to the west of Kitchen Point. Pick up a National Parks Trust mooring just off of the beach and stay for lunch and a snorkel trip. The rocky point is also an excellent 25-30 foot dive for beginner divers.

GREAT DOG

Off of Great Dog there are two possible anchorages depending on the weather. The most common one is on the south side of the island. There are several National Parks Trust moorings you may use with your permit. The depth is between 20-30 feet and the bottom is rocky. The second spot is off the beach on the west coast and it also has National Parks moorings available. The snorkeling is excellent in both locations and for the scuba divers there are a number of excellent sites.

South side anchorage: The reef runs east and west. Over 100 yards of island coral, butterfly fish and scores of other species.

The Chimney (West Bay): A winding canyon leads to a colorful underwater arch. Many coral heads and an unbelievable variety of sea creatures.

GEORGE DOG

GREAT DOG

ISLAND CONNECTIONS

EMERGENCIES
VISAR (Virgin Island Search and Rescue)
VHF channel 16
Tel: 767 (SOS), or 999 or 911 or 284-494-4357 (494-help)
www.visar.org

PROVISIONING
Deliverance
Boat-to-boat delivery service daily. VHF 16.
Tel: 284-542-2181
Deliverance BVI on Facebook

COOPER ISLAND

RESTAURANTS
Cooper Island Beach Club
VHF channel 16
284-495-9084
www.cooperisland-beachclub.com

SHOPS
Sea Grape Boutique

WATERSPORTS
Sail Caribbean Divers
VHF channel 16
Tel: 284-495-1675
www.sailcaribbeandivers.com

NORMAN ISLAND

RESTAURANTS
Pirates Bight
VHF channel 16
Tel: 284-496-7827
Lunch 11am-4pm
Dinner 6:30-9:30pm
Live entertainment
Thursday-Sunday
Reservations requested
www.piratesbight.com

William Thornton
VHF channel 16
Tel: 284-496-8603
Lunch noon – 3pm bar open from noon
www.williamthornton.com

PETER ISLAND

RESTAURANT
Oceans Seven Beach Club
VHF channel 16
Tel. 284-494-2449
www.oceans7online.com

SPRAT BAY

MARINAS
Peter Island Marina
Main Tel. 284-495-2000
www.peterisland.com/yacht_club/harbor_info

HOTELS
Peter Island Resort
Tel: 284-495-2000
www.peterisland.com

FERRY
Peter Island Ferry
Departs from the P.I. Ferry dock in Baugher's Bay, Road Town
Call for schedule
Tel: 284-495-2000
www.peterisland.com

SHOPS
The Boutique
Tel: 284-495-2000

The Dive Shop
284-495-2000
www.peterisland.com/yacht_club/dive_shop

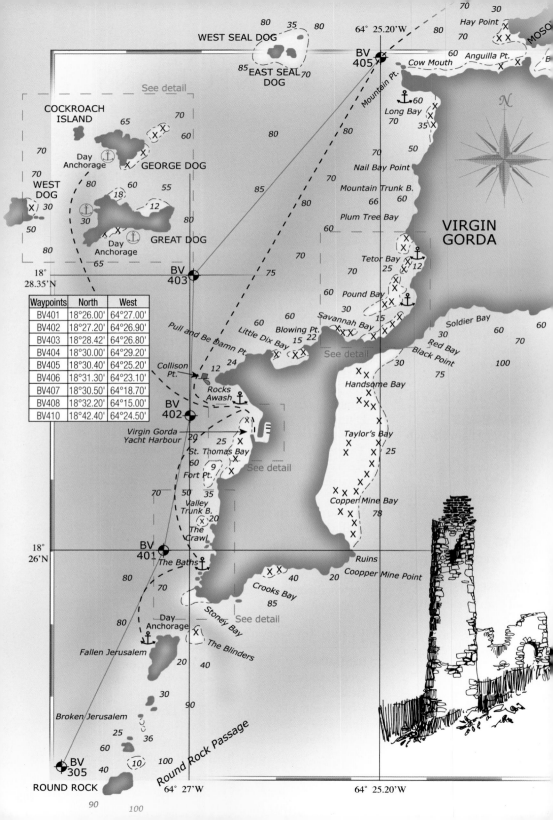

VIRGIN GORDA

The island of Virgin Gorda is approximately 10 miles long with high peaks at the north and central areas. All land over 1000 feet high on Virgin Gorda has been designated National Parks land to preserve its natural beauty. Gorda Peak National Park contains trails you can follow to hike to the summit, but there are many trails to follow including those along and through the Baths. The Baths are a natural collection of slowly eroded boulders that line the south end of Virgin Gorda. Their beauty is iconic. The waters around Virgin Gorda offer the sailor a myriad of delights from the granite caves at the Baths to the deep anchorages at North Sound.

Charts
NV.Charts: St.Thomas to Anegada: Kit C-12,12A,13
NIMA:2561, Imray Iolaire A-231
Admiralty Leisure 5640-2,3,7,8A,9

HISTORY

The first residents in Virgin Gorda history to populate the area were the Ciboney, Arawak, and Carib Indians. They lived by farming the land and fishing its abundant natural resources. Columbus came upon the entire string of Virgin Islands on his second voyage to the New World, in 1493. Seeing so many isles and cays, it is believed he named them after the 11,000 virgin followers of Saint Ursula, who were martyred in the fourth century (as the story goes). Virgin Gorda, the "Fat Virgin," as Columbus irreverently named the island for of its resemblance from seaward to a fat woman lying on her back, was once the capital of the British Virgins with a population of 8,000 people.

Privateers and pirates such as the notorious Bluebeard and the likes of Captain Kidd used Virgin Gorda as a base of operations from which to harass and plunder Spanish galleons that passed through the reef-laced waters carrying home to Europe gold from the New World.

Copper Mine Point

The island is approximately 10 miles long with high peaks at the north and central areas. All land over 1000 feet high on Virgin Gorda has been designated National Parks land to preserve its natural beauty.

VGYH

ST. THOMAS BAY

VIRGIN GORDA

THE BATHS

FALLEN
JERUSALEM

VIRGIN GORDA PANORAMA

THE BATHS

Waypoint: BV401 – 18°26.00'N; 64°27.00'W
Navigation: 4.7nm NE Cooper Island; 1.4nm south of VGYH
Services: Moorings, Restaurant, Beach Bar

Virgin Gorda

When planning a trip around the island, it is essential to include the Baths. Located on the southwest tip of Virgin Gorda, the Baths are a most unusual formation of large granite boulders. Where the sea washes in between the huge rocks, large pools have been created where shafts of light play upon the water, creating a dramatic effect. The beach adjacent to the Baths is white and sandy and the snorkeling excellent. A trail has been established behind the beach, through the boulders, to Devil's Bay to the south.

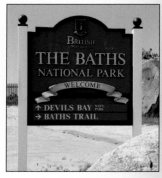

18°
26'N

Valley Trunk Bay

Little Trunk Bay
Rock
The Crawl

Spring Bay

VIRGIN GORDA

SWIM
AREA

The Baths

MOORINGS

TRAIL

Devils Bay

SWIM
AREA

Stoney
Bay

64° 27'W

THE BATHS | SPRING BAY

During winter ground swells, the anchorage is very exposed and at such times it is recommended that you anchor in St. Thomas Bay or take a slip at the Yacht Harbour and take a taxi ride to The Baths. The National Parks Trust has initiated a flag system to warn of dangerous seas in the area of the Baths. There is a flag pole at the top of the Baths, and one on Devil's Bay beach. There are plans to install more along the beach area to ensure that they are clearly visible to boaters.

This information will be provided in the National Parks Trust permit required in order to use National Parks Trust moorings.

Navigation & Piloting:

Approaching from the south (Waypoint BV305 Round Rock Passage North) keep Round Rock, Broken Jerusalem and Fallen Jerusalem well to starboard. The area has numerous uncharted rocks and a 2 knot current that can run northwest or southeast. When approaching from the Sir Francis Drake Channel, the first landmark will be the large rock formations. There are fine, white sandy beaches of varying sizes and the Baths are located at the second beach from the westernmost tip of Virgin Gorda. If there is a ground sea running, it is advisable to keep sailing into the Yacht Harbour and take a taxi to the Baths.

If you are powering or sailing further north towards the Yacht Harbour, be mindful of Burrows Rock, which extends 200 feet out from the small headland at the south end of Valley Trunk Bay.

Anchoring & Mooring

National Park moorings are the only mode of securing the vessel in order to protect the coral as this is in part of the BVI National Park Trust. **There is no anchoring at the Baths.**

There is a dinghy mooring system at the head of the small bay, from there it is an easy swim ashore, or, if you are landing passengers on the beach, no motors are allowed inside of the buoyed areas in order to protect swimmers and snorkelers. If there is a swell evident, use extreme caution landing passengers. It is best to have someone jump out and hold the dinghy in 3 feet of water while passengers and cameras are unloaded safely.

Ashore

Take ashore only those articles that you don't mind getting wet, and wrap cameras and valuables in plastic bags. The entrance to the Baths is unmarked but is at the southern end of the beach under the palm trees. Make your way in between the slot in the rocks and follow the trail. There is excellent snorkeling around the point from the Baths south to Devil's Bay, but the beaches to the north are private. A fabulous trail leads inconspicuously between the Baths and Devil's Bay. Wear reef shoes – it can be slippery, but is well worth the challenge.

Colorful stalls on the beach sell souvenirs, crafts and t-shirts. It is also possible to get a cold drink and sandwiches at the Poor Man's Bar or sandwiches and piña coladas at Mad Dog's, both right on the beach. At the Top of the Baths you can enjoy breakfast, lunch and dinner while enjoying the view of the Baths and the islands to the west or cool off in their fresh water pool. Meal service starts at 8am and dinner service stops at 10pm. Dinner reservations are recommended by VHF Channel 16 or 284-495-5497.

SPANISH TOWN (ST. THOMAS BAY)
VIRGIN GORDA YACHT HARBOUR

Virgin Gorda

Waypoint: BV402 (St.Thomas Bay) – 18°27.20'N; 64°2726.90'W

Navigation: 45.3nm east of Trellis Bay; 1.4nm north of The Baths

Services: Port of entry, Ferry service, Full service 120 slip marina, Restaurants, ATM, Yacht repair facility

Once the capital of the BVI, Spanish Town is still the major settlement on the island. Although opinions vary, it is commonly thought that Spanish Town is so called for the number of Spanish settlers who came to mine the copper ore at Copper Mine Point early in the 16th century. The mines were still working until 1867, and it is estimated that some 10,000 tons of copper ore were exported.

The Virgin Gorda Yacht Harbour is located in the middle of Spanish Town (or the Valley as it is more commonly referred to) and is the hub of shopping and boating activity on the south end of the island.

Navigation

Approaching St. Thomas Bay and the Virgin Gorda Yacht Harbour from the east, head for the northeast corner of the bay. Yachts traveling south from Gorda Sound should give a wide berth to Colison Point (4 sec fl. green buoy) as they have rocks awash at the end of the point.

Yachts not wishing to enter the yacht harbor can pick up one of the available mooring balls (payment should be made ashore at the marina office) or anchor in the lee of the headland in 15 feet of water.

To enter the yacht harbor, you should familiarize yourself with the location of the St. Thomas reef that parallels the shoreline.

Approach the harbor on a line with the prominent jetty in St. Thomas Bay. Leave the first two markers (green) to port.

Immediately to starboard, you will see the first red buoy marking the north end of the reef. As you round the second red buoy, you will turn approximately 90 degrees to starboard and pass between another set of buoys before entering the harbor. Contact the harbormaster via VHF 16 to get your slip assignment before you enter the yacht harbor. A slip reservation the day before is a good idea to ensure you have a slip when arriving. There is no anchoring in the yacht harbor.

When leaving Virgin Gorda Yacht Harbour/St. Thomas Bay and heading north to Gorda Sound, be sure to give Colison Point a wide berth, as the rocks extend well out from the land into the water. There should be a green 4 sec fl. buoy marking this point. Make sure it is on station.

Ashore

Customs and Immigration are located at the town jetty, just a couple of minutes from the Virgin Gorda Yacht Harbour. They are open from 8:30am to 4:30pm Monday through Friday and on Saturday from 8am to 12:30pm. Sundays and holidays incur overtime charges. Upon entry from another country to the BVI proceed to Customs & Immigration. Only the skipper needs to go to present passports of the passengers and the ships papers.

If you arrive after regular hours you must raise your yellow Q flag and call Customs at 284-495-5173 and Immigration at 284-495-5621. You must not leave your vessel until you have cleared in.

The marina has dockage for over 100 yachts and can accommodate 4 – 5 super yachts at any given time. The maximum length is 180 feet and the maximum width is approximately 35 feet. The controlling depth in the harbor is 10 feet.

When entering the marina, the fuel dock is directly ahead on the port side, with a Shell sign. The amenities include water, ice, fuel, oil, Wifi, and power (110v, 220v and 110 amps). Showers and heads are included in the dockage fee. Visit their marine chandlery and while you're there you can also stock up on provisions and use their computers and internet service. Garbage can be disposed of in bins at both ends of the marina.

Complementing the marina is a full service boatyard and dry storage facilities adjacent to the harbor. The boatyard is serviced by a 70 ton Travel Lift that can haul vessels over 100 feet in length with beam up to 22 feet. The boatyard offers complete services including shipwrights, marine mechanics, Awlgrip, and osmosis treatment.

The marina complex offers numerous facilities including a bank, drug store, a market for provisioning, car rentals, taxis, Thee Artistic Gallery and other shops. On the patio is the Bath and Turtle Tavern, a fun, casual place for breakfast, lunch and dinner.

For divers, Dive BVI operates a full service dive shop offering daily tours as well as rendezvous dives from the Virgin Gorda Yacht Harbour.

Little Dix Bay Resort is a taxi ride away and those wishing to look around the grounds are welcome for drinks and luncheon. Reservations are required for dinner. Although jackets are not required, shorts are not allowed in the dining room after 6 pm. Appropriate attire is requested.

Do visit the elegant Chez Bamboo with a specialty bouillabaisse and luscious steak and more. Fischers Cove serves breakfast, lunch and dinner from 7:30am to 10pm daily in a casual, friendly atmosphere by the water. Newly opened, Coco Maya has a cocktail lounge, bar and restaurant, and is open from 4pm every day for drinks and 7pm for dinner. The Rock Café is nestled amongst the fabulous Virgin Gorda boulders and is only a ten minute walk from the yacht harbour. They are open daily for dinner from 4pm until closing. You can dine in air conditioned comfort, or outside on the terrace where you will also find La Tequila Bar. They often have live music.

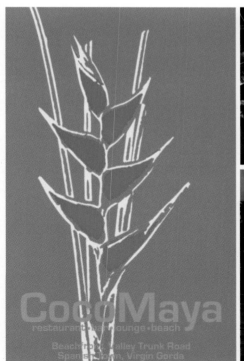

Savannah Bay

Waypoint: BV403 (Gt.Dog) – 18°28.42'N; 64°26.80'W
Navigation: 2.3nm NE of VGYH
Services: None

Virgin Gorda

During the summer months or when the ground swells are down and the weather is calm, there is a delightful anchorage behind the reef in Savannah Bay, however it can be very tricky to get in and navigate over coral heads to the anchorage. When the weather is calm, being anchored in Pond Bay is the quintessential Caribbean experience. If you are chartering this bay may be off limits.

Navigation & Piloting:

The entrance to Savannah Bay behind the reef is at the southern end of the bay, just north of Blowing Point under Minton Hill. It is essential that you have good overhead light in order see the coral heads and a lookout posted on the bow.

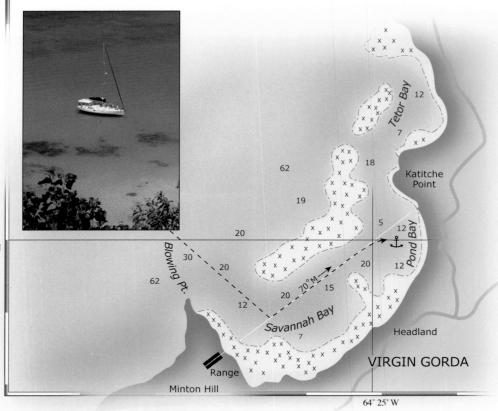

18°
28.20'N

Tetor Bay 12
7
62
18
19
Katitche Point
5 12
20 12 Pond Bay
30
20
Blowing Pt.
62
20 70°M 20 12
12 20 15
Savannah Bay
7
Headland

Range

VIRGIN GORDA

Minton Hill

64° 25' W

Enter the anchorage about 325 yards off the point parallel to the headland. There is a small reef that extends from the headland on your starboard hand. Work your way into the bay until you are abeam of a white range marker painted on the rocks under Minton Hill to starboard. When the range is abeam turn to port (about 70°M) and continue with caution toward the end of the beach under Katitche Point. You will pass over some coral heads but this will take you into Pond Bay where you can anchor in 12-15 feet of water on a sandy bottom. The snorkeling is excellent.

Tetor Bay further north is a complicated channel and should not be attempted except by dinghy. Watch for the small reef that extends from the headland on your starboard hand and work your way around the coral heads that comprise the center reef. Once inside, you can anchor in 7 feet of water.

LONG BAY

Waypoint: BV405 (Mountain Pt.) – 18°30.40'N; 64°25.20'W
Navigation: 3.2nm north of VGYH (Colison Pt.)
Services: None

Situated under Mountain Point, Long Bay is a small, pleasant anchorage that is tenable only when there is no ground sea running. The anchorage is easy to approach and anchoring is on a sandy bottom in 15-20 feet of water. There is a reef that extends from the shore to the northwest.

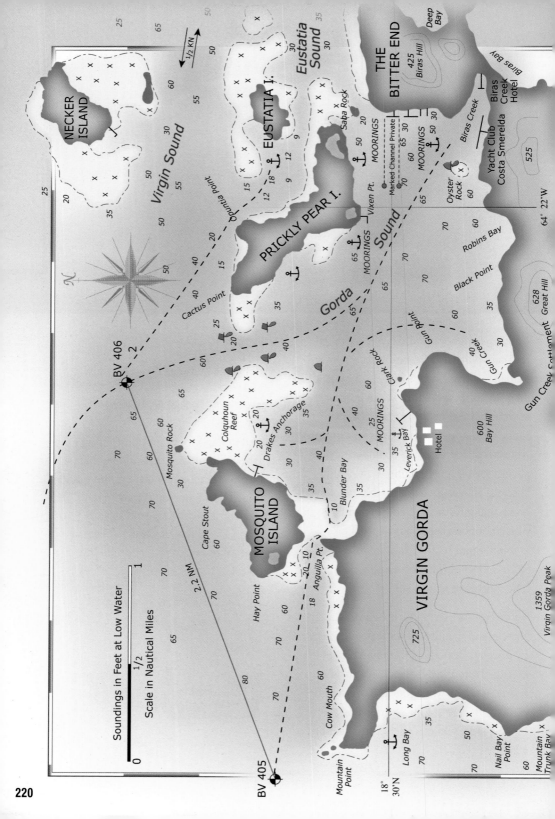

NECKER ISLAND

Virgin Sound

Eustatia Sound

EUSTATIA I.

THE BITTER END

Deep Bay

425 Biras Hill

Biras Bay

PRICKLY PEAR I.

Opuntia Point

Saba Rock

MOORINGS

Marked Channel Private

MOORINGS

Vixen Pt.

MOORINGS

Biras Creek

Biras Creek Hotel

Yacht Club
Costa Smerelda

Oyster Rock

525

64° 22' W

Cactus Point

Gorda

Sound

MOORINGS

Robins Bay

Black Point

628 Great Hill

BV 406

Colquhoun Reef

Drakes Anchorage

Mosquito Rock

Clark Rock

Gun Point

Gun Creek

Gun Creek Settlement

Blunder Bay

MOORINGS

Leverick Bay

Hotel

600 Bay Hill

N

Cape Stout

MOSQUITO ISLAND

Scale in Nautical Miles

Soundings in Feet at Low Water

2.2 NM

Hay Point

Anguilla Pt.

VIRGIN GORDA

725

1359 Virgin Gorda Peak

Cow Mouth

Mountain Point

Long Bay

Nail Bay Point

Mountain Trunk Bay

18° 30' N

BV 405

½ KN

220

GORDA SOUND (NORTH SOUND)

Waypoint: BV406 (Mosquito Rock) – 18°31.30'N; 64°23.10'W

Navigation: 15nm NE Road Harbour; 3.6nm north of VGYH

Services: Moorings, Restaurants, Beach bars, Full service marinas, hotels

Located at the northern end of Virgin Gorda, Gorda Sound or North Sound, as it is sometimes called, is a large bay protected all around by islands and reefs. It is an ideal place to spend several days exploring the reefs and relaxing. There are numerous restaurants and marina complexes here to suit almost everyone's taste and wallet. There are three entrances into the Sound but only one that is well marked. The western entrance via Anguilla Point is tricky and should only be used by those with local knowledge. Most bareboat companies place it off limits.

SABA ROCK

PRICKLY PEAR

BITTER END

BIRAS CREEK

YCCS

GUN CREEK

LEVERICK-BAY

DRAKE'S ANCHORAGE

COLQUHOUN REEF

MOSQUITO ROCK

N

Navigation & Piloting
NORTHERN ENTRANCE
VIA COLQUHOUN REEF

Gorda Sound is best approached from the north. A prominent landmark is Mosquito Rock that extends 25 feet above sea level and marks both the northern extremity of Mosquito Island and the northern tip of Colquhoun Reef that arcs to the southeast into the Sound. The channel between Colquhoun Reef to the west and Cactus Reef to the east is marked with two sets of red and green buoys and the controlling depth is from 15 feet where the buoys are located to 35 feet in the center of the channel.

Leaving Mosquito Rock well to starboard, head for the first green buoy (flashing 6 seconds) that marks the port side of the channel when entering. This will keep you clear of both reefs. There is a red nun (fl.6 sec) to starboard marking the outer (eastern) limits of Colquhoun Reef. Proceed through the second set of markers (fl.5 sec) into clear water and Gorda Sound.

If you are proceeding to Leverick Bay or Drakes Anchorage, continue due south until you are south or east of the third red buoy marking the southern extent of the coral heads extending from Colquhoun Reef. It is imperative that you leave it to starboard in order to avoid going aground. Once past the buoy, you can proceed directly to either anchorage with clear water.

Traveling to the east, past Vixen Point, is a vast mooring field associated with both the Bitter End and Saba Rock. There is a privately marked channel to the docks of Bitter End, and another marking a channel past Saba Rock and into Eustatia Sound.

There is one other navigational hazard in the Sound and that is Oyster Rock, which is to the west of the Biras Creek anchorage. The rock is marked with a red cone buoy.

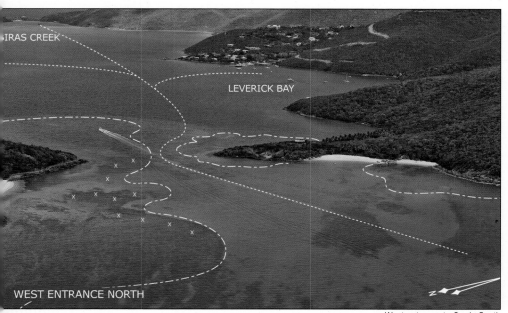

IRAS CREEK

LEVERICK BAY

WEST ENTRANCE NORTH

West entrance to Gorda South

Vixen Point
(Prickly Pear Island)

Navigation: 0.9nm SE Colquhoun Reef Entrance;
Services: Moorings, Beach bar, Restaurant

Anchoring & Mooring

On the west side of Prickly Pear Island, just north of Vixen Point, there is some available room to anchor just to the north of the mooring field. Anchor in about 15 feet of water on a sandy bottom. Closer to Vixen Point several moorings are available off of the sandy beach and you may register and pay for them ashore at the restaurant.

Ashore

The Sand Box serves lunch from 11:00am to 5pm daily and dinner from 6:30 to 11pm in a casual beach bar atmosphere. They also serve a mean margarita! The beach is good for swimming and you have a clear view of the activity in the Sound while you relax. The Sand Box monitors VHF 16 or call 284-495-9122.

Saba Rock

Navigation: 1.5nm NE of entrance channel
Services: Ferry, Wifi hotspot, Marina, Restaurant, Hotel

Originally developed by Bert Kilbride, Saba Rock is a tiny island sitting astride the channel to Eustatia Sound between the Bitter End on Virgin Gorda and Prickly Pear Island. The island boasts an amazing resort for such limited real estate. It includes a marina, gardens, a hotel, restaurant, gift shop, and a beach with hammocks to get rid of that last stubborn bit of stress.

Anchoring & Mooring

Approaching Saba Rock and the moorings from the west it is difficult to know which moorings belong to Saba Rock and which ones to Bitter End. Generally the moorings to the north of the marked channel are those belonging to and maintained by Saba Rock.

Several moorings are available at $25.00 per night (payable in the gift shop) with free 250 gallons of water and a bag of ice. Pull up to the T dock to take on water from 7am until it gets dark. The deep water marina along the shoreline has slips up to 24 feet wide, water, electricity, ice and a place to dispose of garbage. Check your email as Saba Rock provides a free wifi hotspot.

If you plan to anchor, drop your hook to the west of the mooring field, along the coast of Prickly Pear in 15 feet of water.

Ashore

Amazingly spacious, air-conditioned rooms with satellite TV are available with special boater's rates. The restaurant is open daily and has a pub menu served from 12 to 9:00pm. The dinner menu is served from 6:00 to 9:00pm. Check ashore to see when they have live music scheduled.

The Moorings Charter Company has a sub-base here to assist their charterers with anything they need.

Saba Rock offers a free ferry service to collect guests from any dock in the North Sound. Call to arrange a pick up.

BITTER END

Navigation: 1.3nm NE of North Sound Channel Entrance
Services: Moorings, Ferry, Full service marina, Restaurant, Hotel, Watersports

Anchoring & Mooring

Located on John O'Point, the Bitter End is a resort hotel and marina that features water sports and recreational activities. The resort includes restaurants and a marina with overnight dockage, guestrooms and moorings.

There are two sets of lighted buoys marking the approach for the North Sound Express ferryboat. Avoid anchoring near this channel to keep it clear for ferry traffic. The Bitter End channel and mooring field is a no wake zone.

The Bitter End has 70 moorings available for boats up to 60 feet at $30.00 per night that can be paid for at the Quarterdeck Office with cash or credit cards (8am-3pm) or paid to the launch driver every evening from 5pm to 10pm (cash only).

Bitter End has two dinghy docks – both marked with signs that read "Dinghy Dock." One is directly in front of the main lobby at the end of the channel. The other dinghy dock is inside the Quarterdeck Marina to the right of the main lobby building. The Quarterdeck Marina sells fuel and water at the separate fuel dock open from 8am to 4:30pm with a depth at the fuel dock of 12 feet. Vessels taking a berth will also have electricity hookups. Depth in the marina is approximately 10-12 feet and the marina can accommodate yachts with a length of

120 feet and 12 feet of draft. Megayachts 200 feet long and up to 18-foot draft are docked at the concrete "L" dock. Please make arrangements in advance. The Bitter End monitors VHF 16 or can be called by phone at 284-494-2745 ext 315.

Ashore

The Bitter End is a unique nautical village catering to yachtsmen. Ashore you will find the Provisions Emporium which stocks a wide array of meat, fish, breads and pastries baked fresh every day, dairy products, fresh fruits and vegetables as well as beverages including beer, wine, and liquor.

The Clubhouse Steak and Seafood Grille serves breakfast, lunch and dinner. The English Pub serves drinks as well as lunch and dinner daily from 11am until closing. Free wireless internet is available in the Clubhouse and the Pub. Both fax and telephone services are available from the front desk in the main lobby. Bitter End often has entertainment at night. Check ashore to find out what is going on!

For shopping try the Reeftique with clothing, jewelry, sunglasses and Bitter End logo-wear. The Bitter End Outfitters stocks sundries, gifts, local art, books, games and dive gear. For those needing to relax and unwind from a long day on the Sir Francis Drake Channel, the Spa at Bitter End is the place

to do it, with massages, aromatherapy, manicures, facials and private yoga sessions.

Bitter End is known as a watersports center with over one hundred boats to rent, plus windsurfers, stand up paddle boards, kite boarding, fishing, Sunday regattas, and US Sailing certified lessons. Sunchaser Scuba dive center has their base at Bitter End for the divers in your crew. To document it all is Yacht Shots who will photograph you and your crew on board your boat with all sails up, heeling over and gliding through North Sound. Boat supplies can be purchased at the Chandlery.

The Quarterdeck Club and Marina offer private showers and toilets and 24-hour security. They can also accommodate deep draft yachts up to 200 feet. Dockside electricity is available: 30 amp 110V, 50 amp 220V. Garbage pickup is at your boat in the morning between 8 – 9am. Bags must be tied and there is a charge of $2 per bag. Mechanical services are available through the Quarterdeck Marina.

For those on moorings, you may call the dockmaster on VHF 16, Captain Isaac, and request a free ride ashore on the Bitter End launch. The free service is daily from 6:45pm to 10:45pm each evening.

One could stay here for a whole charter and experience something new and exciting every day.

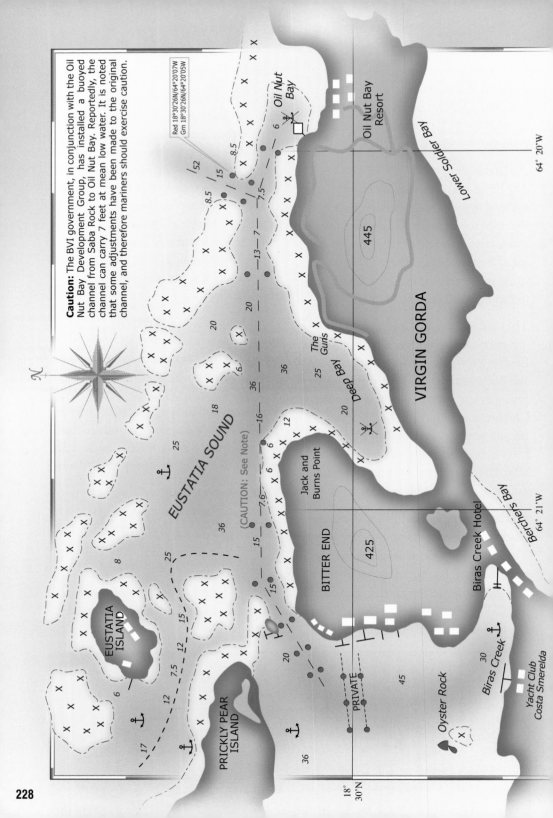

Caution: The BVI government, in conjunction with the Oil Nut Bay Development Group, has installed a buoyed channel from Saba Rock to Oil Nut Bay. Reportedly, the channel can carry 7 feet at mean low water. It is noted that some adjustments have been made to the original channel, and therefore mariners should exercise caution.

Red 18°30'26N/64°20'07W
Gm 18°30'26N/64°20'05W

Oil Nut Bay

Oil Nut Bay Resort

Lower Soldier Bay

VIRGIN GORDA

445

EUSTATIA SOUND

The Guns

Deep Bay

Jack and Burns Point

(CAUTION: See Note)

BITTER END

425

Biras Creek Hotel

Berchel's Bay

EUSTATIA ISLAND

PRICKLY PEAR ISLAND

Oyster Rock

PRIVATE

Biras Creek

30

45

Yacht Club Costa Smerelda

64° 20'W

64° 21'W

18° 30'N

228

EUSTATIA ISLAND AND EUSTATIA SOUND

Waypoint: BV406 (Mosquito Rock) 18°31.30'N; 64°23.10'W

Navigation: 1.7 nm SE of Mosquito Rock (Eustatia Island)

Services: None

Eustatia Sound is a magnificent area, located to the north and east of Bitter End and Saba Rock. The most sheltered overnight anchorage in the area is in behind Eustatia Island, which bounds the western end of the Sound. However, many skippers use the Sound as a day anchorage to enable diving and snorkeling along the stretch of reef that marks the northern extremity of the sound and entrance to the Necker Island Channel.

This area is not well marked and caution should be exercised unless you are very familiar with navigating around and through coral. A good solution is to leave the boat on the mooring at Saba Rock or Bitter End and take the dinghy through the cut and out to the reef.

Navigation

Approaching from the north or west (via waypoint BV406), leaving Mosquito Rock and the entrance to the Sound via Colquhoun Reef well to starboard, continue to the southeast leaving Prickly Pear Island to starboard. To the northeast you will see Necker Island and Eustatia Island will be visible ahead to the southeast. Once you are past Opuntia Point on the northeast tip of Prickly Pear, turn southeast and steer for the eastern tip of Prickly Pear until Eustatia Island is due east. Head for the southwest end of Eustatia where you will see a dock and drop the hook in 15 feet of water in the lee of the island. Do not make your entrance too far north as there is reef to the northwest of the island; favor the Prickly Pear side of the channel.

Eustatia Sound

From North Sound

The B.V.I. government has recently installed a buoyed (red and green) channel from the passage to east of Saba Rock all the way to Oil Nut Bay where a large upscale development is underway. The channel is reported to carry 8 feet and joins a marked channel through the eastern end of the reef to seaward and into the Necker Island Channel. Skippers are encouraged to exercise extreme caution. Anchoring in Deep Bay or Oil Nut Bay is discouraged.

Vessels wishing to transit through the Saba Rock channel and on to the anchorage behind Eustatia Island (Eustatia Sound) should note the location of the reef extending north from Saba Rock toward Eustatia Island. Post a knowledgeable lookout on the bow and proceed with caution. Make sure that you have good light overhead.

Grunt

Bitter End

Looking West from Bitter End

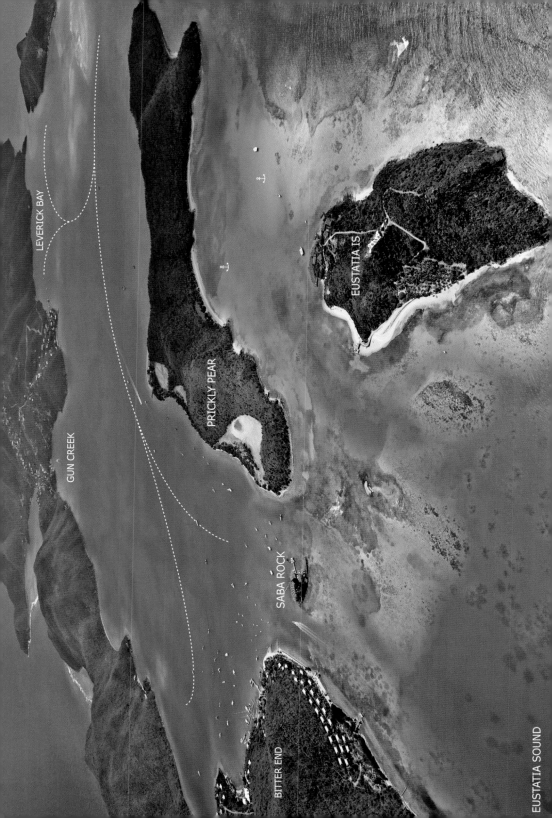

LEVERICK BAY

GUN CREEK

PRICKLY PEAR

EUSTATIA IS

SABA ROCK

BITTER END

EUSTATIA SOUND

BIRAS CREEK

Navigation: 1.8nm NE of Channel Entrance
Services: Ferry, Moorings, Hotel, Restaurant

A very well protected anchorage fringed by mangroves, Biras Creek Resort, at the head of the harbor, straddles a hill with stunning views of the beach on one side and the harbor on the other. The harbor is accessible directly from North Sound where twenty-two moorings are available for a fee of $20.00 per night (free if dining at the restaurant). The mooring field is set up with a 60 foot swinging radius, therefore vessels using a mooring must be under 60 feet in length. An attendant will come to the boat to collect the fee. During a storm these moorings are designated as a hurricane shelter area.

The marina can accommodate vessels not exceeding 50 feet long. To make reservations for dock space, contact them at 284-494-3555 or hail them on VHF channel 16. When slips are available you can pay by the hour, daily or by the month. The dinghy dock is located at the base of the marina dock to your right when facing the resort. Trash is accepted at the fuel dock only, for a fee of $3 per bag.

PRICKLY PEAR

SABA ROCK

BITTER END

N

New Marina:
Yacht Club Costa Smeralda

BIRAS CREEK

BIRAS CREEK

YACHT SHOTS
PHOTOGRAPHY
www.yachtshotsbvi.com

BEYC, North Sound, Virgin Gorda: 284.495.7550

With at least 11 kts of wind, we're out photographing yachts near Seal Dog & Mountain Point, Virgin Gorda and watersports in the North Sound. Get shot now & purchase the digital images or have your photos printed on anything from wallet to poster size prints, T-shirts, mugs & more.
View & order everything online!

Captains! We also shoot interiors. Contact us for your brochure photography.

www.yachtshot-bvi.com

Ashore

Guests from visiting yachts are welcome at the resort's panoramic hilltop restaurant. Breakfast is served from 8 – 10am, lunch is served from 1 – 2pm at the beach five days during the week and the other two days a light lunch is served in the restaurant, dinner is served from 6:30pm to 8:45pm. A private dining room is also available for special occasions. Reservations for dinner are required and must be guaranteed with a credit card. In order to maintain a calm, stress-less holiday environment, children under eight years old are not allowed at the resort.

The Biras Creek Restaurant is well-known for its superb meals served in a romantic atmosphere. The resort requests that after 5:30pm men wear trousers and a collared shirt and ladies wear suitable resort attire and please no shorts, jeans or tennis shoes. The grounds, beach and swimming pool are reserved for resort guests guests but visitors are welcome to use the trails to the beach.

On your starboard side as you enter Biras Creek are the service buildings for the resort and also the location of the Fat Virgin Café and Boutique. This is a casual, fun establishment serving from 10am for sandwiches, burgers, chicken and roti.

Bitter End Resort, Saba Rock, and Leverick Bay Resort are all within dinghy range of Biras Creek and they all have gift shops, restaurants and bars.

YACHT CLUB COSTA SMERALDA

Opened in late 2011 the Yacht Club Costa Smeralda (YCCS) has been designed and built to the highest standards. Targeted to the owners of high end luxury yachts, the facility is attracting berthing memberships and eventually will become a members-only club. In the near term the facilities are open to the public and transient berthing is available.

The central T shape dock is 2,500 feet long and accessible from both sides with 38 slips available for yachts up to 100 meters (328 feet) and a draft of up to 9 meters (30 feet). To their credit, YCCS has installed one of the first marine pump-out stations in the area and has a strong commitment to the preservation of the environment. All marina services are available. Call the dockmaster on VHF 16.

The restaurant and bar are also open to the public and beautifully situated up the hill, overlooking Gorda Sound.

GUN CREEK

Navigation: 1.2nm due south of Colquhoun Reef Entrance; 1.2nm SE of Leverick Bay
Services: Provisions, Ferry, Restaurant, Taxi, Garbage Disposal, Customs & Immigration Clearance

To the east of Leverick Bay around Gnat Point, Gun Creek provides a protected anchorage in 18-20 feet of water. Ashore there is the local settlement of Creek Village. Should you need provisions check out the Gun Creek Convenience Center and Eatery. You may tie your dinghy up to the ferry dock and find the store about two hundred yards up the main road. Taxi and island tours can be arranged.

Leverick Bay Resort

LEVERICK BAY

Navigation: 1nm SSW of the Colquhoun Reef entrance channel

Services: Moorings, Ferry, Full service marina, Restaurant, Dive shop, Hotel, Provisions

Anchoring & Mooring

Leverick Bay Resort and Marina is one of those destinations that make North Sound a water sports haven. Heading for the marina from North Sound the water is fairly deep with a minimum 16 feet at the marina. Leverick Bay monitors VHF 16 or you may call 284-495-7275. Pull in to the T dock for water, fuel and ice. There are approximately 36 moorings in the bay available to pick up and pay the $25 per night fee at the marina.

On the southern side of the marina you will find the dinghy dock. The marina has 25 slips with electricity, fuel, ice, showers, trash disposal and laundry facilities. Both moorings and dock customers are entitled to 100 gallons of fresh water and a free bag of ice along with use of the resort's swimming pool. The marina can also accommodate up to three mega-yachts for overnight stays. The deepest part of the marina is 24 feet and has room for a 300 foot mega-yacht.

Ashore

Located on the northern shore of Virgin Gorda, Leverick Bay is an entertaining water sports recreation center. You will find all the amenities you need including a pool, grocery market, 24 hour laundry, wifi, and air conditioned rooms and villas.

The Yacht Club Costa Smeralda
Looking North to Bitter End

For the shoppers, the Pusser's Company Store carries a unique line of nautical and tropical clothing, watches and luggage presented as if you're in an antique nautical shop. Palm Tree Gallery has an extensive collection of Caribbean art, jewelry and ceramics. The Chef's Pantry and Deli has a wide selection of mouth watering gourmet foods. All the resort facilities are available to both villa and visiting boat guests.

The Leverick Bay Restaurant has open air dining on the second story terrace or dining at Jumbies Bar on the beach. It offers a breezy view of North Sound. Lunch and dinner are served, with reservations for dinner recommended. Friday nights feature a beach barbecue with the lively mocko jumbies show (Caribbean stilt dancers). Live music starts at 7pm until!

Leverick Bay is a good base for exploring by land or by sea. Dive BVI is a full service dive shop servicing divers in Virgin Gorda since 1975. They provide a good opportunity for diving on some of the unique dive sites around North Sound. Leverick Bay Water Sports have power boats, dinghies, Sunfish and kayak rentals for exploring North Sound.

If fishing is your passion, Charter Virgin Gorda will arrange to take you to the Sea Mount or the North Drop. Both are renowned fishing areas by anyone's standards.

DRAKE'S ANCHORAGE
(SOUTH BAY)

Tucked up to the east behind Colquhoun Reef and to the north of Blunder Bay, Drake's Anchorage as it is known is a delightful spot and a little off the beaten path. The breeze flows across the anchorage but the reef breaks up any chop.

Approaching the anchorage from the east, make sure that you are south of the red buoy marking the southern tip of the coral heads extending from Colquhoun Reef. Once past the buoy, continue west a short distance before turning northwest toward the docks. Anchor off the docks in 15 feet of water on a sandy bottom.

Ashore

Mosquito Island has reportedly been purchased by world renowned adventurer and entrepreneur Richard Branson. Plans are being made to build an eco-friendly, carbon-neutral, "green" resort are not surprising from this long time friend to the environment. At this time, no details of the resort have surfaced except that the island will be private. This will be one of many projects in the B.V.I. to use renewable resources, recycle, reduce carbon output and go green.

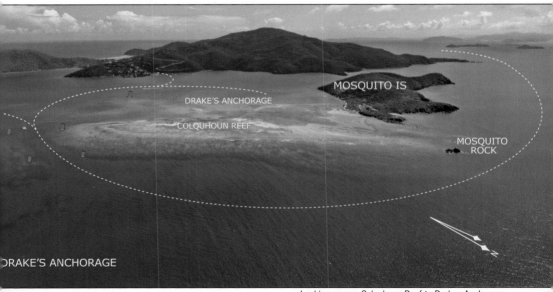

DRAKE'S ANCHORAGE

MOSQUITO IS

DRAKE'S ANCHORAGE

COLQUHOUN REEF

MOSQUITO ROCK

DRAKE'S ANCHORAGE

Looking across Colquhoun Reef to Drakes Anchorage

EMERGENCIES
VISAR (Virgin Island Search and Rescue)
VHF channel 16
Dial 767 (SOS), 999, or 911 or 284-494-4357
(494-help)
www.visar.org

TAXI, CAR RENTAL
Speedy's
284-495-5235/40
Speedy's can take you by taxi or rent you a car to discover Virgin Gorda by yourself
www.bviferries.com

THE BATHS

Top of the Baths
Breakfast and lunch, dinner may resume in the future
Opens at 8am till 6pm
Reservations recommended
VHF channel 16 or
284-495-5497
http://topofthebaths.com

Mad Dog
284-495-5830
Funky West Indian bar located at the roundabout
9-6 daily
maddogbvi.net

BIRAS CREEK

Biras Creek Marina
VHF channel 16
or email ga@biras.com
to reserve a mooring or dock space. 284-494-3555
www.biras.com/docking-and-mooring.html

Biras Creek Hotel and Restaurant
284-494-3555
Serves breakfast 8-10am, in the Hilltop Restaurant, lunch 1-2pm at the beach, and dinner back at the Hilltop from 6:30-8:45
Reservations required, dress code for dinner
www.biras.com

Fat Virgin's Café
VHF channel 16
284-495-7052
Open from 10am to 9pm
Serving casual fare on the waterside
www.fatvirgin.com

BITTER END

MARINAS
Bitter End Marina
VHF channel 16
284-494-2745
www.beyc.com/index.php/marina-facilities.html

PROVISIONS
Provision Emporium
284-494-2745
www.beyc.com/index.php/provisioning.html

RESTAURANTS
Clubhouse Steak and Seafood Grille
Serves breakfast (8-10am) lunch (12:15-2pm) and dinner (6:30-9:30pm) daily
www.beyc.com

The Crawl Pub
Serves drinks as well as lunch and dinner daily from 11am until closing.

SHOPS
Reeftique
Bitter End Outfitters
www.beyc.com/index.php/amenities.html

LEVERICK BAY

MARINAS
Leverick Bay Marina
VHF Channel 16
Tel: 284-495-7421
Cell: 284-542-4010
www.leverickbay.com/
Leverick_Bay/marina.php

RESTAURANTS
Leverick Bay
Tel: 284-495-7154/
346-5238. Open daily
8am-midnight. Lunch is
served at the beach bar
The Cove & dinner on
the upstairs terrace The
Restaurant at Leverick
Bay. Friday night BBQ at
the Jumbies Beach Bar.
Happy hour 5-6pm
www.leverickbay.com/
Leverick_Bay/restaurant
.php

PROVISIONS
**Chef's Pantry
Supermarket/Deli**
Open 8am to 5:50pm
Tel: 284-495-7372

Bucks Marketplace
Tel: 284-495-7368
Open daily 7am-7:50pm,
Sundays 7:30am-6:50pm

**Watersports
Dive BVI**
Tel: 284-495-5513
Dive tours, lessons and
rendezvous dives
www.divebvi.com

**Leverick Bay
Water Sports**
Tel: 284-495-7376
Rent water toys, Hobie
cats, snorkel equipment,
power boats and dinghies
www.watersportsbvi.com

Charter Virgin Gorda
Tel: 284-541-0465
For a fishing adventure

SHOPS
Pusser's Leverick Bay
Tel: 284-495-7369 or
495-7370
Check out this great shop
with nautical and tropical
items, clothing, jewelry, and
assorted interesting gifts.
www.pussers.com/
t-leverick-bay.aspx

Thee Nautical Gallery
Tel: 284-495-7479
Includes hand crafted
jewelry, art and gifts

YACHT CLUB COSTA SMERALDA

Yacht Club Costa Smeralda
Tel: 284 346-2000
VHF 08,
www.yccsmarina.com/
more_info.aspx

OIL NUT BAY

Oil Nut Bay
Private Resort
Community
Tel: 800-761-0377 or
284-495-5400
www.oilnutbay.com/home

SABA ROCK

MARINAS
Saba Rock Marina
VHF channel 16
284-495-7711
www.sabarock.com/
marina.php

RESTAURANTS
Saba Rock Restaurant
Tel: 284-495-9966
Happy hour daily 4-6pm
Reservations Requested
www.sabarock.com/
restaurant.php

SPANISH TOWN

CUSTOMS & IMMIGRATION
Virgin Gorda Customs
Tel: 284-495-5173
Virgin Gorda Immigration
Tel: 284-495-5621

MARINAS
Virgin Gorda Yacht Harbour
VHF channel 16;
working channel 11
Tel: 284-495-5500
Slip reservations info@
virgingorday-
achtharbour.com

MARINE REPAIRS
Virgin Gorda Yacht Services
Tel: 284-495-5685

TAXI SERVICE
Ask for Das, he is very
dependable for taxi
service and tours

RESTAURANTS
Bath & Turtle
Pub & Rendezvous Bar
Tel: 284-495-5239
Patio tavern open
7:30am -10pm
www.bathandturtle.com

CocoMaya
Tel: 284-495-6344
cocomayrestaurant.com
Fusion of Asian and
Latin cuisines

Chez Bamboo
Tel: 284-495-5752
Tapas Bar, Creole cuisine
Open daily from 4pm
Reservations requested
www.chezbamboo.com

Fischer's Cove
Tel: 284-495-5252
Waterside serving breakfast,
lunch and dinner
Specializing in island cuisine
Reservations requested
www.fischerscove.com/
hotel/restaurant.html

Little Dix Bay Hotel
Tel: 284-495-5555
Dining terrace serving
buffet luncheon 12:30-
2:30 daily, Dinner 7-9pm,
dress code required
Beach Grill serves lunch
from 12-3pm
www.rosewoodhotels.com
/en/littledixbay/dining/
the_sugar_mill/

Rock Café
Tel: 284-495-5482
VHF channel 16
Serving Italian and
Caribbean cuisine
amongst the boulders
Open daily from 4pm
Rock Café BVI on FB

Wheelhouse Restaurant
Tel: 284-495-5230
Serving local West
Indian fare
Breakfast, lunch & dinner

ANEGADA The Drowned Island

In contrast to the mountainous volcanic formation of the remainder of the Virgin Islands, Anegada is comprised of coral and limestone, at its highest point the island is 28 feet above sea level. Created by the movement between the Atlantic and Caribbean plates, which meet to the northeast of the island, Anegada is 11 miles long and fringed with mile after mile of white sandy beaches.

Horseshoe Reef, which extends 10 miles to the southeast, has claimed over 300 known wrecks, which provide excitement and adventure for scuba diving enthusiasts who descend on them to discover their secrets. The reef also provides a home for some of the largest fish in the area, as well as lobster and conch. The numerous coral heads and tricky currents that surround the island, along with the difficulty in identifying landmarks and subsequent reef areas, make it off limits for many charter companies. Since a marked channel into Setting Point has been established, daily traffic to Anegada has increased dramatically. Plan on spending at least two nights on Anegada. It is one of those special places.

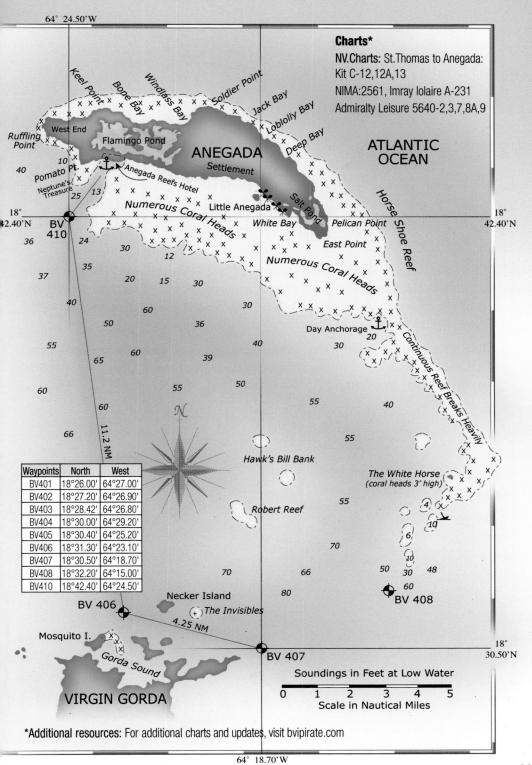

64° 24.50'W

Keel Point
Bone Bay
Windlass Bay
Soldier Point
Jack Bay
Loblolly Bay
Deep Bay

West End
Ruffling Point
Flamingo Pond
ANEGADA
Settlement

ATLANTIC
OCEAN

Pomato Pt.
Neptune's Treasure
Anegada Reefs Hotel

Numerous Coral Heads

Little Anegada
Salt Pond
White Bay
Pelican Point
East Point

Horse Shoe Reef

18°
42.40'N

BV
410

Numerous Coral Heads

Day Anchorage

Continuous Reef Breaks Heavily

18°
42.40'N

Charts*

NV.Charts: St.Thomas to Anegada:
Kit C-12,12A,13
NIMA:2561, Imray Iolaire A-231
Admiralty Leisure 5640-2,3,7,8A,9

N

The White Horse
(coral heads 3' high)

Hawk's Bill Bank

Robert Reef

Waypoints	North	West
BV401	18°26.00'	64°27.00'
BV402	18°27.20'	64°26.90'
BV403	18°28.42'	64°26.80'
BV404	18°30.00'	64°29.20'
BV405	18°30.40'	64°25.20'
BV406	18°31.30'	64°23.10'
BV407	18°30.50'	64°18.70'
BV408	18°32.20'	64°15.00'
BV410	18°42.40'	64°24.50'

Necker Island
The Invisibles

BV 408

BV 406

Mosquito I.

Gorda Sound

4.25 NM

BV 407

18°
30.50'N

VIRGIN GORDA

Soundings in Feet at Low Water

0   1   2   3   4   5
Scale in Nautical Miles

***Additional resources:** For additional charts and updates, visit bvipirate.com

64° 18.70'W

SETTING POINT

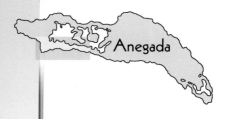

Anegada

Waypoint: BV410 (Setting Point) – 18°42.40'N; 64°24.50'W

Navigation: 11.4 nm north of Virgin Gorda (North Sound Entrance)

Services: Moorings, Restaurants, Tours, Car rentals, Ice, Fuel, Dive tours, Gift shops, Hotels

Additional resources: For additional charts and updates, visit bvipirate.com

Because of its low profile and surrounding coral heads, Anegada should be approached only in good weather conditions and with the sun overhead in order to see the bottom. Leave North Sound between 8 and 9:30am to arrive at the west end of Anegada with good light overhead in order to see the coral heads.

Day excursions from Marina Cay, Leverick Bay and Virgin Gorda Yacht Harbour are operated by Dive BVI's high-speed catamaran several times a week. Double "D" Charters also operate day trips from Virgin Gorda Yacht Harbour.

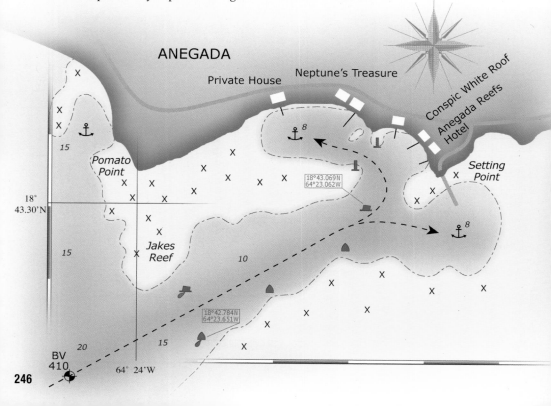

ATLANTIC OCEAN

FLAMINGO POND

NEPTUNE'S TREASURE

ANEGADA REEF HOTEL

POTTERS BY THE SEA

SETTING POINT

JAKE'S REEF

Navigation & Piloting

Departing from Gorda Sound (Waypoint BV406) steer a course of 008°m, which will take you from Mosquito Rock to Waypoint BV410 south of Pomato Point. The 1-2 knot current will set you down to the west and some compensation may be required as you approach the island. The 11.5 mile sail is usually a close reach. Approaching the island, you will see coral patches, but if you are on course, they will have 10-20 feet of water over them. Owing to the low elevation of the island, the palm trees and pines will be sighted before the land. Do not turn off course until you have identified Pomato and Setting Points or verified your waypoint. (Before the buoys were in place we would line up the eastern tip of Jost Van Dyke, and head in towards Setting Point). From BV410 to Setting Point the course is 076°m. Depending upon weather conditions you should be able to visually identify the outer red buoy marking the channel into Setting Point.

There are reported to be five channel markers, three reds and 2 greens, but at the time of the last survey one of the red buoys was missing. The outer port hand green buoy marks the southern end of Jakes Reef. Continue through the channel toward the dock until you reach the inner green marker leading you into the anchorage. If in doubt, call Anegada Reef Hotel, or Neptune's Treasure on VHF channel 16 for assistance.

POMATO POINT ANCHORAGE

When the weather is calm and the main anchorage is crowded, there is an anchorage in the small bay northwest of Pomato Point. The anchorage is due north 1.2 nautical miles of waypoint BV410. Anchor in 12-15 feet on a sandy bottom. Pomato Point Restaurant is a tranquil spot for dinner although they do not have a dock to land the dinghy.

Anchoring

Yachts drawing over 7 feet should anchor off the commercial dock, which is in line with the green buoy in 10-15 feet of water. All others can make their way into the inner harbor where numerous moorings are available. Skippers should take note of the reef that extends east into the anchorage between the southernmost dock (Potter's) and the large concrete commercial dock at the end of the point. Drop the hook in 8-10 feet of water on a good sandy bottom. Moor-Seacure has ten mooring buoys in the anchorage (white/blue and marked Moor-Seacure). After picking up one of these buoys, please go ashore and pay the $25.00 fee to the Anegada Reef Hotel.

There are ten more buoys painted orange in front of Potters by the Sea. A dinghy will come around to pick up mooring fees from the boats using these buoys. Again, the fee is $25.

Continue west of the Setting Point anchorage towards Neptune's Treasure. There are ten moorings in front of Neptune's Treasure. Approach these moorings from the east passing between the privately maintained red and green channel markers. Draft is around 6-7 ft. Fees for these moorings are $25. Please go ashore and pay at Neptune's Treasure. Note the coral head to the north between the red marker and the dock belonging to Neptune's Treasure. There is usually a fender marking the end.

Ashore

There is an abundance of things to do on Anegada. It is a unique island with its own unique culture. If time and schedule permits, plan on spending at least two nights here and settle into the low key atmosphere that makes Anegada a favorite destination for sailors from around the world.

One of the first things to do is decide where to eat dinner and make a reservation. The Anegada Reef Hotel specializes in fresh lobster on the grill, served under the stars in a very casual environment. The old honor bar still exists and they will organize taxis and tours.

Mark & Dean from Neptune's Treasure supply fish to numerous restaurants around the BVI from their fishing boat. Their first stop at the end of the day is home to Neptune's Treasure so you know the evening menu at Neptune's will feature fresh swordfish and conch served outside when weather permits.

Anegada has both interesting and fun activities to offer the visiting yachtsman. For exploring this unique island on your own, there are several car rental companies to select from: DW Jeep Rentals, Anegada Reef Hotel (Garfield's Rentals), and Egbert Wheatley Car Rentals. Additionally, there are bicycles and Kenny's motorized bike located on the main government dock at Setting Point.

For those preferring to use a bus shuttle service or taxi, there are services at Potter's by the Sea, Anegada Reef Hotel and Neptune's Treasure. It is advisable in all cases to ask what the rates are before accepting a ride. There is always transport available here, just come ashore or call ahead on VHF channel 16. Also the other establishments with dinghy docks will assist you with obtaining a taxi.

There are dinghy docks at Potter's, Anegada Reef, Lobster House, Lobster Trap, Whistling Pine, and Neptune's Treasure. Anegada Reef Hotel and Neptune's cater to the larger boats with approximately 4 feet 6 inches draft and 46 feet in length.

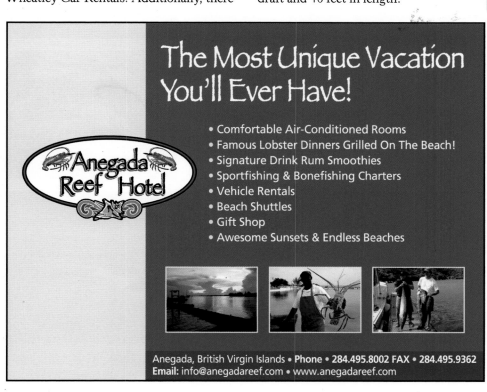

You can obtain fuel from Kenneth's Gas Station at Setting Point, just a few steps from Potter's and Anegada Reef docks. *Note:* This is the only place to buy gas on the island. If you wish you can bring your boat, or dinghy around to his dockside and there you are close to Lil Bit Cash & Carry, Sue's Boutique at the Purple Turtle, Potter's by the Sea, VnJ's, Angelina's and Anegada Reef Hotel.

Lil Bit Cash & Carry at Setting Point offer groceries, and also a laundry. Sue's Boutique at the Purple Turtle is also on the dockside and offers some groceries, including cheeses, paté, and wines together with a wide selection of gift items, tee shirts, etc. Here you can use the internet for checking and sending email, and a mailing service is offered. There are three grocery markets in the village (called the Settlement), Faulkner's Country Store, Vanterpool's Grocery Store and Cap's Grocery Store.

Gifts and boutique items: visit Sue's Boutique at the Purple Turtle at Setting Point, Anegada Reef Shop, VnJ's and Angelina's. These stores are situated at Setting Point which is now developing into a small shopping area.

Heading east towards the Settlement, at Nutmeg Point, visit VnJ's and next door, Henny's Gift Shop and DW Car Rentals. Pat's Pottery is also situated here on the ocean side of the road. Several restaurants will sell t-shirts and gift items at their various locations.

Visitors must experience the wonderful north shore beaches, particularly Loblolly where the snorkeling is spectacular. For

251

those wishing to "lagoon swim" and beach walk, Bones Bight and Cow Wreck beaches are some of the best in the world. For a very long beach walk, walk from the anchorage westwards and enjoy the idyllic beaches down to the west end. However, remember, most of the beaches are deserted and have little shade, so it is important to take some cold drinks with you, sun screen, a hat and a t-shirt for sun protection.

For the avid fishermen, the island has excellent bone fishing flats from Setting Point eastwards towards the end of the island. There are several guides who will take you by boat to the flats. They also rent fishing gear and will assist fishing

novices. The boat ride in itself is stunning and some guides will take you to their special little snorkeling areas within the Horseshoe Reef. For diving the stunning reefs and wrecks surrounding the island, call We Be Divin'.

The salt ponds in the center of the island are the habitat for many migrating birds and also the home of a flock of Caribbean

flamingoes, reintroduced to Anegada. Eighteen birds were brought from the Bermuda Zoo in March, 2002 and have successfully bred. These birds are thriving and now the flock far exceeds 100 birds. The habitat is perfect for them.

Heading west, look for the fields of wild orchids and also the endangered Anegada Rock Iguana, sometimes seen around the Bones Bight area. There is now an iguana "head-start" facility in the Settlement where visitors can view young iguanas being raised safely in captivity so they may grow to a suitable size before being released into the wild.

Accommodation ashore includes rooms and guest houses at Anegada Reef Hotel, Neptune's Treasure (both at Setting Point anchorage), and Ocean Range Guest House (in the Settlement). There are various beach cottages for rent, but generally this is for periods of longer term accommodation.

Beach restaurants that offer perfect day facilities are Cow Wreck Beach Bar & Restaurant, Big Bamboo and Flash of Beauty. Just order lunch and go for a swim and your lunch will be ready when you come back. They also offer dinners and will arrange transportation from the anchorage.

For dinner at Setting Point, if you prefer not to drive so far, Potter's, Anegada Reef, Lobster House, Lobster Trap, Whistling Pine and Neptune's Treasure are all very pleasant places to eat, offering lobster and seafood as their specialties. A little further west at Pomato Point is the Pomato Point

Restaurant. This is a lovely tranquil setting for dinner. Although they do not have a dinghy dock, they will arrange for transportation to and from Pomato Point.

Most restaurants need to have your dinner reservations by 4 pm at the latest. Dinners are by order only, so don't just show up and expect dinner without a reservation. The majority of restaurants monitor channel 16.

In the Settlement, there is a medical clinic, school, police and fire station, and a post office. As mentioned earlier, there are three grocery stores and a couple of bakeries/restaurants for local food. There are also several churches situated in the village.

Only some establishments accept credit cards, so it is advisable to check ahead. Most businesses do accept travelers checks in U.S. dollars and of course, U.S. currency. Euros are not accepted in the Virgin Islands. There is no ATM or bank in Anegada at present.

Build a Buoyage System and They Will Come

During the late '70s and early 1980s when the charter trade in the BVI was starting to expand, Lowell Wheatley was, as ever, busy developing, planning and re-building the Anegada Reef's Hotel. About this time the first edition of the *Cruising Guide to the Virgin Islands* was to be published.

Sitting at the bar with Lowell talking about how to get more boats into the anchorage we determined that a reasonable system of markers into the anchorage would certainly encourage sailors to make the passage and perhaps persuade the charter operators to relax the "off limits" approach. With private markers in place a planned approach route, all described in the upcoming guide, we had a plan!

At that same meeting we pulled out a chart and plotted the proposed approach. Then we jumped into Lowell's boat and surveyed the channel into Setting Point to determine where the buoys should be placed. I sent Lowell the proposed chart, he in turn made some changes and eventually between us we got it to press.

Some time later the BVI government placed permanent markers and GPS became mainstream. Now, every time I sail into Anegada, I marvel at the number of yachts sitting at anchor and remember the good old days.

Here's to you, Lowell!

SS

Setting Point

Looking across ponds to Neptune's Treasure

ISLAND CONNECTIONS

EMERGENCIES
VISAR (Virgin Island Search and Rescue)
VHF channel 16
Tel: 767 (SOS), 999 or 911
or 284-494-4357 (494-help)
www.visar.org

RESTAURANTS
Anegada Reef Hotel
VHF channel 16
Tel: 284-495-8002
Serving breakfast 8:30-10am, lunch 12:30-2pm, dinner 7:30 pm
Waterside at Setting Point
Reservations by 4pm
www.anegadareef.com

Potter's by the Sea
VHF channel 16
Tel: 284-495-9182
Serving lunch 10am-2pm and dinner 7:30
Waterside at Setting Point
Reservations by 4pm

Lobster Trap
VHF channel 16
Tel: 284-495-9466
Serving lunch 11am-2pm and dinner at 7:30
Waterside, specialty is BBQ Lobster
Reservations by 4pm

Neptune's Treasure
VHF channel 16
Tel: 284-495-9439
Serving lunch and dinner on the water
Specializing in conch, swordfish, and other local seafood
Dinner reservations by 4pm
www.neptunestreasure.com

Whistling Pines
Tel: 284-495-9521
Casual serving local conch, lobster, fish, steak
Open 11am-2pm, dinner from 6pm
Reservations by 4pm

Pomato Point
VHF channel 16
Tel:284-495-9466
Overlooking the beach
Serves local food for lunch and dinner
Reservations by 4pm

Lil'Bit Taz
Tel: 284-495-9932
Snack Bar open all day
Also has some provisions

Dotsy's Bakery
Tel: 284-495-9667
In the Settlement, serves fresh bread and pastries, and local cuisine
Lunch at 12-2pm, dinner 7-8pm

Big Bamboo
VHF channel 16
Tel: 284-499-1630

At Loblolly Bay on the north shore
Lunches specializes in Anegada lobster, conch, fish, chicken and more
Dinner on request
www.bigbamboo.vg

Cow Wreck Beach Bar
VHF channel 16
Tel: 284-495-8047
Cow-wreck-beach on Facebook

HOTELS
Anegada Reef Hotel
Tel: 284-495-8002
www.anegadareef.com

Neptunes Treasure
Tel: 284-495-9439
www.neptunestreasure.com

DIVE OPERATORS
We Be Divin'
Tel: 284-541-2835 or 541-0489
www.bviscubadive.com

RESOURCES
For additional charts and updates, visit bvipirate.com

Jost Van Dyke & Tobago

A large, high island, Jost Van Dyke lies three miles to the northwest of Tortola and becomes visible to yachtsmen sailing from St. Thomas upon entering Pillsbury Sound. With a population of less than 225, the island remains relatively unspoiled. The largest settlement is Great Harbour, which is also a port of entry into the BVI.

Claimed to be named after a Dutch privateer, Joost Van Dyke, the island is known as the birthplace of Dr. John Lettsom, born into a Quaker community on Little Jost Van Dyke in 1744. Dr.

Lettsom (also spelled Lettsome) later returned to his father's native England where he attended medical school and founded the London Medical Society and became a founding member of the Royal Humane Society. A philanthropist, abolitionist and humorist Dr. Lettsom wrote the following:

> *I, John Lettsom,*
> *Blisters, bleeds and sweats 'em*
> *If, after that, they please to die,*
> *I, John, lets 'em!*

As with many other islands in the region, Jost Van Dyke and the BVI in general saw steady economic decline throughout the 18th century.

From the emancipation era forward, the community of Jost Van Dyke subsisted mainly on small scale fishing and subsistence agriculture. Charcoal making was a practice that began during the plantation era, when strong fires were

West End Poi

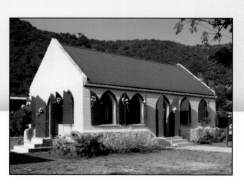

vital for sugar and rum production, and charcoal making emerged as a primary industry for the BVI during the post-emancipation years.

Maritime resources were also extremely important historically to the people of Jost Van Dyke, and the island has emerged as a fishing village. The desire for trade and social interaction with nearby islands stimulated the development of seafaring skills. Small, locally constructed sailing vessels like the "Tortola Sloop" flourished in the BVI until about the 1960s when they were replaced with motorized craft.

Waypoints	North	West
BV201	18°26.60'	64°42.75'
BV202	18°25.90'	64°43.05'
BV203	18°26.10'	64°45.00'
BV204	18°26.30'	64°45.80'
BV205	18°26.00'	64°49.50'
BV206	18°26.75'	64°50.00'

Charts
NV Charts: St.Thomas to Anegada: C-14
NIMA: 25641, Imray-Iolaire: A-231
Admiralty Leisure: 5640-5

LITTLE JOST VAN DYKE
DIAMOND CAY, GREEN CAY AND SANDY CAY

Jost Van Dyke

Waypoint: BV201 18°26.60'N 64°42.75'W
Navigation: 23nm from Anegada – 6.7nm from Guana Island (North WP)
Services: Long Bay only: Ice, Restaurant & Bar

Connected by a shallow channel on the northeast extremity of Jost Van Dyke, Little Jost Van Dyke is a small uninhabited island approximately 370 feet high. To the east is the small iconic islet of Green Cay and one mile to the south is Sandy Cay.

From the waypoint located between Green Cay and Sandy Cay, traveling to the northwest you will enter Manchioneel Bay. On the southeast of Little Jost Van Dyke is a delightful anchorage where you can stay away from the crowds, or

a little further east, is the idyllic Green Cay and Sandy Spit.

Traveling to the northwest, the anchorage shown on the chart as East End Harbour, is not recommended since it is exposed to the east.

Nestled between the eastern end of Jost Van Dyke and Little Jost Van Dyke, northeast of Diamond Cay, and west of Long Bay is the anchorage known as Diamond Cay, where Foxy's Taboo Bar and Restaurant is located.

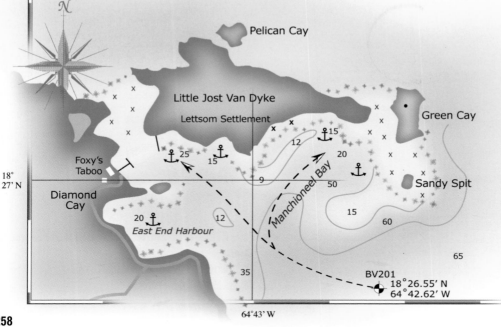

GREEN CAY
SANDY CAY
FOXY'S TABOO

Little Jost Van Dyke

DIAMOND CAY / LONG BAY

The approach is straightforward entering from the south and deep water. Moderate and deep draft vessels should anchor adjacent to the mooring field in 15-30 feet of water on a sandy bottom. Moorings (10 available) should be paid for ashore at Foxy's Taboo. If the wind is from the south, the anchorage becomes very sloppy and during northerly ground swells the surge can become excessive.

Dinghies and smaller powerboats can tie up at the dock, but care should be taken to identify the shoal water extending from the north where the two islands meet.

Ashore

Foxy's Taboo, a charming restaurant with a marina, is just north of Diamond Rock on Jost Van Dyke facing east towards Green Cay and Sandy Spit. This is a fun spot with an open air bar and dining area serving lunch and dinner. The food is

LITTLE JOST VAN DYKE

259

excellent and the atmosphere is breezy and light. The marina has depths of 8 to 15 feet and several slips. There are no facilities for garbage disposal here, so please hang on to it until you are somewhere that has garbage bins.

The "Bubbly Pool," a natural pool surrounded by large rocks at the ocean's edge, is about half a mile from the marina. The trail will take you along the beach and over a rocky pathway; reasonable footwear is recommended as flip-flops can be dangerous. At high tide, waves tumble in through a hole in the rocks creating a bubbling salt water pool. During periods of northerly swells, the water rushes in through the opening and surges up the small beach. Hang on to young children and beware of manchioneel trees! Ask for directions at the restaurant.

LITTLE JOST VAN DYKE / SOUTH SHORE

Once again the approach from the south is straightforward. If you are transiting from Diamond Cay, be aware of and identify the shoal area extending from Little Jost Van Dyke to the south. There are two good spots to drop your anchor, one at the Green Cay end of the headland and the other further along to the east. You will find sandy beach areas separated by rocks, providing ideal conditions for a day anchorage. Drop your anchor in 12-15 feet of water on a sandy bottom.

The Jost Van Dykes Preservation Society

The Jost Van Dykes Preservation Society has undertaken the building of a traditional island sloop designed by local residents who have sailed these traditional wooden vessels in days gone by. The purpose is to teach high school students lessons on boat building as well as to preserve a piece of history. Both Tessa and Foxy Callwood are very involved in the Preservation Society and will show you where to see the building of the sloop, Endeavour II, behind their restaurant. This is only one part of the mission of the Jost Van Dykes Preservation Society who are honoring, and creating an awareness of the island's maritime heritage, history of the island and its culture, and working to save the island environment. You can check the progress of the sloop project at www.jvdps.org and read about the many other projects they are working on in order to preserve the history of the islands. It is an interesting website describing the plants, living creatures, and salt ponds, some of which exist only in Jost Van Dyke. If you feel inclined, you may help them out with a generous donation.

GREEN CAY/SANDY SPIT

Green Cay is the quintessential Caribbean anchorage. Light turquoise water, a small sand island with a few palm trees and no services. It doesn't get better than this! Green Cay and Sandy Spit provide a safe comfortable anchorage in most conditions, but in unsettled weather or during a northerly ground swell, we suggest that you move to one of the more protected anchorages for overnight.

Anchor on a sandy bottom in 10-15 feet of water. Take the dinghy ashore or swim from the boat. The island is a perfect setting for a picnic.

SANDY CAY

To the southeast of Jost Van Dyke, Sandy Cay is a postcard setting and a perfect daytime stop for swimming and relaxing. For this reason the anchorage is usually crowded so anticipate company.

Sandy Cay is a national park, thanks to the efforts of Laurence Rockefeller, and a botanical tour on the small trail will afford you magnificent views of the surrounding islands.

The anchorage is on the southwest side close to shore, in the lee of the island. Anchor in 10-15 feet of water, the holding ground is excellent (sand) but be careful to avoid coral heads.

Extreme caution should be exercised during winter ground swells as the swell makes its way around both sides of the island, causing waves to break on the beach, making the landing of a dinghy difficult if not disastrous.

Bubbly Pool

LITTLE HARBOUR

(GARNER BAY)

Waypoint: BV202 18°25.90'N 64°43.05'W
Navigation: 3.4nm from Cane Garden Bay;
3nm due north of West End
Services: Restaurants, Bars, Ice, Provisions, Water

Little Harbour, or Garner Bay as it is sometimes called, lies to the east of Great Harbour. Once used as careenage for island sloops, the local skippers would lay their vessels alongside the beach (where Sidney's Peace and Love stands today), secure a block and tackle from the masthead to the palm trees and careen the boat in order to scrub or repair the bottom. The harbor now caters to the vibrant yacht trade with three restaurants and limited provisioning available. Little Harbour is easy to access and reasonably well protected.

Navigation & Piloting

The entrance to Little Harbour is straightforward and deep. The entrance is marked by red and green buoys, but use caution, since one or both of these buoys have been noted as missing on recent visits to the area. In transit from Great Harbour, be mindful of the shoal area to your port upon entering the bay, should the green buoy be off station.

Anchoring & Mooring

The traditional anchorage is in the northwestern end of the bay in 15 feet of water. In recent years, as the number of visiting boats has increased, mooring balls have been laid limiting the available room to lay an anchor. If you are anchoring, pick a spot in the northeastern end of the bay and anchor in 30 feet on hard coral sand. Make sure your anchor is well set before heading for shore.

Jost Van Dyke

To
Little Jost Van Dyke

Fuel
30   15   Abe's
36

Sidney's
Harris'
Place

Gregory Hole Pt.

Sandy Cay

70

10

Black Point

Little Harbour
Garner Bay

50   60

18°
26.10'N

BV202
18°25.90' N
64°43.05' W

Pick up a mooring on the west side of the bay and pay for it at Harris' Place, or Abe's if you pick up one to the east.

Ashore

On the western end of the bay is the Little Harbour Marina where you may purchase water and ice. There are three restaurants in the bay. On the eastern side is Abe's By the Sea, serving lunch and dinner with reservations. Abe's also has a little grocery store where you can buy ice and some provisions for the boat. Inflatable dinghies are available for rent next door to Abe's.

The western side of Little Harbour is home to Sidney's Peace and Love Restaurant (cheerfully decorated with hanging colored t-shirts), and Harris' Place. Sidney's is open at 9am for breakfast, lunch and dinner (specializing in seafood) with live music on some nights. Sidney's daughter Strawberry will be there to welcome you with her famous smile. If your party is four or more, the captain eats free. Harris' can provide you with ice, fax, telephone, and a dock with electricity. They serve breakfast, lunch and dinner daily. Check to find out which nights they will have live entertainment. Monday through Friday is all-you-can eat lobster! All restaurants monitor VHF 16.

For those who enjoy hiking, there is a small track that takes you about 1000 feet up the mountain. For those ambitious enough to make the climb, the views are spectacular – bring your camera!

GREAT HARBOUR

Jost Van Dyke

Waypoint: BV203 - 18°26.10N 64°45.00'W

Navigation: 5.5 nm from Cane Garden Bay: 4nm from West End : 5.3nm from Durloe Passage, USVI St. John

Services: Port of Entry BVI, Ice, Garbage disposal, Provisions, Restaurants & Bars, Shops, Fuel & Water at North Latitude Marina

This normally sheltered harbor nestled at the foot of 1,000 foot high peaks, Great Harbour is a port-of-entry into the BVI and is the largest settlement on the island. Access to the anchorage is straight forward, however, shoal water near the beach restricts anchoring room and on a weekend or holiday, it is advisable to arrive early. Great Harbour is serviced by ferry from West End, Tortola and the USVI.

Navigation & Piloting

Your approach should be approximately 351°. On your port side, upon entering the bay, there are two sets of red and green buoys designating a channel for ferries and official government business only. This channel carries a depth of 12 feet. Most pleasure

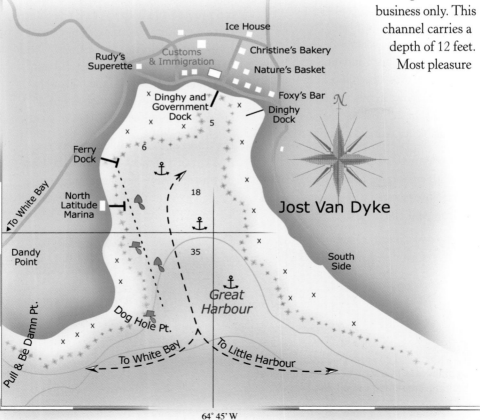

craft head down the middle of the harbor giving the shoreline on either side a reasonable berth. There is a large reef extending out 300 yards from the inner shoreline, be sure to identify the shoal before you reach it.

Anchoring & Mooring

Shoal water extends from both the east and west shorelines and you will need to be at least 300 yards from the beach. Since a limited number of mooring balls have been laid in this anchorage, swinging room can be limited depending upon the size of the fleet. The most favored spot would be to tuck yourself up is the east end of the bay under the reef in 10 feet of water. Normally, you will be anchoring in 15-30 feet of water. Make sure your anchor is well set and adequate scope laid out.

Ashore

Great Harbour is a port of entry with a customs and immigration office. Take the dinghy ashore through the break in the reef and head directly for the dock, in order to avoid shallow coral heads. The customs officer for Jost Van Dyke will clear vessels

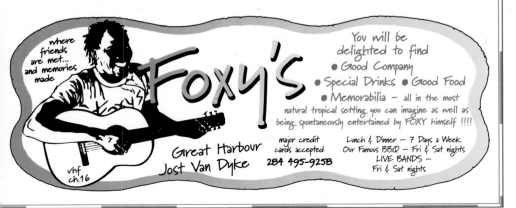

in or out of British Virgin Island waters for both customs and immigration, however, they cannot give immigration extensions, which must be done at the Road Town immigration office. Customs and immigration are open seven days per week from 8:30 to 4:30 and are closed briefly to deal with the ferry arrivals and departures. The office for customs, immigration and the JVD police are all located just at the base of the government dock. Across from the police station at the base of the dock is a dumpster for garbage disposal.

At the ferry dock on the western end of the harbor is the Sugar and Spice Snack Bar, where you can grab a bite to eat while waiting for the ferry. Ferries are available to West End, Tortola.

North Latitude Marina is located just south of the ferry dock and offers diesel, gasoline, water, ice in addition to a small convenience store. There is 12 feet of water at the dock and they stand by on VHF 16 daily from 7am to 5pm (9-5pm on Sunday).

Great Harbour has a worldwide reputation for having great beach parties! The atmosphere is casual with flip-flops and shorts welcome everywhere. You can stroll down the beach and take your pick of fun beach bars and restaurants and dance to the sounds of reggae, calypso, steel pan music and maybe even a fungi band.

At the west end of the beach is Rudy's Mariner Inn with five rooms along with

Corsairs Restaurant, Great Harbour

Strawberry from Sidney's, Little Harbour

Jost Van Dyke Scuba, Great Harbour

Rudy's Superette for necessities. The Jost Van Dyke Health Service is situated near Rudy's. Continuing toward the police station is Corsairs Restaurant and Bar, known for its excellent fare, Corsairs serve breakfast, lunch and dinner. The open air restaurant faces the beach – it is fun and casual, serving excellent northern Italian dishes and TexMex with a Caribbean flair - thanks to their chef, Roger! Ask Vinney for a pirate punch or a voodoo juice, to name two of their potent specialty drinks or try some absinthe. Next down the beach is Ali Baba's restaurant – great for local food and it is open for breakfast, lunch, and dinner and features free wifi. Wendell's World is on the beach near the Jost Van Dyke grocery store. The Ice Cream Parlor will cool you down, and Kisses, sells casual, tropical clothing.

A & B Bar and Restaurant features local West Indian food from 8:30am for breakfast, lunch and dinner.

On the road perpendicular to the beach, near the Customs House, you will find Nature's Basket with locally grown fresh fruits and vegetables and Christine's Bakery with her delectable fresh baked bread. Further up the road the Ice House can replenish the ice aboard. Around the corner next to the fire department is a small gas station.

Cool Breeze Restaurant offers large screen televisions so you won't miss any of your favorite sports! On the eastern end of the waterfront you can't miss the colorful JVD Water Sports and BVI Eco-Tours to discover the island on and off the beaten path.

WATER FRONT CHURCH, JOST VAN DYKE

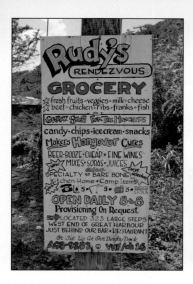

White Bay

Sidney's Little Harbour

Foxy's Bar

Tucked into the corner on the far eastern end of the beach is Foxy's dock in front of the restaurant. Foxy and his wife Tessa, have been welcoming sailors for over 40 years and it has grown in popularity and is now legendary. Foxy's hosts the annual Foxy's Wooden Boat Race held in May, as well as their New Year's Eve celebration. It is amazing the countries and places you will see someone with a Foxy's t-shirt strolling by! The restaurant and bar are open for lunch and dinner and they often have live entertainment. It might be a good idea to make dinner reservations when the harbor is full of boats!

Stop in at their extensive gift shop and sport your own Foxy t-shirt. You won't walk out of the shop empty handed – they have a lot of interesting items. On rare occasion you may catch Foxy singing calypso and playing his guitar – he is the one with the twinkle in his eye and a crowd around him!

WHITE BAY

Jost Van Dyke

Waypoint: BV204 18°26.30'N 64°45.80'W
Navigation: 6.1nm Cane Garden Bay;
3.4nm West End
Services: Ice, Garbage Disposal, Restaurants and Bars

White Bay is the westernmost harbor on the south side of the island, aptly named for its beautiful stretch of white sandy beach. White Bay is an excellent anchorage under normal sea conditions. During the winter months however, ocean swells can make it an untenable overnight anchorage, suitable for day stops only. On the weekends, many small craft make their way over from both Tortola and the USVI, often crowding the western end of the anchorage.

Navigation & Piloting

White Bay is a relatively small anchorage with limited maneuvering room once inside the reef, however, there is room for a number of boats if anchored properly. Although there are three entrances through the reef, it is highly recommended that only the middle entrance and the eastern entrance be considered since both of these channels are marked.

The middle channel is considered the main channel and once you have visually located the red and green markers proceed through the reef leaving red to starboard on a course of approximately due north. **Caution:** The red buoy is hard to see due to bleaching by the Caribbean sun (as of April 2012).

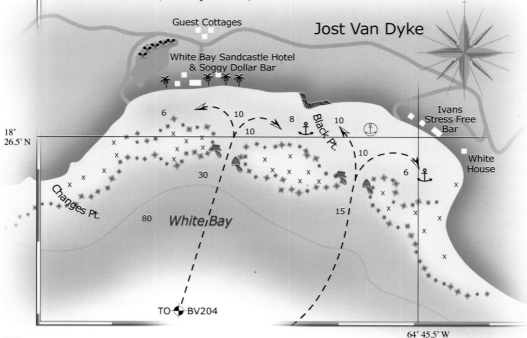

The eastern pass is also marked with red and green buoys, however on our previous two visits, the green marker was high and dry, relaxing near Ivan's Stress Free Bar. This entrance is straightforward, but once again, make sure that you have identified the marker before starting your approach.

Anchoring and Mooring

The middle channel will take 10-12 feet of draft. Once inside the reef, anchor either side of the channel in 7-10 feet on a sandy bottom. **Do not anchor in or obstruct the channel.** Since the anchorage is narrow, you can swim ashore or if you take the dinghy, pull it well up on the beach and use your dinghy anchor to secure it. It is not recommended that dinghies be landed during a northerly ground swell.

The eastern anchorage is also narrow so tuck yourself up behind the reef either side of the pass and anchor in 8-12 feet of water on a sandy bottom. **Do not drop the anchor on coral.** There are a few moorings available, these are on a first come basis and fees should be paid at Ivan's Stress Free Bar.

Ashore

White Bay Sandcastle is a small delightful resort that serves breakfast, lunch and four course gourmet dinners with reservations. The Soggy Dollar Bar is a great spot to swim ashore for a *Painkiller* and to while away the afternoon in a hammock under a palm tree. The *Painkiller*, a delicious but potent rum drink was originally invented at the Soggy Dollar Bar (named for the soggy state of dollar bills used to pay for drinks after swimming ashore from an anchored vessel).

To the west down the beach is One Love Bar & Grill serving lunch and cold drinks daily. Jewel's Snack Shop serves light bites during the day, White Bay Superette is a small market where you can pick up a few essentials. Ivan's Stress Free Bar and Restaurant, lavishly decorated with shells from the beach, is on the eastern end of the bay and is where you pay for your moorings.

GREAT TOBAGO

Waypoint: BV206 18°26.75'N 64°50.00'W
Navigation: 4.5nm White Bay JVD; 7.9nm West End
Services: None

Great Tobago is the westernmost of the British Virgin Islands, situated approximately 2.5 miles to the west of Jost Van Dyke and 525 feet in elevation. A favorite of divers, the island is remote and exposed. The small anchorage on the west side of the island is large enough to accommodate two vessels only. Generally used as a daytime stop, Great Tobago is unpopulated but home to a large nesting seabird population, protected by The National Parks Trust.

Navigation & Piloting

Approaching Great Tobago, there are three hazards that need to be understood. If your approach from the east takes you to the north of the island, Mercurious Rock lies half a mile to the east and is covered by 6 feet of water. A better approach is to the south end of the island, sailing close enough to avoid King Rock which is just awash and situated due south of the southwest tip of the island and due east of the northern tip of Little Tobago. Make your approach between Cable Rock, due west of the southwest point and easy to identify, and Great Tobago. The anchorage is a small bay halfway up the western face with a rocky beach landing.

Anchoring

Since there is limited room, anchor in 15 feet of water on a sandy bottom. It has been reported that entering the anchorage, there is a submerged rock to starboard about 25 feet from shore with 4-5feet of water over it.

Ashore

You can hike up the hillside to gain a commanding view of the surrounding islands.

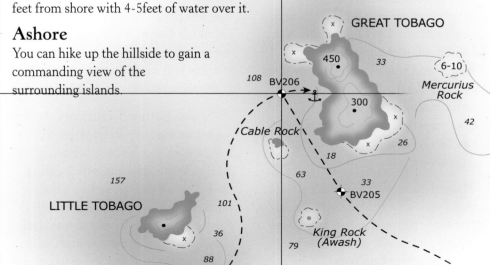

GREAT HARBOUR

IMMIGRATION
VHF channel 16
Tel: 284-495-9374

CUSTOMS
VHF channel 16
Tel: 284-494-3450

MARINAS
North Latitude Marina
VHF channel 16
Tel: 284-495-9930
http://northlatitude
marina.com

FERRIES
New Horizon Ferry
Tel: 284-495-9278
West End/Great Harbour

Inter Island Ferry
Tel: 340-776-6597
St. Thomas/St.John to
Jost Van Dyke
www.interislandboat
services.vi

PROVISIONING
JVD Grocery
Rudy's Superette
VHF channel 16
Tel: 284-495-9282

RESTAURANTS & BARS
Foxy's
VHF channel 16
Tel: 284-495-9258
Reservations requested
www.foxysbar.com

Ali Baba
VHF channel 16
Tel: 284-495-9280
www.alibabasrestauran-
tandbarbvi.com

A&B Bar and
Restaurant
VHF channel 16
Tel: 284-495-9352

Corsairs
VHF channel 16
Tel: 284-495-9294
www.corsairsbvi.com

Rudy's
VHF channel 16
Tel: 284-495-9282

WHITE BAY

RESTAURANTS
Ivan's Stress-Free Bar
& Restaurant
VHF channel16
Tel: 284-495-9312 or
495-3489
www.ivanscampground.
com

Soggy Dollar Bar &
White Bay Sandcastle
Restaurant
VHF channel 16
Tel: 284-495-9888
www.soggydollar.com

One Love Bar & Grill
Tel: 284-495-9829
www.onelovebar.com

Jewel's Snack Shop
Tel: 284-495-9286

Gertrude's
Beach bar that serves
tropical drinks

PROVISIONS
White Bay Superette

LITTLE HARBOUR

RESTAURANTS
Abe's By the Sea
VHF: channel 16
284-495-9329

Harris' Place
VHF channel 16
Tel: 284-495-9302
Harris Place JVD on FB

Sidney's Peace and Love
VHF channel 16
Tel: 284-494-9271

LITTLE JVD/ DIAMOND CAY

RESTAURANTS
Foxy's Taboo
VHF channel 16
Tel: 284-495-9891
Reservations requested

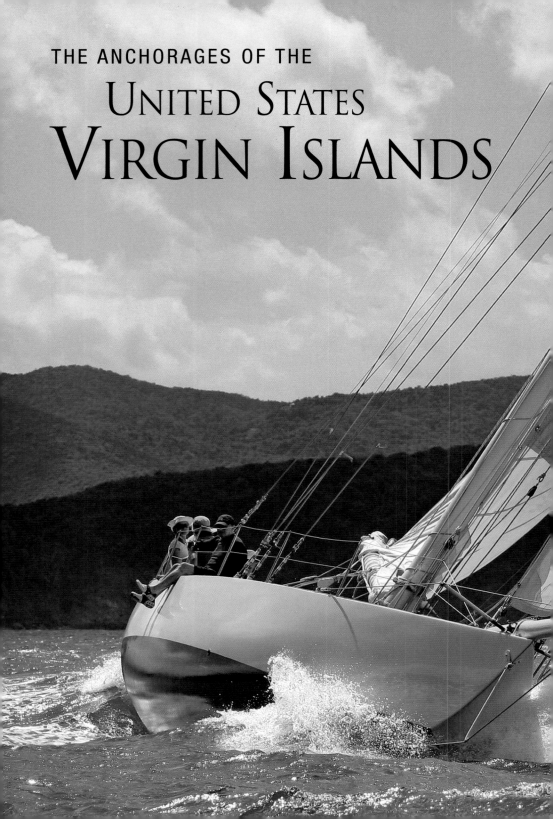

THE ANCHORAGES OF THE
UNITED STATES
VIRGIN ISLANDS

THE UNITED STATES VIRGIN ISLANDS
OFFICE OF THE GOVERNOR
GOVERNMENT HOUSE
Charlotte Amalie, V.I. 00802

340-774-0001

MESSAGE FROM THE GOVERNOR

Welcome to my home, the beautiful United States Virgin Islands! Our islands are blessed with an abundance of beauty – wide, white beaches; translucent turquoise water; year-round warm weather and sunny days, punctuated with cool tropical breezes; and lush, colorful vegetation on our hills and mountains. Our islands offer so much to visitors as you will quickly learn

The United States Virgin Islands is a premiere destination for travelers from around the globe. Surrounded by some of the finest cruising waters, it's no wonder that the Virgin Islands is recognized as the Yacht Charter Capital of the World. The dozens of islands and cays that make up the Territory have an unspoiled beauty and accessibility unmatched anywhere else.

Since Christopher Columbus first arrived on St. Croix more than 500 years ago, our islands have been a haven for free-spirited seafarers. That spirit still lives today and can easily be found by cruising our waters and mooring in isolated harbors and bays; fishing for the elusive Blue Marlin, snorkeling and diving through living coral reefs and world-famous shipwrecks; and relaxing on the beaches that hug our tropical shoreline. Your options for a perfect visit are many — from enjoying the solitude of an isolated cove, to fine harbor side dining, to legendary waterside parties. The choices are yours.

And when you step on shore, you'll find more new experiences waiting to be discovered. Our history and culture are rich and varied, and our architecture reflects the influence of the seven nations which at one time or another claimed these islands as their own. Because our favorable customs regulations were originally established under Danish rule, our retail shops offer quality items that are less expensive than found elsewhere.

As a proud Territory of the United States of America, U.S. passports are not required to visit our islands.

On behalf of the residents of the United States Virgin Islands, I welcome you to our islands, our home, and a place where families and friends can truly experience paradise! Enjoy your stay and come back again!

John P. de Jongh, Jr.
Governor

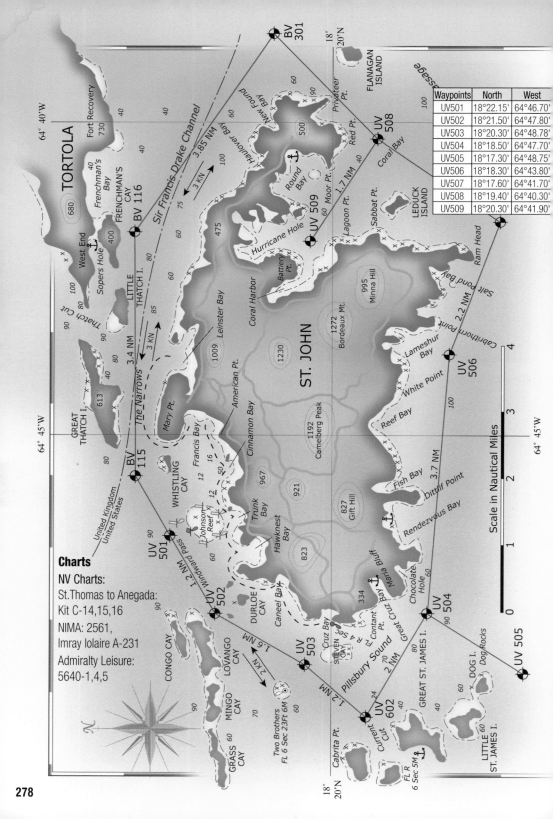

Waypoints	North	West
UV501	18°22.15'	64°46.70'
UV502	18°21.50'	64°47.80'
UV503	18°20.30'	64°48.78'
UV504	18°18.50'	64°47.70'
UV505	18°17.30'	64°48.75'
UV506	18°18.30'	64°43.80'
UV507	18°17.60'	64°41.70'
UV508	18°19.40'	64°40.30'
UV509	18°20.30'	64°41.90'

Charts

NV Charts:
St. Thomas to Anegada:
Kit C-14,15,16
NIMA: 2561,
Imray Iolaire A-231
Admiralty Leisure:
5640-1,4,5

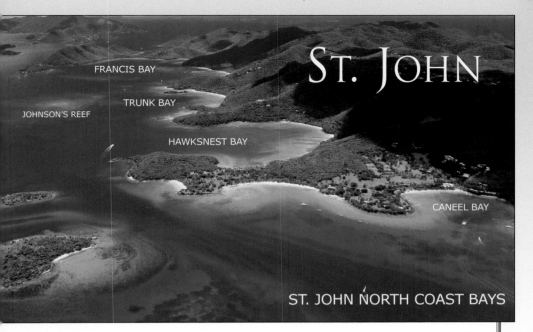

ST. JOHN

FRANCIS BAY

TRUNK BAY

JOHNSON'S REEF

HAWKSNEST BAY

CANEEL BAY

ST. JOHN NORTH COAST BAYS

Two-thirds of this fabulous island is under the auspices of the National Park Service, maintaining its pristine appearance. The Park Service has taken great efforts to provide moorings in most of the anchorages in order to help preserve the underwater reefs and sea beds from the damage of anchors. The Park has stringent guidelines that have helped to keep this island from the abuse of overuse. It is well worth a visit.

There are only a few roads on St. John and most wind up at one or another of the island's gorgeous white-sand beaches, framed by the tropical forests of Virgin Islands National Park, which cover more than half the island. Trails wind through the ruins of Danish-colonial sugar plantations dating to the 18th century, when sugar, rum and slavery ruled St. John and the rest of the Caribbean.

Denmark sold the islands in 1917 for $25 million to the United States.

The town of Cruz Bay is charming with excellent restaurants tucked away and commanding spectacular views. You don't compete with the cruise ships for bargains, but the same duty free status applies here. With the thriving artist community in St. John there are some original and interesting treasures to see and buy. You may even wish to check into villa rentals for your next trip.

It is highly recommended you stop at the National Park Service Headquarters in Cruz Bay for information on the park as a national monument, tours, things to see and regulations. Please read the section on the National Park at the beginning of this guide before visiting St. John for essential information.

CRUZ BAY

St. John

Waypoint: UV503 -18°20.30'N; 64°48.78'W
Navigation: 6.5nm SW Soper's Hole, BVI;
2.3nm NE Current Cut (Gt. St. James)
Services: U.S. Port of Entry, Ferry Service, Island Tours, Ice, Water, Fuel, Provisions

Cruz Bay, a port of entry, is the main town on St. John and, without doubt, the best place to clear customs. Serviced by ferries to St. Thomas on an hourly basis, many charterers elect to leave their vessels in Cruz Bay or anchored under Lind Point and take the ferry across the sound to Red Hook. Cruz Bay offers the yachtsman all of the basic services, including banks, post office, grocery markets, etc. Often crowded, the anchorage, though protected, is not necessarily a good overnight stop, as the movement of the ferries tends to make it uncomfortable. Vessels under sixty feet may anchor in the Cruz Bay Creek area near the boat ramp for a maximum of three hours for the purpose of clearing customs and immigration or other business in Cruz Bay.

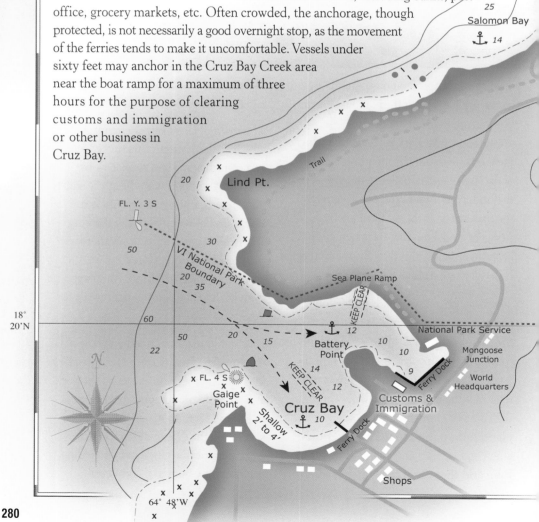

NATIONAL
PARK SERVICES
BUILDING

CUSTOMS &
IMMIGRATION

Navigation & Piloting

Approaching Cruz Bay from the north, pass through the Windward Passage (waypoint UV502) or the Durloe Channel leaving Henley and Ramgoat Cay to starboard. Head SW toward the north end of Steven Cay, before turning east into Cruz Bay. A flashing yellow buoy to the west of Lind Point marks the boundary of The National Park. Follow the markers into the inner harbor.

Making your approach from the southwest or Great St. James, it is not recommended to pass between Stephen Cay and St. John, as there are numerous coral heads. Leave Steven Cay to starboard.

The Two Brothers, a set of rocks marked by a flashing yellow at 6 seconds and standing 20 feet above sea level, are always visible in the middle of Pillsbury Sound, and have good water all around. Entering Cruz Bay, there is a reef extending out from Gallows Point to starboard, marked with a red flashing marker. Stay well to the north of it, as it is in very shallow water. There are two marked channels within the harbor, one servicing the ferry dock to starboard, and one servicing the National Park dock and customs to port.

This is a busy harbor so be aware of ferry traffic at all times.

Anchoring & Mooring

Shoal water extends from the marker on the end of the reef about 50 to 60 feet toward the ferry dock, so be careful when anchoring. Be sure to avoid obstructing both channels or you will incur the wrath of the ferry boat captains. Do not tie up to the dock as it is reserved for commercial traffic. A public dinghy dock has been built on both sides at the base of the pier. Tie up on the west side of the dock using a short scope so that the dinghy doesn't get caught under the dock. Dinghies are not permitted on the beach.

All moorings in Cruz Bay, Great Cruz Bay and Coral Bay are private and subject to stiff fines for unauthorized use. There is an anchoring zone under Lind Point / Salomon Bay where you can leave the vessel and dinghy around into Cruz Bay. There is also a dinghy channel onto Salomon Beach and trail that joins the Lind Point Trail (1.1 miles).

Ashore

Customs & Immigration: In Cruz Bay, a U.S. Port of Entry, you must anchor in Cruz Bay and all come ashore with passports and the vessel's documents. If there are no other boats or ferries at the Customs dock, you may tie up there.

The customs house is on your right in the northern section of the bay known as the Creek. The depth at the dock is 9 feet. There is a dinghy dock pier off the ferry dock for those anchored out in the bay that are coming ashore to clear customs. If coming ashore this way, turn left along the waterfront to the customs building.

When entering the U.S. Virgin Islands from a foreign port, the skipper and passengers as well as any crew aboard must all report to Customs and Border Protection with passports and the ship's documents, wearing proper attire (tops, bottoms, and shoes for both sexes; wearing a bathing suit is not acceptable).

Customs and Border Protection is open in Cruz Bay seven days a week from 7am to 5:30pm. If you arrive before or after those hours, you must remain on your vessel, raise your quarantine flag

and report to the authorities when they open. Cruz Bay Customs telephone number is 340-776-6741.

Caneel Bay Shipyards, across from customs, is a full service facility offering repair services for fiberglass, sails, refrigeration, woodwork and storage, as well as ice, fuel and water.

Several shops and offices are located within the waterfront area. Jeep rentals are available and a tour of the islands is a must if you don't have time to sail to all the anchorages. Also this gives you a chance to visit some of the beautiful beaches St. John has to offer. Connections offers mail, internet access, fax and telephone answering services both in Cruz Bay and in Coral Bay as well as how to find a tour for hiking, where to rent a car and anything else you can think of, they probably know the answer. Islandia Real Estate can make your dream come true if you are ready to trade it all in and move to the islands. They are located on Centerline Road. Or check out Holiday Homes of St. John, a complete real estate firm including commercial property.

For medical emergencies dial 911. There are doctors and clinics in St. John – see our Island Connections section at the end of St. John for information on hospitals and clinics.

To replenish the galley, Starfish Market is open daily from 7:30am to 9:00pm, and they do provide provisioning. Check out their wine room and the walk-in humidor. Marina Market is open from 7am to 8:45pm on Sunday.

St. John is an artistic community boasting painters, musicians, song writers and writers. For information on art galleries, restaurants, accommodation and happenings contact the Tourist Office near the post office, which is open on week days only. The last Saturday of every month is St. John Saturday with music, crafts, special food in the park, and other activities.

Scheduled taxi buses leave from Cruz Bay to many of St. John's exquisite beaches. You can also ride the bus all the way to Coral Bay or round trip to anywhere on the island for a very inexpensive fare – a real bargain.

Chris Simmons

Cruz Bay

MONGOOSE JUNCTION

Just past the Park Service Center is a charming shopping arcade built of natural stone, known as Mongoose Junction. Visitors should stop by and browse in the quaint, interesting shops. You will find it hard not to part with some money here! There are a few restaurants in this romantic tropical setting. Sun Dog Café/Gecko Gazebo bar overlooks the courtyard and has an eclectic menu and can cool you with tropical drinks. The Ocean Grill serves lunch and dinner. The Paradiso Restaurant opens at 5:30 daily. The Tap Room is a microbrewery and bar and the home of St. John Brewers. They also serve non-alcoholic drinks.

Island Fancy Gallery and Gifts features tropical gifts and St. John specialties.

Bamboula is a favorite that features a collection of primitive art, clothing, beads, baskets and textiles. Rent or buy your snorkel gear at Just Beach; it is the perfect place for casual wear, sandals, and t-shirts for the entire family.

R&I Patton Goldsmithing designs and crafts stunning gold and silver jewelry. The Friends of the Park store carries unique gifts for sustainable environment that will inspire and educate as well as crafts, and logo t-shirts.

These are just a sampling of the shops at Mongoose Junction. There are shops for clothing, furnishing, jewelry, art galleries, environmental sustainability and more. Even if you visit just to look around, you will find it a lovely group of shops.

WHARFSIDE VILLAGE

Adjacent to the ferry dock is a wonderful collection of shops and restaurants overlooking the action in Cruz Bay. From clothing to fine jewelry it is a great place to walk around if you've got some time and some extra pocket money!

There are many choices for dining at Wharfside Village like the new Waterfront Bistro. This sophisticated restaurant features interesting appetizers, delicious entrees and luscious deserts. Joe's Rum Hut is just what it says with a tin roof and a beachside hut for some fantastic concoctions. Joe has an exotic collection of different rums that he mixes to make some very interesting flavors. Cruz Bay Deli and Pizzeria makes a mouth-watering pizza and a variety of sandwiches, wraps and salads. You may eat in or take out

your meal to the picnic beach. The Mojo Café will start your day off with a grilled breakfast sandwich. Or later come back for lunch. The Beach Bar suggests you wear wet bathing suits and sandy feet. This casual beach bar is open early and closes very late! They have live music during the weekends. This is just a smattering of the many restaurants and bars.

Shops are just as numerous and run the gamut of possibilities to interest passersby for an afternoon. There are eclectic boutiques such as Freebird Creations, which carries locally crafted items, duty-free watches, island jewelry, and much more. Cruz Bay Trading Post has "everything for everybody", there are stores that carry solely beach accoutrement, and some that carry only fine jewelry. There are numerous shops to investigate; one has but to take a stroll.

The National Park Service

One of the first stops you should make is to visit the National Park Service Visitor's Center next to Caneel Bay Shipyard. It is open from 8am to 4:30pm. There are many new rules and regulations that you should be familiar with before spending time sailing and boating in the park. Besides the boating you should familiarize yourself with the fishing and diving regulations. See our section on National Parks at the back of this book for many of these important regulations.

Almost two thirds of the island of St. John is protected as a National Park. Park rangers schedule hikes and tours throughout the park on both land and sea trails, identifying flora and fauna. Annaberg Sugar Mill can be toured on your own with the assistance of a pamphlet.

Any beach in the USVI can be used by anyone according to USVI law. However, you cannot gain access to that beach by crossing private property, or go beyond the beach onto private property. Some beaches therefore, are accessible only by sea.

Courtesy of Virgin Islands National Park

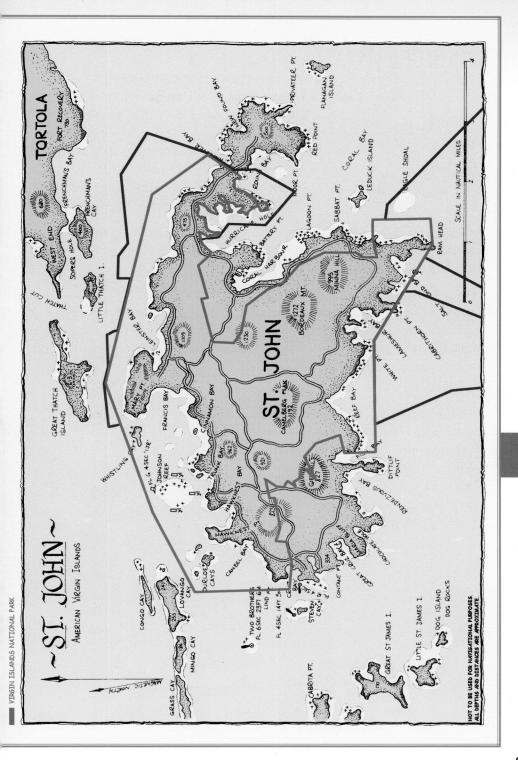

~ ST. JOHN ~

AMERICAN VIRGIN ISLANDS

MAGNETIC NORTH

TORTOLA

ST. JOHN

CAMELBERG PEAK 1192

NOT TO BE USED FOR NAVIGATIONAL PURPOSES.
ALL DEPTHS AND DISTANCES ARE APPROXIMATE.

SCALE IN NAUTICAL MILES

Caneel Bay

St. John

Waypoint: UV503 -18°20.30'N; 64°48.78'W
Navigation: 0.6nm NE Cruz Bay; 3.2nm NE Redhook, St.Thomas
Services: Moorings, Caneel Bay Resort & Restaurant

Caneel Bay is the home of the resort of the same name, which is built on the site of an 18th century sugar plantation. The property extends to the east side of the bay, to Turtle Bay, including the Durloe Cays.

Visiting yachtsmen are welcome in the bay, but are requested to keep noise to an acceptable level and to refrain from hanging laundry on the lifelines.

Navigation & Piloting

Traveling north from Cruz Bay around Lind Point and Salomon Bay, there is a marked channel for small craft allowing access to the beach and the Lind Point Trail. This is a designated anchoring zone (see section on mooring use) and public moorings are available.

Eastbound

If you are sailing east to Hawksnest or Trunk Bays, care should be taken when negotiating the small channel between the Durloe Cays and Hawksnest Point on St. John. The wind direction can change rapidly around the headland and strong currents (2 knots in either direction) can create a choppy sea. It is prudent to start the motor while negotiating this passage.

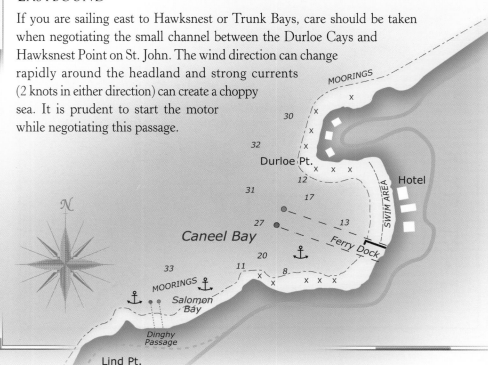

HAWKSNEST BAY

CANEEL BAY

DURLOE CHANNEL

Anchoring & Mooring

Once inside Caneel Bay, there is a marked ferry channel that services the small jetty in the middle of the bay. Stay outside of the line of buoys off the beach that designates the hotel guest swimming area. There are several NPS moorings available to pick up. If the moorings are taken, anchoring is only permitted 200 feet to seaward of the mooring field. Payment is made ashore at the "iron ranger" kiosk. There is no charge for daytime usage, overnight starts at 5.30pm.

Ashore

During the day, visitors may go ashore and are welcome to visit the old plantation ruins, gift shop and the Beach Terrace. Outside guests may make reservations for lunch and dinner at the charming Equator Restaurant. Check with the restaurant regarding dress codes. There may be times when the hotel must request that outside guests return at another time if the hotel management feels their visitor capacity has been reached. Uniformed hosts and hostesses

are stationed throughout the complex to give directions and answer questions.

Hawksnest Bay

Waypoint: UV501 (Johnson Reef) - 18°22.15'N; 64°46.70'W

Navigation: 1.5nm NE Caneel Bay; 1.8nm SW Whistling Cay Passage

Services: Moorings

This lovely, peaceful bay is great for swimming and snorkeling. Hawksnest has 13 NPS moorings installed for overnight use. If the moorings are taken, or if your vessel is over 60 feet, anchor 200 feet seaward of the mooring field.

Navigation & Piloting

Approaching from the southwest via Durloe Channel, identify Hawksnest Rock to the north of Hawksnest Point before making your turn into the anchorage.

If your approach is from the north, special note should be taken of the buoyage system around Johnson Reef. If your transit is south of the reef, you will be leaving the yellow buoy "JC" marking the southern extremity to starboard.

TRUNK BAY

(JOHNSON'S REEF)

Waypoint: UV501 (Johnson's Reef) - 18°22.15'N; 64°46.70'W

Navigation: 1.3nm SW Whistling Cay Passage

Services: Moorings, Underwater Trail

St. John

One of the more spectacular beaches in the Virgin Islands, Trunk Bay is the site of an underwater snorkel around Trunk Cay, a small islet about 48 feet high. During the winter months or when a ground sea is running, it is not recommended as an overnight mooring area because of the bad swell.

JOHNSON'S REEF

A large reef a half mile to the north of Trunk Bay, Johnson's Reef, although well marked, continues to claim its share of wrecks due to negligence. The reef is marked at the northern end by a green flashing (JR-1) buoy, further north is a yellow 4 sec fl. National Park boundary buoy, marking the northern extremity of the National Park. The reef is surrounded by an additional five yellow buoys marked JA-JD, three of which are flashing. Do not go between them. If sailing south of the reef, identify the southernmost (JC) marker. Care should be taken to give the reef a wide berth.

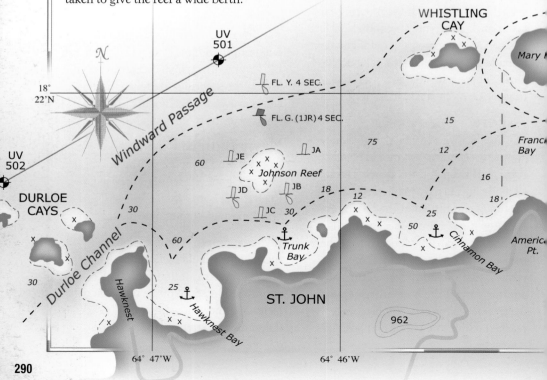

CANEEL BAY

HAWKSNEST BAY

TRUNK BAY

JE

FL G "1"

JD

JOHNSON'S REEF

JA

JC

JB

N

JOHNSON'S REEF NORTH WEST COAST ST. JOHN

Navigation

The approach to Trunk Bay is straight forward with the exception of Johnson's Reef, as previously noted. If approaching from the west, there is a small cay (Perkins Cay) north of the headland to watch for. When departing to the east, you can proceed between Trunk Cay and the yellow marker (JC) marking the southern tip of Johnson's Reef, taking care to stay at least 200 yards off the shoreline. When a heavy ground swell is running, there will be considerable surface action and it is recommended to go around the outside, once again giving the reef a good offing.

Mooring

There will be a line of marker buoys off the beach, which indicates the swimming area. Dinghies going ashore must use the channel marked with red and green buoys toward the western end of the beach. A field of National Park Moorings are available on a first come basis (payment ashore at the kiosk).

During ground seas, the surf on the beach can make the landing of dinghies a difficult, if not a dangerous, task.

Ashore

The National Park Service maintains an underwater snorkel trail at Trunk Bay. Picnic grounds and facilities are also maintained by the Park Service and snacks and cold drinks are available.

CINNAMON BAY

Navigation: 0.7nm E Trunk Cay;

Services: Moorings, Trails, Restaurant, General store

The site of the National Park Campground, Cinnamon Bay provides a good daytime spot to pick up a mooring for lunch and a snorkel. Being exposed, it can be uncomfortable as an overnight anchorage and largely untenable during northeast ground seas. The NPS has provided 8 mooring buoys for day or overnight use. To the east end of the bay is Cinnamon Cay. A reef extends to the southwest and is marked by private buoys. A dinghy landing area is provided by the National Park Service building.

Accommodations at the campground include cottages, tents, and bare sites. The watersports center offers snorkel gear and beach chairs for rent, as well as diving, sailing and windsurfing. There are also two short trails (0.5 to 1.5 miles) that are well signposted and intertwine, offering great views of the coastline and the ruins of an old sugar mill. There is a restaurant called T'ree Lizards on the terrace of the Cinnamon Bay Campground that serves American/Caribbean cuisine for breakfast (8:30-10am), lunch (11:30am-2:00pm) and dinner (5:30-8pm). Their menu includes vegetarian selections as well as selections from the bar. Hours are seasonal so they ask that you please check with the front desk for current hours of operation.

The General Store, also found on the terrace, carries essential groceries and toiletries. From the beach, take the path to the left of the watersports center to find the Front Desk, the General Store, and the T'ree Lizards Restaurant.

MAHO BAY

Navigation: 0.6nm East of Cinnamon Cay
Services: Moorings, Trails, Watersports Rentals, Bar & Restaurant

To the northeast of American Point (525 feet high) and less than 0.5nm from the Fungi Passage, between Whistling Cay and St. Mary's Point is Maho Bay, a delightful anchorage fringed with white sand. The head of the bay is shoal. To the east is Maho Point marking the northeast extremity of the bay. There are 28 moorings provided for day or night use.

Maho Bay Camps, an eco friendly resort, welcomes boaters and has a well stocked store, as well as available showers. Camping accommodations include canvas covered cottages hidden on a hillside in the National Park. There are three places to eat on the grounds, but depending on the season, some may be closed. These include Café Concordia, Maho Pavilion Restaurant, and Beach Café. There is a lot to do here so check with the activity desk and see what's going on. Make sure if you dinghy in from Cinnamon Bay or Francis Bay, you do so through the marked channel.

FRANCIS BAY

Waypoint: UV501 (Johnson Reef) - 18°22.15'N; 64°46.70'W
Navigation: 3.7nm NE Cruz Bay
Services: Moorings, Trails

Located on the northern shore of St. John, Francis Bay is the large bay, extending to the very southeast of Whistling Cay.

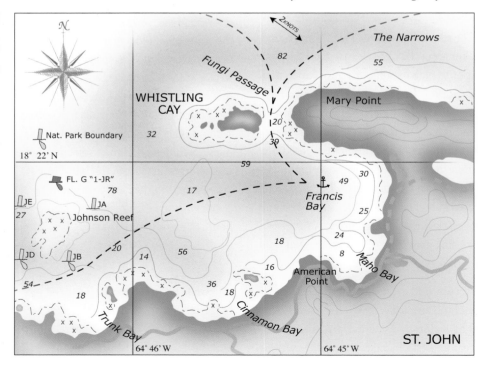

Protected from the north by Mary's Point, Francis Bay is fairly deep (50 feet) until close to shore where it shelves to 15 feet.

Navigation

If you are making your approach from the west, you will be rounding Johnson's Reef. Favor the northern end leaving the large green buoy to starboard. There is also a channel between Trunk Cay, and the yellow buoy "JC" (leave to port or north). If you are approaching from the north, there is plenty of water through the Fungi Passage that lies between Mary Point on St. John and Whistling Cay. A small shoal area extends south from Whistling Cay, where the decaying ruins of an old customs house can still be seen.

Anchoring & Mooring

This bay is the only bay in the National Park that allows yachts from 125 - 210 feet to anchor following the NPS guidelines.

All vessels over 125 feet and less than 210 feet in length must anchor in sand at depths of 50 feet or greater, in Francis Bay, at least 200 feet shoreward of a line from Mary Point to America Point according to NPS regulations. Yachts 60 feet or under in length may pick up a NPS mooring. 29 moorings are provided in Francis Bay.

When the wind is light, it may get buggy if you are close to shore. A small sandbar lies in the northeastern corner. Stay outside the buoys designating the swimming area.

Ashore

For those who feel like taking a healthy walk, the National Park Service maintains a trail that extends from the picnic site to an abandoned plantation house. From there you can follow the road to the Annaberg Ruins. The National Park Service maintains garbage facilities ashore.

Departing

If you are heading east, you will find yourself in the Narrows with the wind and current against you. Many of the local skippers prefer to lay a tack toward Jost Van Dyke, and then tack back through the cut between Great Thatch and Tortola, rather than fighting the Narrows with its strong adverse currents.

MAHO BAY

FRANCIS BAY

CINNAMON BAY

TRUNK BAY

ST. JOHN NORTH WEST COAST BAYS

LEINSTER BAY

St. John

Waypoint: BV116 (Frenchman's Cay) -
18°22.70'N; 64°41.90'W
Navigation: 1.7nm east of Fungi Passage;
2.1nm SSW Soper's Hole
Services: Moorings, Trail to Annaberg Ruins

Located on the north coast of St. John, Leinster Bay lies directly to the south of the westernmost tip of Little Thatch. The bay is well protected and quite comfortable.

Navigation & Piloting

Leinster Bay is open and straightforward whether your approach is from the west or east. Approaching from the east, leaving Waterlemon Cay and the marked restricted area to the west of Waterlemon Cay, to port; work yourself up into the eastern end of the bay, known as Waterlemon Bay. It is not allowed to transit between Waterlemon Cay and St. John.

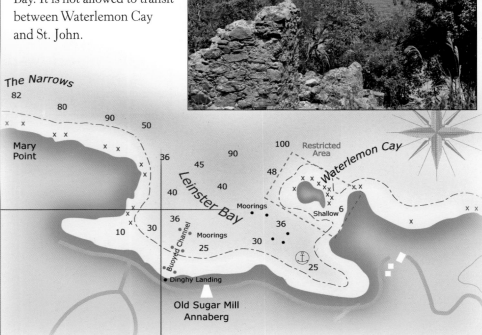

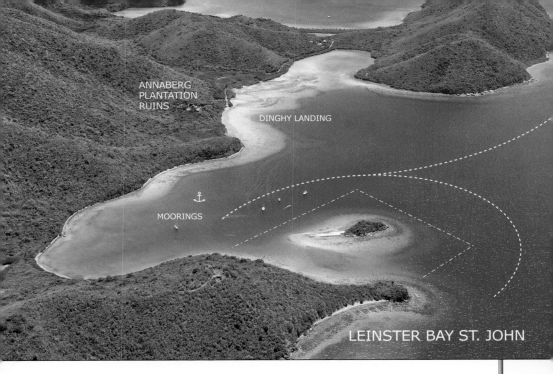

ANNABERG
PLANTATION
RUINS

DINGHY LANDING

MOORINGS

LEINSTER BAY ST. JOHN

Anchoring & Mooring

Leinster Bay has 20 overnight moorings provided by the National Park Service.

As is the case throughout the National Park system, anchoring is discouraged because of the impact to the sea bed over time. Only anchor in sand 200 feet from the mooring field if there are no moorings available.

Ashore

Dinghies are not permitted to land on Waterlemon Cay. Dinghy moorings are provided just inside the restricted area. Dinghies may also be landed to the southwest end of the anchorage, where a short channel has been marked. This is also the entrance of the trail to the ruins of the Annaberg Sugar Mill, which have been restored by the Park Service.

LEINSTER BAY

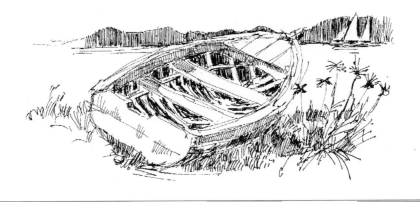

The Ruins of the Annaberg Plantation

Years before the United States purchased the US Virgin Islands from Denmark in 1917, sugar cane was the raison d'être for plantation life on St. John. Above the anchorage at Leinster Bay, the Annaberg ruins offer a brief insight into the island's history. Walk around the stone-and-coral remains of the old slave quarters, windmill and horsemill used to extract the juice from the sugar cane. Close your eyes and conjure up the sweet heavy scent of crushed cane, molasses and rum. If your timing is right, you will detect the aroma of fresh bread baking; follow your nose to the kitchen and you might be lucky enough to taste a slice of "dumb bread" as it comes out of the traditional oven. Wandering through this historic site it's easy to see

what led to the slave revolt against the plantation owners in 1733. It was thwarted, but in 1848 a second uprising heralded the end of slavery and the economic collapse of the sugar

plantations. Cultural demonstrations, including baking "dumb bread" takes place Tuesday through Friday from 10 a.m. to 2 p.m. In August to November the demonstration also includes subsistance gardening.

OUR ACTIONS AFFECT THE REEF'S FUTURE;
THE REEF'S FUTURE AFFECTS YOURS. . .

Protect Our Coral Reefs

PROTECT OUR FUTURE BY
PRACTICING THESE
FRIENDLY TIPS

NEVER feed marine life

Put on fins WHILE floating in water

Anchor in sand OR use a mooring

Stay OFF the bottom to avoid damage

Look, but NEVER touch coral

Throw your TRASH in bins

Snorkel ABOVE corals to protect them & you

LEAVE coral & marine life in paradise

Know & FOLLOW your local fishing rules

University Virgin Islands   Virgin Islands National Park

Windmill

If there was a steady breeze, cane was brought to the windmill. Revolving sails turned a central shaft, rotating the rollers and crushing the stalks. Juice ran down the rollers into the gutter and flowed downhill to the factory.

The windmill, as well as the rest of the factory, was built between 1797 and 1805. It could produce more juice than the horsemill, and involved fewer people and no draft animals.

The now-missing turret carried axle and sails, and could be turned into the wind.

For Your Safety
DO NOT
Stand or climb
on Ruins or Walls

CORAL BAY
CORAL HARBOR, ROUND BAY, HURRICANE HOLE

St. John

Waypoint: UV508 (Coral Bay) - 18°19.40'N; 64°40.30'W

Navigation: 9.7nm E Cruz Bay; 7.5nm SE Leinster Bay

Services: Coral Harbor: Provisions, Chandlery, Bars, Restaurants, Trails

Comprised of a series of bays, coves, and fingers of land, Coral Bay contains Coral Harbor, Hurricane Hole and Round Bay, and they are located on the southeast corner of St. John and are generally open to the southeast. Hurricane Hole is now part of the Coral Reef National Monument and anchoring is strictly prohibited. However, the park service maintains 8 moorings for day use only – overnight use is prohibited. Hurricane Hole/ Coral Reef National Monument

N

SAINT JOHN

See detail

15   15

36

See detail

Hurricane Hole

Coral
Harbor

18°
20.38'N

UV
509

Round Bay

20   50   30

50

Moor Pt.

1272
Bordeaux

Lagoon Pt.

Red Pt.

995
Minna Hill

60

UV
508

LEDUCK
ISLAND

64° 41.85'W   64° 40.30'W

is a no-take zone, so fishing, and collecting are not permitted. At the time of the slave days, when the sugar mills were at their peak, Coral Harbor was the main anchorage on St. John. There are some interesting ruins still in existence.

Navigation & Piloting

If you are approaching from the north or east or northeast, the route is straight forward. Leave Flanagan's Island to port and proceed to waypoint UV508 or make your entry into the bay midway between Red Point on St. John and Leduck Island (85 feet high) to the south. It is wise to give all headlands in this area a wide berth as most have rocks and coral extending out from them.

Approaching from the south or west, care must be exercised to avoid Eagle Shoal, situated about 0.7 nm south of Leduck Island. The shoal is very difficult to see and has about 2 feet of water over it. When rounding Ram's Head, it is possible to hug the shoreline, passing midway between Sabbat Point and Leduck Island via the Sabbat Channel in 50 feet of water, however, given the fact that this route puts you on a lee shore, the more prudent route is to stay south of a line drawn between Ram's Head and Water Point on the northern tip of Norman Island until Leduck Island bears northwest. Then enter Coral Bay midway between Leduck Island and Red Point.

CORAL BAY

ROUND BAY

Waypoint: UV508 (Coral Bay) - 18°19.40'N; 64°40.30'W
Navigation: 1.8nm E Coral Harbor
Services: None

St. John

Round Bay is really a series of smaller bays comprised of Long Bay, Hansen Bay and Elk Bay. Open to the south, the anchorages at times can be rolly and uncomfortable. The most protected of the bays is Hansen Bay, which, when tucked in behind and to the north of Pelican Rock makes a delightful anchorage.

Navigation & Piloting

Approaching Coral Bay from the southwest between Red Point to the north and Leduck Island to the south, you will round Moor Point (Long Point) that extends to the west. Long Bay extends north from the point and you can anchor in 10-15 feet of water on a shell bottom. We have always found this bay uncomfortable as it is exposed to the south and the surge tends to find its way around the point. Continuing north to Hansen Bay, do not pass between the shore and Pelican Rock. Leave Pelican Rock (7 feet high) to starboard and anchor to the north of the rock in 25 feet of water on a grassy bottom.

Further to the north is Limetree Cove and Elk Bay. Both are exposed and not recommended.

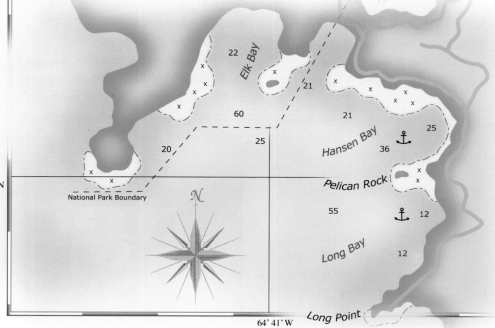

CORAL HARBOR

HURRICANE HOLE

ROUND BAY

LONG PT

D PT

PRIVATEER PT

N

CORAL BAY ST. JOHN

PELCAN ROCK

Hansen Bay, St. John

HURRICANE HOLE

Hurricane Hole is now part of the Coral Reef National Monument and anchoring is strictly prohibited. However the park service maintains 8 moorings for day use only– overnight use is prohibited – for vessels not exceeding 60 feet (length on deck).

Navigation & Piloting

Departing Round Bay and heading toward Hurricane Hole, you will be leaving Turner Point to starboard, there is a small reef that extends to the southeast so allow a reasonable offing as you round the point.

Working your way up into Hurricane Hole, the depth will be around 60 feet and the shoreline lined with thick mangrove growth. Water Creek is the first finger that opens to the northeast with a secondary bay to starboard that is about as protected as you can be. The depth is 15 to 20 feet.

Further north is Otter Creek (15 feet) and Princess Bay (22 feet) heading off to the northeast. Bork Creek (18 feet) is at the head of the bay to the northwest. All of these bays provide excellent protection.

ROUND BAY

CORAL HARBOR

HURRICANE HOLE

CORAL BAY | HURRICANE HOLE   N

CORAL HARBOR

Waypoint: UV509 (Hurricane Hole) - 18°20.30'N; 64°41.90'W

Navigation: 3.4nm N Ram's Head; 2.2nm NW Moor Point (Long Point)

Services: Provisions, Chandlery, Bars, Restaurants, Trails, Gift Stores

St. John

Coral Bay historically was the center of plantation life in the early 18th century. It still bustles with the sailors who anchor in the bay, and many of them flock to Skinny Legs for a libation or two. Coral Harbor in particular has a truly laid-back character reflecting the iconoclastic nature of the inhabitants, craftsmen and artists preferring to be perched on the other side of the great divide of the bustling town of Cruz Bay. The anchorage is open to the southwest.

Navigation & Piloting

The entrance to Coral Harbor is straight forward but narrow. The anchorage is usually crowded with cruisers and private moorings, which makes it difficult to find room to anchor. Stay mid-channel until the stone house on the eastern side of the bay bears northeast. The channel is marked by two sets of red and green buoys that are privately maintained. You should then be able to anchor in 10-15 feet of water. Keep the channel clear for fishing boats, and do not pick up the private moorings you will see here. Ashore there is a small dinghy landing area, which usually reflects the high density of the anchorage.

Coral Bay

Dingy Dock

10

10

390

20

18

18

Harbor Pt.

35

Coral Harbor

18°24.30'N

18

Sanders Bay 10

Johnson Bay

64° 42.28' W

CORAL HARBOR ST. JOHN

Ashore

There is no customs service at Coral Harbor. There are a number of buildings left over from slavery days, including the Moravian Mission and the ruins of an old sugar mill and a fort. Coral Harbor has become the place to eat in St. John. Try the Shipwreck Landing, Island Blues Seaside Bar and Grill, and Skinny Legs Bar and Grill. Sputnik's is open for breakfast and pizza on Wednesdays and a couple of other days - best to check with them first. The Jolly Dog Island Outpost at Shipwreck Landing has "stuff you want". The Coccoloba Center is the home of Lily's Gourmet Market with full deli items, liquor and beer along with meats and seafood. Or, if you prefer to eat out, try the Aqua Bistro with its circular bar or the Big Belly Deli. For a bit of fun shopping (for women anyway) check out the Sugar Apple Boutique with gems and jewelry, accessories and sarongs.

Coral Bay Marine monitors VHF 16 from 9am to 5pm Monday through Friday and 9am to 1pm on Saturday. Sunday they are closed. They provide engine repairs, sail repairs, ice and miscellaneous items.

Coral Harbor is home to some wonderfully eccentric and dedicated cruising sorts. It is considered more of a haven from the tourists, rather than a tourist destination.

THE SOUTH COAST BAYS

SALT POND BAY & LAMESHUR BAYS

St. John

Just a half mile beyond the point of Ram's Head, there are a number of bays, less frequently visited by the cruising yachtsman. We have listed below several of these anchorages, along with any pertinent information. In the south bays no anchoring is permitted by the National Park Service, however, there are some moorings available to pick up that are maintained by the park service.

SALT POND BAY

Waypoint: UV507 (Ram's Head) - 18°17.60'N; 64°41.70'W
Navigation: 0.5nm NW Rams Head
Services: Moorings, Trails

When the weather is settled, Salt Pond Bay is an excellent spot to pick up an NPS mooring. It is easy to enter, although there

are rocks awash at the entrance. You can pass on either side of them; however, there is more room if you leave them to starboard. Both channels have a minimum of 12 feet of water.

When approaching and leaving Salt Pond Bay, Booby Rock is easy to see (35 feet) with good water all around to the north and a small reef extending to the south-southwest. Anchoring is forbidden. The snorkeling around this anchorage is excellent.

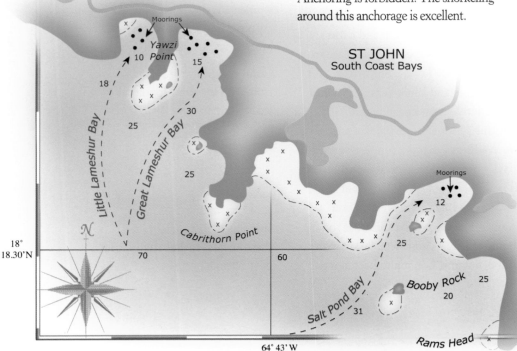

GREAT LAMESHUR BAY

LITTLE LAMESHUR BAY

LAMESHUR BAYS ST. JOHN

There are several trails, varying from .25miles to 1.4 miles long, that can be accessed from this anchorage.

A word of caution is that this bay has been subject to some petty thievery. Sunbathers, rental cars and boats all seem to be fair game.

GREAT & LITTLE LAMESHUR BAY

Waypoint: UV506 (Lameshur Bay) – 18°18.30'N; 64°43.80'W

Navigation: 1.5nm NW Ram's Head; 5.1nm SE Cruz Bay

Services: Moorings, Trails

Making your approach from Ram's Head to the southeast, stay well to the south of Cabrithorn Point as there is a reef that extends to the south. Once past the point, turn northeast toward Yawzi Point that separates the two bays. Be aware that shoal water extends southwest from Yawzi Point so do not cut the point close transiting from one bay to the other. When entering either side, favor the middle of the channel.

Great Lameshur Bay carries 15 feet almost all the way to the shoreline and Little Lameshur has 10 feet of depth.

GREAT LAMESHUR BAY

Another well-protected bay, Great Lameshur Bay is easy to gain access to. Once inside, pick up a Park Service mooring. Anchoring is forbidden.

LITTLE LAMESHUR BAY

To the west of Great Lameshur, Little Lameshur offers good protection except when the wind is in the south. This is another bay with restricted anchoring. Pick up a mooring and head for the water. Snorkeling here is excellent.

EMERGENCIES

At sea call for mayday on
Channel 16
Ashore dial 911
www.rosewoodhotels.com
/en/caneelbay

CANEEL BAY

Caneel Bay Resort
340-776-6111

CINNAMON BAY

**Cinnamon Bay
Campground**
340-776-6330 or
340-693-5654
www.cinnamonbay.com

National Park Service
340-776-6201
www.nps.gov/viis/index
.htm

Supervisory Ranger
340-776-6451

Clinic
340-693-8900

**T'ree Lizards
Restaurant**
340-776-6330
www.cinnamonbay.com/
treelizards.html

CORAL BAY

BOAT REPAIR

Coral Bay Marine
VHF Channel 16
Open Monday-Friday
and 9am to 1pm Sat
www.coralbaystjohn.com/
CBMarine.htm

PROVISIONS

Lily's Gourmet Market
Tel: 340-777-3335

RESTAURANTS

Shipwreck Landing
Serves lunch and dinner
Live music
Tel: 340-693-5640
www.shipwrecklanding
stjohn.com

**Island Blues Seaside &
Grill**
Open 10am to midnight
Tel: 340-716-6800
www.island-blues.com

Skinny Legs
Nightly band, serves
burgers, hot dogs, salads
Tel: 340-779-4982
www.skinnylegs.com

Aqua Bistro
Tel: 340-776-5336
www.aquabistrostjohn.
com

Big Belly Deli
Serves breakfast, lunch
and dinner
Coccoloba Plaza

Tourist Trap
Fun restaurant
340-714-0912
www.wedontneedno
stinkingwebsite.com/
The_Tourist_Trap/
Welcome.html

SERVICES

**Connections East
Business Services**
Telephone, mail,
computer usage, etc.
Coral Bay
Tel: 340-779-4994
www.connectionsstjohn.
com

SHOPS

Now & Zen Shop
Clothing and more

Sugar Apple Boutique
Tel: 340-799-0009

ISLAND CONNECTIONS

There are many other restaurants and shops too numerous to mention!

CRUZ BAY

Customs and Border Control
340-776-6741
7am-5:30pm 7 days a week

Schneider Regional Medical Center
340-776-8311

CONNECTIONS WEST BUSINESS SERVICES
Telephone, mail, computer usage, etc.
Cruz Bay
Tel: 340-776-6922
www.connectionsstjohn.com

Virgin Islands National Park Service
Visitors Center in Cruz Bay
Open from 8am-4:30 pm
Tel: 340-776-6201 ext. 238

Virgin Island Ecotours
Professional guides
Hike or paddle
Tel: 340-779-2155
www.viecotours.com

RESTAURANTS
Fish Trap Restaurant
Seafood specialty
One block from the ferry dock
340-691-9994
www.thefishtrap.com

Cruz Bay Prime
At the Westin Great Cruz Bay
340-776-6234
www.starwoodhotels.com/westin/property/dining/attraction_detail.html?attractionId=1004853278&propertyID=1098

Deli Grotto
Soups, Salads, Pastries
7am-6pm M-F
8am Saturday,
Closes 3pm Sunday
Tel: 340-777-3061
FB Deli-Grotto

La Plancha del Mar
Serving Dinner 5-10pm M-F, closed Wed.
Weekend brunch 10-2pm
Tel: 340-777-7333
www.laplanchadelmar.com

There are many more restaurants in Cruz Bay, but this will get you started if you want a night on the town!
www.mongoosejunctionstjohn.com

MAHO BAY

Maho Bay Campground
340-715-0501
Activities
340-693-5722 ext. 212
www.maho.org

RESTAURANTS
Café Concordia
Open Tuesday-Saturday
Dec-May
4:30-5:30pm Happy Hour
5:30-8:30pm dinner
www.maho.org/MealsMenu.cfm

Maho Pavilion Restaurant
Open every day
Breakfast 7:30-9:30am
Happy Hour 4:30-5:30pm
(Nov through May)
Dinner 5:30-7:30pm

Beach Café
Open every day mid-Nov through mid-June
11am - 3pm
www.maho.org/MealsMenu.cfm

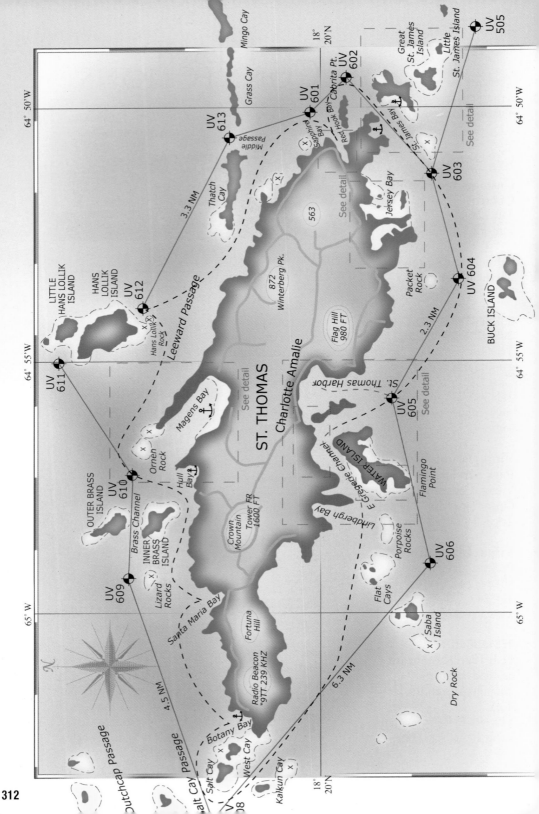

ST. THOMAS

Charts

NV Charts:
St.Thomas to Anegada:
Kit C-14,14A,16

NIMA 2561,
Imray Iolaire A-231

Admiralty Leisure:
5640-1,4,10

Waypoints	North	West
UV601	18°20.00'	64°50.00'
UV602	18°19.30'	64°49.60'
UV603	18°18.20'	64°51.30'
UV604	18°17.60'	64°53.40'
UV605	18°18.60'	64°55.60'
UV606	18°18.10'	64°59.00'
UV607	18°16.80'	65°06.30'
UV608	18°22.00'	65°04.20'
UV609	18°23.40'	64°59.65'
UV610	18°23.40'	64°57.50'
UV611	18°24.75'	64°55.00'
UV612	18°23.40'	64°53.70'
UV613	18°21.50'	64°50.70'

A Brief History

St. Thomas was made a free port in 1815 and in the years following it became a shipping center and distributing point for the West Indies. Charlotte Amalie flourished commercially. A large part of all West Indian trade was channeled through the harbor. The population and atmosphere was very cosmopolitan, particularly in comparison to its sister island of St. Croix where plantation life was the norm. It is on St. Croix that a slave revolt in 1848 prompted the abolition of slavery in the Danish West Indies.

With the increase of steamships in the 1840's St. Thomas continued forward by becoming a coaling station for ships running between South and North America. Shipping lines made Charlotte Amalie their headquarters. Later advancements in steam and political climate made it possible for Spanish and English islands to import directly from producers, therefore skipping St. Thomas. By the 1860's the end of prosperity loomed on the horizon. Coaling however, would continue until about 1935.

In the late 1800s through early 1900s, several major natural disasters including hurricanes, fires and a tsunami left Charlotte Amalie wanting for major re-building. On St. Croix, plantations were suffering with labor issues and low market prices on sugar. The Danish West Indies became more and more dependent on Denmark, and its treasury, during these difficult times.

Negotiations between the United States and Denmark were initiated on several occasions between 1865 and 1917 when the final deal was struck and the United States bought the Danish West Indies for $25 million.

The United States flag was hoisted on the three "Virgin Islands of America" on the 31st of March 1917.

COLD Beer
TOURIST INFO →
DON'T WORRY
BE HAPPY :)
PUERTO RICO
40 MI →

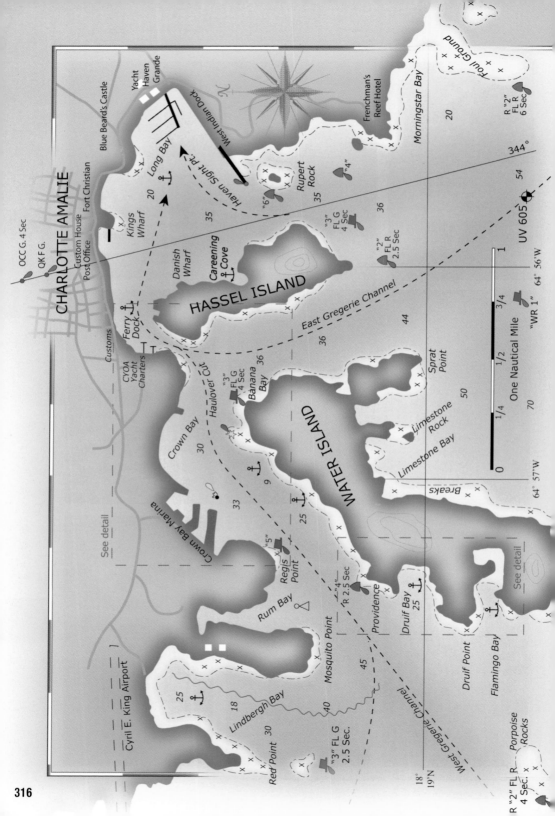

CHARLOTTE AMALIE

Blue Beard's Castle
Fort Christian
Custom House
Post Office

OCC G. 4 Sec
QK F.G.

Yacht Haven Grande

Frenchman's Reef Hotel

Foul Ground

Morningstar Bay
20

R "2" FL R 6 Sec

344°

UV 605
54

"6"

Rupert Rock
35

"4"

"3" FL G 4 Sec
36

"2" FL R 2.5 Sec

1

3/4

"WR 1"

64° 56'W

Long Bay
20

West Indian Dock

Haven Sight Pt.

Kings Wharf

Danish Wharf
35

Careening Cove

HASSEL ISLAND

East Gregerie Channel
36

44

Sprat Point

Limestone Rock
50

Limestone Bay

One Nautical Mile

0   1/4   1/2   3/4

70

64° 57'W

Ferry Dock

Customs

CYOA Yacht Charters

"3" FL G 4 Sec

Haulover Cut

Banana Bay
36

Breaks

See detail

Crown Bay
30

Crown Bay Marina

33

9

25

WATER ISLAND

See detail

"5"

Regis Point

Rum Bay

R 2.5 Sec

"4"

Providence

Druif Bay
25

Druif Point

Flamingo Bay

Mosquito Point

45

West Gregerie Channel

Cyril E. King Airport

25

Lindbergh Bay
18

40

Red Point
30

"3" FL G 2.5 Sec.

Porpoise Rocks

R "2" FL R 4 Sec.

18° 19'N

316

St. Thomas Harbor

Named after a Danish Queen, Charlotte Amalie is the capital city of the U.S. Virgin Islands and historically a major seaport. Used extensively over the centuries as a haunt of pirates and privateers, St. Thomas was declared a free port by the Danes thus enabling the sale of goods, livestock and ships acquired in honest trade or under the flag of piracy.

The town still has many of the original Danish buildings and mansions on the hillside overlooking the harbor. Picturesque alleys and stairways will lead you from large mansions to traditional West Indian houses surrounded by gardens.

Sheltered in all weather, St. Thomas Harbor tends to have a surge, especially when the wind moves around to the south, making it uncomfortable for small boats. Since it is a commercial harbor, swimming is not recommended.

Approaches

There are three approaches to Charlotte Amalie and St. Thomas Harbor. If your approach is from the west you will be using the West Gregerie Channel. Leaving Water Island to starboard and Crown Bay Marina to port then on through Haulover Cut into the main harbor.

Approaching from the east, via Current Cut and St. James Bay; leave the exposed rocks (Cow and Calf) west of the cut to port (waypoint UV603). You will pass the red nun buoy (#2) marking the southern end of Packet Rock (waypoint UV604), which lies approximately one mile due north of the easily distinguishable Buck Island (115 feet).

At the mouth of the harbor a red buoy "R2" marks the shoal ground that extends south from Morningstar Bay under the recognizable Frenchman's Reef Hotel. To the west is the green flashing 4sec. buoy (WR1).

From here you can approach the harbor via the main commercial channel to the north, or if proceeding on to Frenchtown, Crown Bay Marina or Water Island then via The East Gregerie Channel to the northeast leaving Hassel Island to Starboard.

Navigation & Pilotage
St. Thomas Harbor & Yacht Haven Grande

From waypoint UV605 head 370°m toward the red ("4"fl.4sec.) and green ("3" fl.4sec.) markers. Continue in on the same course and you will pass red marker ("6" fl.4sec.) marking the western extremity of Rupert Rocks. There is also flashing red on the western end of the West Indian Dock (cruise ship). Leaving them to starboard, you can head directly for the anchorage.

There is also a range that brings you into the harbor. From a point west of the red buoy ("2" fl.6sec.) at the entrance, the range aligns two green lights on Berg Hill,

ST. THOMAS HARBOR

one at 300 feet the other at 200 feet. The range is 344° (358°m).

Once inside the harbor, you will note several buoys off the West Indian dock. These designate the turning area for the many cruise ships that come and go on a daily basis and the anchorage lies to northeast of them. Yacht Haven Grande is at the head of the harbor at the foot of the cruise ship dock.

Vessels wishing to clear customs and immigration, or anchor/moor in close proximity to the arriving and departing ferries should head for the Frenchtown anchorage located in the far western end of the harbor, north of Hassel Island just inside of Haulover Cut. Moorings may be available from CYOA Yacht Charters who monitor VHF16.

Anchoring & Mooring

The traditional anchorage for yachts in St. Thomas is off the Yacht Haven Grande Marina complex. Take care not to foul any of the private moorings that have been placed by the charter yachts operating out of the harbor. It is not recommended to tie up to the quay in Charlotte Amalie, as the surge is both dangerous and uncomfortable.

Customs & Immigration

Customs clearance can be carried out wharf-side at the ferry dock at the west end of the harbor; the hours are from 8am to noon and 1pm to 4:30pm, Monday through Saturday. Sundays the hours are from 10am to 6pm. The telephone number is 340-774-6755. You may also clear in at the Yacht Haven Grande 7 days a week by appointment. Their telephone number is 340-774-9500. Cruisers planning to stay on the east end of St. Thomas may find it easier to clear in at Cruz Bay, St. John. They do not monitor the VHF radio.

When clearing at customs, bear in mind the dress code ashore calls for shirts and shoes, as wearing just bathing suits is deemed generally inappropriate.

U.S. Virgin Island Customs and Border Control law requires that all people on board must accompany the skipper while clearing. Non U.S. citizens or residents arriving by private or chartered boat must have a visa and passport in order to clear into the U.S. U.S. citizens must have a passport to check in to the U.S. Virgin Islands from other countries, including the British Virgin Islands. U.S. resident aliens must have a green-card. For questions call immigration at 340-774-4279.

Yacht Haven Grande

Yacht Haven Grande is situated in Long Bay, near the cruise ship docks. This state of the art marina has 5200 linear feet of dock designed for luxury yachts and can accommodate mega-yachts over 600 feet in length with a depth of 15 feet and a beam of 54 feet. High speed fueling is from a pedestal right at your slip – no need to move to a fuel dock. Also provided are cable television, telephone service, and WiFi! They will also dispose of oil, black water etc.

The marina complex has everything you need and want including fine dining in several restaurants, catering, laundry, a florist, provisioning, and ships chandlery.

Adding to the experience is an elegant upscale group of shops on the premises at duty free prices.

If you need some time off the boat, relax in the pool, use the tennis courts, or hone your skills on the putting green. Yacht Haven Grande has included some fantastic condominiums in their complex if you want to stay and live the dream! In the center of the marina is an exclusive, private yacht club.

Security is a priority in the marina complex. Your personal safety and the security of your vessel will be assured. The marina can be reached on VHF channel 16 or 340-774-9500.

YACHT HAVEN GRANDE

Nearby, within walking distance are a number of helpful shops such as a grocery store, bank, car rentals and more. You will also come across various restaurants, bars and fast food for those craving a burger and fries.

Near Yacht Haven Grande is a tramway that will carry you to the top of Flag Hill to Paradise Point presenting incredible vistas of Charlotte Amalie and the harbor. You can get a variety of tropical drinks and food as you gaze out on this spectacular view, as well as finding some interesting things to buy to remind you of your trip. Don't forget your camera!

A short walk from the marina brings you to Havensight Shopping Mall full of gift shops like A.H. Riise, Royal Caribbean and Little Switzerland, and a collection of glamorous jewelry shops like Cardow, and Amsterdam Sauer. Many other shops of all descriptions provide for more than a few hours of shopping gluttony!

HASSEL ISLAND

Hassel Island, just minutes from the Charlotte Amalie waterfront, is under the domain of the National Park Service. You can still see some 18th and 19th century fortifications, as well as some private homes and the ruins of an old shipyard visible at the north end of the island.

The park has a limited trail system at this time, amongst the cactus and orchids. Green iguanas can be spotted from time to time. There is a small anchorage in the Careening Cove on the eastern side of the island, often full of local boats.

FRENCHTOWN/HAULOVER CUT

Navigation: 0.8nm NW Main Harbor Entrance
Services: Marina, Moorings, Slips, Garbage, and Showers

Frenchtown Marina, near the ferry dock in the far western section of St. Thomas Harbor, is the base for the CYOA Yacht Charters and their fleet of power and sailboats. The marina is open from 8am to 5pm daily and monitors VHF 16. The water is from 6 feet to 18 feet deep and they can accommodate vessels from 30 to 150 feet long, stern to the dock. Water, electricity, showers and garbage drop off are all available. Moorings just off the marina can be picked up and paid for at the marina.

Frenchtown is quaint, steeped in history and is home to some really great restaurants such as Hook Line and Sinker, Oceana,

Craig and Sally's, and the Frenchtown Deli. It is worth the stop for that alone! Frenchtown is also a convenient spot to get to the ferry terminal if you are planning to go to St. John or the British Virgin Islands, or it is only a very short walk to the Main Street shops and restaurants.

HAULOVER CUT

Traveling west from Frenchtown you will pass through the Haulover Cut in 12 feet (3.6 meters) of water. The high speed ferry traffic uses this channel and therefore extreme caution should be exercised and a sharp lookout for traffic. There are no lights or markers, but the reef on both sides at the western end is easy to see.

French Town Marina

CUSTOMS

CROWN BAY
MARINA

HAULOVER CUT

HASSEL ISLAND

EAST GREGERIE CHANNEL

WATER ISLAND

ST. THOMAS HARBOR LOOKING WEST

ASHORE IN CHARLOTTE AMALIE

Main Street, or Dronningens Gade (which means Queen Street) with its Danish buildings and stone alleys is laced with shops and restaurants. Known as a free port, St. Thomas bustles with shoppers from the cruise ships, and visitors from all parts of the Caribbean and many other parts of the world.

U.S. citizens are allowed a $1600 duty-free exemption on imports purchased in the USVI Excellent values can be found on such luxury items as perfumes, camera gear, liquor, jewelry and other treasures.

Charlotte Amalie has many historical buildings steeped in a myriad of cultures. A tour of the town will take you through many fascinating labyrinths of old stone buildings and wooden houses.

Across Tolbod Gade from the brightly colored Vendors Plaza is the office of the V.I. Government Visitors Bureau and the Native Arts and Crafts Cooperative. This was once the old customs building and is a good place to get your bearings before shopping.

Emancipation Park, named for the freed slaves, borders the vendors market on the seaside of the park. You can easily find it by looking for the rainbow of umbrellas with vendors selling local handicrafts and assorted other mementos. Next to the park, Fort Christian, now a museum, is the oldest building in St. Thomas, having been built in the 1600s.

Market Square, just west of the busy shopping district of Main Street, was a slave market in earlier days, and later became a market for local farmers. Note the wrought iron roof, which came from a European railway station at the turn of the century.

The second oldest synagogue in the United States is located on Crystal Gade. The sand floors in the synagogue are characteristic of Sephardic Carib Synagogues.

On Norre Gade stands the Frederick Lutheran Church, the official church of the Danish Virgin islands. It was rebuilt in 1826 after a fire. You may visit the church Monday through Saturday from 8am to 5pm and on Sunday from 8am to noon.

Above Main Street, the Governor's House and other government buildings are painted with traditional bright red roofs to be easily spotted from sea. This lovely building has housed both the governor's residence as well as his offices. The spacious second floor reception room can be viewed by appointment.

Bluebeard's Castle tower guarded the harbor and the Danish settlers, with the help of Fort Christian and Blackbeard. The hotel and grounds command an excellent view of the entire harbor.

CROWN BAY MARINA

Navigation: 1.75nm west of Haulover Cut
Services: Fuel, Water, Provisions, and Restaurant

Navigation

Located immediately west of the historic Charlotte Amalie Harbor and Hassel Island and north of Water Island, Crown Bay lies within the area known as Sub Base. Yachts may approach via either West Gregerie Channel or East Gregerie Channel; both of which are well marked, as is the reef extending northward from Water Island. While in Gregerie Channel, yachtsmen may approach Crown Bay Marina by leaving the cruise ship dolphin piling to port. The signed entrance to the marina is immediately north of the northernmost cruise ship dock. The tall Texaco sign on the fuel dock marks the entrance to the marina.

Upon entering, the marina's 315-foot fuel dock with high volume pumps lies hard to starboard and is open from 8am to 5pm daily. Water, diesel, gasoline and a pump-out station are available. There is ample maneuvering room inside the turning basis with a controlled depth of 20 feet. The wet slips have a depth of 15 feet. The marina monitors VHF channel 16.

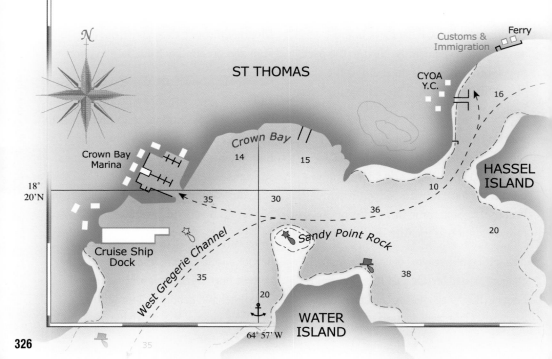

Ashore

Situated on four acres of landscaped grounds, the facilities at Crown Bay Marina are exceptional. There are 99 slips available ranging from 25 to 200 feet, including 16 alongside and stern-to-berths catering to megayachts up to 200 feet in length.

The slips have metered power, water, telephone hookups, satellite TV service and wifi high speed broadband internet service. The marina office is open from 8am to 5pm and provides on-site security, specialized ship's agent service for port clearance and wire transfer banking assistance. Crown Bay Marina is in close proximity to the airport.

Dockside retail shops include Island Marine Outfitters, a chandlery, and Gourmet Gallery for provisioning with an extensive selection of wine, specialty cheeses, choice meats, fresh seafood, fruits and vegetables. Tickles Dockside Pub, with a casual atmosphere is open daily serving dinner until 10pm with the bar staying open for late night drinks.

Blue Island Divers and Water Sports is a full service scuba diving facility that caters to an international clientele from beginners to more challenging dive experiences. They also rent out water toys such as kayaks, snorkels etc. Your Choice Laundry offers self-service washers and dryers or the convenience of making an appointment. Le Face By Zina is a day spa that provides the full spectrum of face and body pampering services. Monica's Hair Studio can help tame that wind-blown hair look offering a full range of services.

Messages, Mail and More can assist with mail, courier service, mail boxes, notary services, photocopying and more. Yacht captains and owners without Caribbean

bank accounts are able to transfer money via the marina account to facilitate with emergency funds.

The Water Island Ferry Service provides several round-trip runs daily between the marina and Water Island. Check with the operators for schedules and fares.

More and more luxury yachts today are utilizing the services of United Yacht Transport to facilitate the movement of yachts to and from the Caribbean region. Crown Bay Marina's close proximity to the United Yacht Transport staging area is advantageous for yachtsmen utilizing UYT which ferries dozens of luxury yachts across the Atlantic in dry-dock cradles secured to the deck.

CROWN BAY MARINA

SUB BASE

Dry Docks

On the western side of Crown Bay is the Sub Base Dry Docks and Shipyard, providing a complete repair facility including yacht repairs, machining, welding, painting, fiberglass work electrical and carpentry

shops, as well as a sail loft and rigging facility. Sub Base Dry Docks has a 100 ton crane and 100 foot long dry-dock.

Quantum Sails, Island Rigging and Offshore Marine are all located at the marine center. They are open from 8am to 5pm Monday through Friday and on Saturday as needed. Sub Base Dry Docks monitors VHF 16.

WATER ISLAND

St. Thomas

Water Island gets its name from the fact that it was one of the few places in the Caribbean with fresh water ponds where sailing vessels could replenish their fresh water casks. Both the pirates and merchantmen were accustomed to coming to Water Island for water.

It is known that the pirates used to anchor in its bays out of range of the guns of the Danish Fort on St. Thomas and lie in wait for merchant vessels that were entering or leaving the port of St. Thomas.

Water Island is two and one half miles long and one half mile wide. It can be reached via the ferry that leaves from Crown Bay Marina on St. Thomas. Water Island divides the east and west Gregerie channels. On the southern most part of the island is an old lookout tower on the top of Flamingo Hill.

From Haulover Cut, transiting to the southwest along the West Gregerie Channel, Sandy Point Rock, marking the northern point of Water Island, will be seen to port standing 15 feet above water level. South of the point is Ruyter Bay and there are usually several boats anchored here in 15 feet of water. Further to the south is Elephant Bay, where once again yachts can be seen at anchor.

R '4' FL R 2 1/2 Sec.

47 Providence Pt.

40

Druif Bay
(Honeymoon Bay)

10

47

WATER ISLAND

60

N

Flamingo Bay   16

58

235
Flamingo Hill

30   30

18°
19'N

64° 57'60 W   Flamingo Pt.

HONEYMOON (DRUIF) BAY

Navigation: 1.5nm SW of Haulover Cut, West Gregerie Channel
Services: None

Just south of Providence Point, Honeymoon Bay, or Druif Bay, is a favorite anchorage with local sailors and the beautiful white sand beach attracts day-trippers from St. Thomas. The designated swimming area is well marked so you can avoid motoring through. Dinghies may be beached on either side. The anchorage has a sandy bottom in 15 to 20 feet of water. Good snorkeling can be found along the southern shore.

FLAMINGO BAY (WATER ISLAND)

Navigation: 0.5nm south of Honeymoon Bay
Services: None

Flamingo Bay is situated at the southwest end of Water Island. When the wind works its way round to the south, the anchorage can be subject to a surge and therefore not suitable for an overnight anchorage. The inner harbor is shallow and therefore suitable only for small boat traffic. The outer harbor is fairly deep and under normal conditions you can tuck yourself up in the northeast corner and drop the hook in 15 to 20 feet on a sandy bottom. The island is privately owned and therefore consideration shown to the homeowners ashore.

LINDBERGH BAY (ST.THOMAS)

Navigation: 2.3nm west of Haulover Cut
Services: Restaurant

Lindbergh Bay, situated east of the terminal and south of the runway at the Cyril E. King Airport is a pleasant bay with no obstructions. At the mouth, depths are about 30 feet, gradually reducing to 15 feet inside the bay. A beautiful beach lines the inner bay and the adjacent hotel provides beach services. Lindbergh Bay is open to the south and the occasional sea swell makes its way into the anchorage. Being so close to the airport you will also have to contend with the noise of jet traffic during the day. A submerged cable runs up the east side of the bay, so when anchoring favor the west and center of the bay.

Departing from Lindbergh Bay for the west, make sure that you continue out to the green marker #3 before making your turn to starboard in order to avoid the shoal area south of Red Point.

Image labels:
CYRIL E. KING AIRPORT
LINDBERGH BAY
MOSQUITO PT.
RED PT.

WESTWARD BOUND

Heading west from Lindbergh Bay and the green marker #3 you will pass to the north of Flat Cays, a small group of rocks surrounded by reef, they are easy to see. To the north tucked up behind the head of the airport runway, is Brewer's Bay. There is an anchorage in about 20 feet of water, but the noise from the airport traffic makes this less than an idyllic tropical escape from civilization.

Heading toward Waypoint UV608 (Salt Cay Passage) located just west of the tip of Salt Cay, the recommended route is to leave Saltwater Money Rock and Kalkun Cay to port with West Cay and Salt Cay to starboard. Do not attempt to pass between the western extremity of St. Thomas and West Cay named Big Current Hole. Although there is 7 feet of water, the narrow channel is best negotiated by those with local knowledge.

From Waypoint UV608 you will be heading west toward Puerto Rico or turning northeast toward Waypoint UV609 (Lizard Rock) to explore the north shore bays of St. Thomas.

BOTANY BAY

(WEST END OF ST. THOMAS)

Waypoint: UV608 (Salt Cay Passage) 18°22.00'N; 65°04.20'W

Navigation: 6.5nm NW of St.Thomas Harbor: 1.5nm SE Salt Cay

Services: None

Less than 1.5 miles SE of Salt Cay on the northwestern tip of St. Thomas is a delightful anchorage known as Botany Bay. The bay itself is separated into two smaller bays by a point of land that has some coral heads extending to the west. Although the various charts mark these bays differently, for the purpose of this document we will assume Botany Bay to be the anchorage to the south of the point separating the two bays. The bay to the north of the small point and directly south

of Botany Point is also a suitable anchorage; however there is a ledge of patch coral that extends across the entire bay.

Although suitable as an overnight in settled weather, during times when the northeast trade winds are at their peak, or a NE swell is present, these anchorages should be treated with extreme caution.

Approaching from the west, after rounding Salt Cay (waypoint UV 608), continue east until you can identify Botany Point and Sandy Bay to the south, then proceed due south. The recommended anchorage would be in 15-20 feet of water on a sandy bottom. At the time of the last survey no services were available, however it should be noted that development has been is underway for some time and therefore changes should be anticipated.

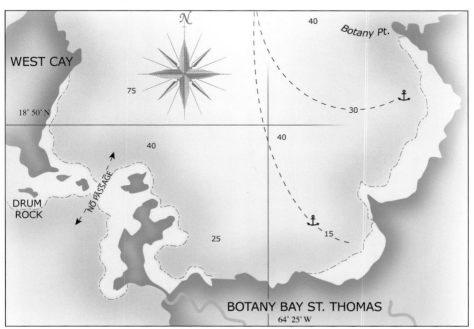

BENNER BAY
(THE LAGOON)

Waypoint: UV603a (Jersey Bay) 18°18.50'N; 64°51.50'W

Navigation: 5.5nm east of St.Thomas Harbor

Services: Full Service Marina, Repair, Travel Lift, Chandlery, Provisions, Restaurants

Benner Bay, locally known as The Lagoon is probably the most protected anchorage for small craft on the island. There are several marinas and services available once inside. Yachts drawing up to 6 feet have access to the Lagoon, yachts drawing over 5 feet should enter on a high tide. Independent Boatyard and Compass Point Marina both monitor VHF16

Navigation & Pilotage

When making your approach into Jersey Bay and the Lagoon, from the west, it is imperative that you not confuse it with the tricky "False Entrance" to the west of Red

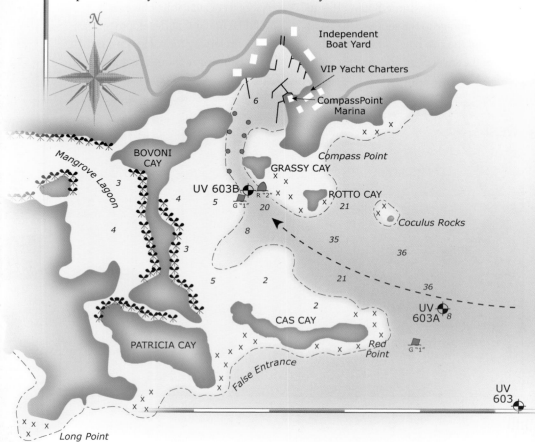

NO PASSAGE

FALSE ENTRANCE

RED POINT

Fl G "1"

UV603A

COCULUS ROCKS

UV603B

N

THE LAGOON | BENNER BAY

Point. As its name implies, there appears to be a direct passage when approaching from the south or west, and boats at anchor can be seen at the head of the bay, but beware, there is a reef extending all the way across the false entrance. A good rule of thumb would be to say: if you can't see a green "1" buoy on the port side of the channel, marking the eastern end of Cas Cay (Red Point), don't go in! That being said, the channel into the Lagoon is well marked and provides no problems once you have identified Rotto Cay and its relationship to other landmarks.

Approaching from the east from Current Cut, you will see a set of rocks named Cow & Calf (north of Deck Point), leaving them to port you will be able to identify the green "1" buoy. Waypoint UV603a marks the approach to the channel and a shallow (7 feet) spot east of the green buoy.

Leaving the green "1" buoy on the tip of Cas Cay to port, and Coculus Rocks to starboard, proceed to Grassy Cay (waypoint UV603b). You will pick up a green buoy on your port hand and red nun marking the southern tip of Grassy Cay. Leave it to starboard. Take Grassy Cay to starboard by 25 feet, and round the red buoy on the northwest side. Leave the anchored boats to port and follow the channel. The channel is marked with red and green buoys and is easily followed leaving the red nuns to starboard when entering from the sea.

Ashore

Independent Boatyard and Marina provide a full-service boat yard, complete with a 50-ton Travel Lift and a 10-ton crane. The boat yard maintains a group of private contractors to accommodate boats requiring services, including: Bruce Merced's Marine Repair, Benner Bay Marine (outboard repairs), Carpentry Plus, Dave Gott Refrigeration, Mike Sheen's Fiberglass Shop, Island Marine Outboards, and Tim Peck Enterprises (Awlgrip work).

Adjacent to Independent Boatyard is Caribbean Inflatables. They can service life rafts and sell and repair inflatable boats, along with selling emergency gear. They are open from 8:30 to 5pm.

The marina includes 85 slips, with full services for both transients and live-aboards. The depth is 7 feet. Daily hours are from 8am to 5pm.

At anchor behind "false entrance" at Benner Bay

Boater's Haven Marina (formerly called Compass Point Marina), across the Lagoon, has over 100 slips and will accommodate boats up to 60 feet in length, with a 19-foot beam and 5 foot draft. The marina provides electricity, water, showers, storage, marine services, and a public dinghy dock on the southeast side of the marina. The marina is conveniently close to restaurants and shops.

Skippers must contact the marina by telephone (340-775-6144) to make a reservation before coming to the marina. Most slips are rented on a yearly basis, but occasionally there is a slip available for a night or two. Boater's Haven Marina is the headquarters for VIP Yacht Charters with their fleet of late model power and sailing yachts.

Located at the marina are two restaurants, with three other restaurants within dinghy distance. St. Thomas Yacht Sales along with a dive shop and several marine repair businesses are based at Compass Point.

Pirate's Cove Marina has 24 slips with depths from 3 to 7 feet. The marina primarily rents slips on a yearly basis. They sell gas and diesel, provide water, ice and electricity and have internet access. You can purchase provisions from the General Store and items from the Pirate's Cove Gift Shop and Boutique. The Pirate's Cove Bar and Grill is a casual, breezy spot for breakfast, lunch and dinner daily. The marina monitors VHF 16.

Fishhawk Marina is a small, shallow marina mostly used for local sports boats.

Nazareth Bay (Jersey Bay)

Nazereth Bay or Secret Harbor as it is also known is tucked away in the northeast corner of Jersey Bay and can be a pleasant anchorage in settled weather. The approach from the south is straightforward from Waypoint UV603 (Cow & Calf 18°20.00'N; 64°51.30'W) proceed due north leaving Coculas Rocks to port. Approaching from the east head towards the entrance to the Lagoon and look for the white buildings of Secret Harbour Beach Hotel on the right.

The east side of the bay is full of coral heads, so head to the west side and anchor in about 20 feet of water. Do not use the moorings, as they are private.

Do not attempt to bring your boat in to the dock, as it is extremely shallow. You may tie your dinghy up to the hotel dock. The dock to the right of the hotel dock is private.

Ashore

The Blue Moon Café and Aqua Action Dive Center are located on the property of the Secret Harbor Beach Hotel. The restaurant, with a stunning view of the sea, is open daily and serves breakfast, lunch and dinner with reservations.

Cowpet Bay

Navigation: 6nm east of St. Thomas Harbor; 0.25nm east of Current Cut
Services: Restaurants

Cowpet Bay, located in the northwest region of St. James Bay and just to the west of Current Cut, is home to the St. Thomas Yacht Club. Much of the bay is occupied with member moorings, which makes this a difficult choice for an anchorage. When the wind is from the south the bay can get quite choppy, exacerbated at times by the wash from fast moving ferry traffic to and from St. John via Current Cut.

If room to anchor can be found without fouling the surrounding moorings, you will be in 15-18 feet on a sandy bottom.

Ashore

Cowpet Bay is the home of the St. Thomas Yacht Club on the western end of the bay. Moorings and the dock are reserved for yacht club members only. The anchorage can be quite crowded at times.

There are a few restaurants ashore; Robert's American Grill is on the beach with a perfect view of the bay. It is an open-air restaurant on the eastern section of the bay at the Elysian Beach Resort. Arthur's Café is near the Anchorage Condominium complex.

CURRENT CUT/CHRISTMAS COVE
(GREAT ST. JAMES ISLAND)

St. Thomas

Waypoint: UV602 (Cabrita Point) 18°19.30'N; 64°49.60'W
Navigation: 2.4nm SW Cruz Bay
Services: Moorings

Navigation & Pilotage

Current Rock "4" sits astride the channel, easily identified at 20 feet above sea level and marked with a flashing 6 sec. light. The eastern most channel is recommended, although the west channel can carry 8 feet but is narrow and fringed with coral.

As the name implies, there can be a strong current of up to 4 knots running in either direction depending upon the tide. If approaching from the west start your engine in advance, as the island of Great St. James tends to blanket the wind. The Cow and Calf, a group of rocks awash to the southwest of Current Cut, are easy to see.

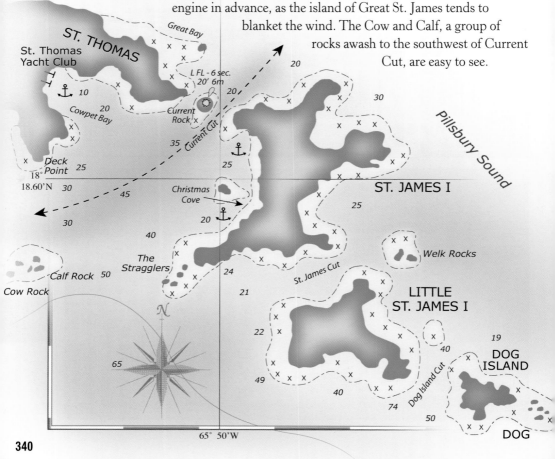

GREAT ST. JAMES

CHRISTMAS COVE

COWPET BAY

Christmas Cove is to the east of the cut and sheltered in the lee of Great St. James. Making your approach to Christmas Cove, you will notice it is divided north/south by Fish Cay. There is a reef extending from the Cay southeast toward the shoreline of St. James. Although there is 6 feet of water between the shore and the cay, it is recommended that you transit via the west end of Fish Cay.

Anchoring

Anchor on either side of Fish Cay in 15 feet of water. Do not anchor too far out as the wind tends to become erratic. Do not pass between Fish Cay and the shore. If anchoring to the north of Fish Cay, ensure that you are anchored close enough to the shore in order to be out of the current flow. There are 10 mooring balls available.

Ashore

There is good snorkeling toward the southern tip of the island. When the weather is calm, take the dinghy and explore the waters and reefs around the south end of St. James Island. When diving and snorkeling in this area always be mindful of the current and ferry traffic.

RED HOOK BAY

Waypoint: UV601 (Red Hook) 18°20.00'N; 64°50.00'W

Navigation: 2.1nm NW Current Cut; 3nm E Cruz Bay

Services: Two Marinas, Provisioning, Dive Shop, Restaurants, and Ferry Service

Just to the north and west of Cabrita Point on the eastern end of St. Thomas, Red Hook Bay is a busy harbor with ferries departing for Cruz Bay, St. John on the hour. American Yacht Harbor, on the north side of the bay provides yachtsmen with all services and Vessup Point Marina to the south is a 30-slip full-service marina. Because of its exposure to the east, Red Hook is often a choppy anchorage.

Navigation & Pilotage

From the south, once around Cabrita Point, Green Marker "1" (UV602), follow the coastline around to the west but favor the middle of the channel. There is a buoyed ferry channel to the north of the bay, but most private vessels make their approach just to the south of the buoys in 12 feet of water. Keep an eye out for ferry traffic and stay out of its way. There is a marked channel into Vessup Bay.

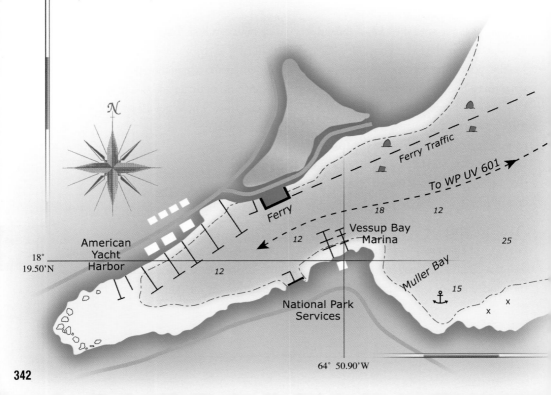

RED HOOK BAY

Anchoring & Mooring

As there are numerous private moorings and a considerable amount of ferry, and other traffic to contend with, a favorable anchorage for yachts can be found at Muller Bay on the southern side of Red Hook. Care should be taken when laying an anchor (15 feet) not to foul a vacant mooring. If you are looking for a slip or taking on water, Vessup Point Marina to port stands by on VHF 16 and further into Vessup Bay, the unique architecture of American Yacht Harbor will be evident to starboard. Don't go too deep into the bay, as it shoals off rapidly past the last set of docks. The marina monitors VHF16.

Ashore

American Yacht Harbor is part of the International Global Yachts (IGY) group of luxury marinas. It has far more than just the basic marina amenities. This includes dockage, ice, water, showers, fuel, electricity, cable TV, and free wifi! The marina can accommodate vessels up to 110 feet in length with a 10 foot draft and a 30 foot beam. Mail, telephone, fax and internet services are also provided at the marina office. A mobile pump-out service is available in the marina. The marina monitors VHF channel 16.

Several sport fishing charters, power boat rentals and sailing charters are based here. American Yacht Harbor hosts some very well known billfish tournaments and is located across from the Virgin Islands Game Fishing Club.

The marina complex includes a shopping village, with convenient stores and businesses for provisioning, Island Marine Outfitters, a bank, laundry service, movie rentals and a host of gift shops and boutiques. Several restaurants are in the marina complex as well as many in the Red Hook vicinity.

In the marina you can have a beer at Island Time Pub, Mexican food at Burrito Bay Deli, and Molly Malone's serves an excellent shepherd's pie. For fish try Whale of a Tale or for steak the Caribbean Steakhouse and Saloon. East End Café serves Italian food and Asian Lotus Grill is a combination of Chinese, Thai and Japanese flavors.

There are many shops in the center including Harbor Laundry, Chris Sawyer Dive Center, a realty company, First Bank, Island Marine Outfitters, Neptune's Fishing Supplies, Red Hook Video and Rhiannon's Unique Gifts.

Just to the east of the marina is the ferry dock, convenient for a trip to St. John or the British Virgin Islands. Across the street is Red Hook Plaza with a grocery store, mail services, restaurants (including the popular Duffy's Love Shack), and a chiropractor. The Marina Market is less than a block away and is a very well stocked market with an excellent selection of wines and champagne, meats, seafood and more.

These are among many other shops and businesses in the Red Hook area.

On the southern part of the bay is the Vessup Point Marina. They offer water, ice and electricity at every slip. Near to them is the National Park dock. Even if it looks like a perfect place to put your boat, don't do it!

The Latitude 18 Restaurant & Bar is close to the marina as well as a car rental place.

Red Hook is a busy center for bareboat charters, crewed boat charters, fishing charters and many other marine oriented businesses. For more information and directions, check ashore at the marina office. The ferry to St. John leaves from Red Hook every hour and ferries to and from the British Virgin Islands stop here as well. Rental cars and taxis are readily available.

Coki Point around the corner from Red Hook is the home of Coral World Marine Park. Situated on four beautifully land-scaped acres, this marine park offers incredible views of the ocean coral reef life twenty feet below the sea through a unique underwater observatory. Feedings for the fish and the sharks are scheduled during the day. The park is complete with gift shop, dive shop, and restaurant. It is well worth a visit.

SAPPHIRE BAY MARINA

Waypoint: UV601 (Red Hook) 18°20.00'N; 64°50.00'W
Navigation: 2.9nm east of Cruz Bay
Services: Marina, Water, and Restaurants

To the north of Red Hook Bay and the American Yacht Harbor is the Sapphire Bay Marina, a part of the Sapphire Bay Resort complex. The marina has 67 slips, water, electricity and fresh water showers. The depth is 10 feet. The resort has several beachfront restaurants, a fresh water pool, ATM and car rentals are available. The entrance is narrow and the marina is generally full of local boats. Call ahead on VHF16 for slip availability,

Navigation & Piloting

Approaching from the northeast, leave Shark Island to starboard and head for the southern end of Red Bay under Red Hook Hill. There is a set of red and green buoys marking the channel entrance and the extremity of the reef on the port side. The marina entrance is narrow and you will be making a 90-degree starboard turn once inside the breakwater.

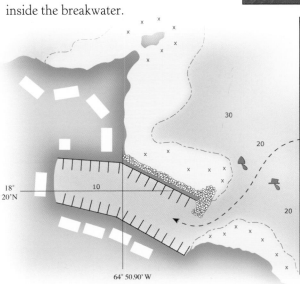

THE LEEWARD PASSAGE/ NORTH COAST

Many of the anchorages along the north coast could be subject to the NE swell when the trade winds are heavy. In fair settled weather, there are some beautiful anchorages to explore.

Traveling northwest via the Leeward Passage from Pillsbury Sound, there is generally a one- to two-knot current that flows either to the NW or to the SE.

There are two obstructions that skipper's should note; Shark Island, northeast of Prettyklip Point and SE of Cabes Point. The second is Turtle Rock that lies between Coki Point to the NW and Cables Point to the SE. Favor the Thatch Cay side of the channel until you are past Coki Point. Favor Lee Point on the western end of Thatch Cay as there are two small inshore reef areas around the points of Sunsi and Mandel Hill. From here you have clear water to Hans Lollick Island or to Picara Point. Both have obstructions. Hans Lollick Rock at the southern extremity of the island is awash. Picara Point has a reef that extends north from the point some 30 yards so give it a wide berth. Ornen Rock is an unmarked hazard 0.5nm northeast of Picara Point. Yachts traveling into Magens Bay can round Picara Point in 50 feet of water, however those that are heading to the Brass Channel between Inner and Outer Brass Islands should exercise caution.

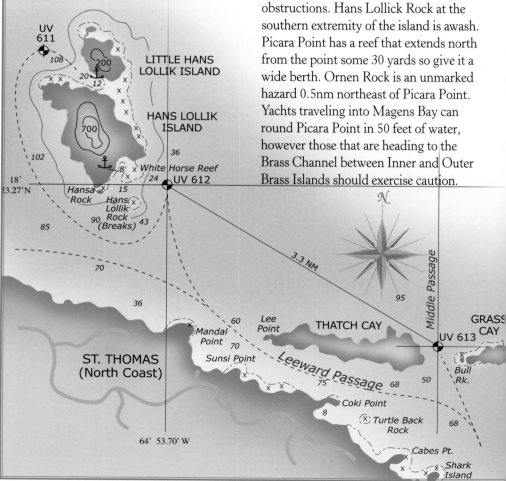

HANS LOLLICK ISLANDS

Waypoint: UV612 (Hans Lollick) 18°23.40'N; 64°53.70'W;
UV611 (Little Hans Lollick) 18°24.75'N; 64°55.00'W
Navigation: 5nm NW Red Hook Bay
Services: None. Good snorkeling

Both of the anchorages on Hans Lollick Island are considered day anchorages only except in very light weather. During the winter months when the trade winds are at their heaviest and there is a NE swell present, we recommend extreme caution.

There are two possible anchorages, one at the southern end of Hans Lollick, known as Coconut Bay and exposed to the east. The other, approached from the west, is south of Little Hans Lollick behind the reef that connects the two islands.

Navigation & Piloting

Approaching from the east to waypoint UV612 there are three obstructions. Hans Lollick Rock will be to the southwest. This rock is awash and will be breaking in a swell. To the northwest is Whitehorseface Reef and to the west is Hansa Rock. Assuming weather is calm, anchor in 15 feet on a sandy bottom. Smaller, shallow-draft vessels can make their way inside the reef to Coconut Beach.

Approaching from the west via waypoint UV611 head for the south end of Little Hans Lollick and work your way into the saddle between the two islands. Anchor in 15 feet of water to the west of the reef between the two islands.

HANS LOLLICK

HANS LOLLICK

LITTLE HANS LOLLICK

PELICAN CAY

MAGEN'S BAY & HULL BAY

St. Thomas

Waypoint: UV610 (Ornen Rock) 18°23.40'N; 64°57.50'W
Navigation: 8nm NW Pillsbury Sound
Services: Moorings, Restaurant, Gift Shop

A deep bay on the north coast of St. Thomas, Magen's Bay is 1.5 miles deep and 0.5 miles wide. To the east is a beautiful beach that logically attracts many daily visitors from the cruise ships berthing daily in Charlotte Amalie on the south side. To the north of the bay is a long tongue of land extending to the NW that ends at Picara Point. To the west is Tropaco Point looking out toward the Brass Islands. During periods of heavy ground swell, Magen's Bay can be rolly and uncomfortable.

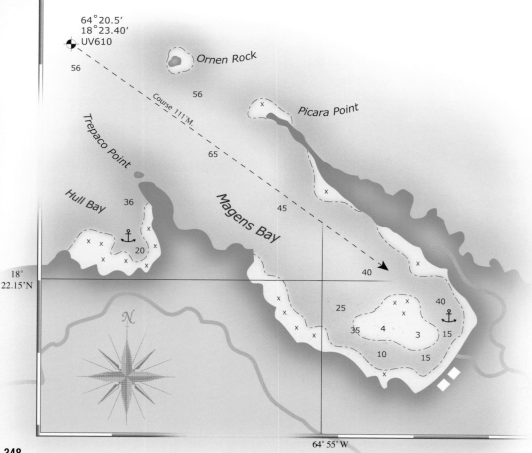

TROPACO POINT

HULL BAY

MAGENS BAY

Navigation & Piloting

Approaching Magen's Bay from the east and Picara Point, care should be taken to keep a minimum of 50 yards off the point, as there is a reef that extends to the north and during the winter months the seas can be very confused in this area. Further to the northwest (0.5nm) is the unmarked Ornen Rock.

Approaching from the Brass Channel between the two islands, and waypoint UV610 leaving Ornen Rock to port, steer 111° magnetic, which will bring you to the anchorage near the head of the bay in 30-35 feet of water.

Anchoring

At the southwestern end of the bay there is a shoal with about 3-4 feet of water over it. There is deep water all around but the safe approach is to head for the anchorage up in the northeast section of the bay in 30-35 feet of water on a sandy bottom.

Ashore

Magen's Bay Beach, under the auspices of the Magen's Bay Authority, is arguably one of the most beautiful and popular beaches in St. Thomas. Try to visit either before or after the cruise ship passengers go back to the ship! There are bathroom facilities, a snack bar and a gift shop.

A nominal entrance fee is collected for those arriving by land. The prices are determined by whether you are a local resident or a visitor. The fee is only charged if you enter the beach by road; anchoring and coming ashore is free. The fee helps to keep the grounds and beach clean and maintained.

HULL BAY

Navigation: 0.8nm SE Boulder Point (Inner Brass Is.)
Services: Restaurant, Dive Shop

When the weather is calm, Hull Bay is a delightful small anchorage under Tropaco Point. Caution is recommended since there are coral reefs to the SW and at the head of the bay.

From Boulder Point, off the southern end of Inner Brass Island, head for Tropaco Point before turning to the SE and paralleling the coastline into the anchorage. Anchor in 25 feet of water on a sand bottom.

Ashore

This lovely bay is often frequented by local fishermen, many of whom are descendants of the French settlers who escaped to St. Thomas over 200 years ago. Their small fishing boats are anchored in the bay and their fishing nets are often drying on the trees. The bay is tranquil and shady – a good place to relax with a book or just watch the fishermen and do nothing at all.

Ashore you will find a casual restaurant/bar, the Hull Bay Hideaway, who specialize in fresh fish dishes. They have a dart room, pool table, computer with internet and a television for watching those sports games you thought you would have to miss.

The restaurant is open from 10am to 10pm on week days and 10am to 11pm on weekends

TROPACO PT.

18   ⚓   15

Hull Bay, St. Thomas

Magen's Bay

351

COWPET BAY

RESTAURANTS
Robert's American Grill
Serving breakfast, lunch
and dinner
340-714-4049

Arthur's Café
Near the Anchorage
condo complex
340-775-4049

St. Thomas Yacht Club
340-775-6320
www.styc.net/index.php/
dining.html

CROWN BAY

MARINAS
Crown Bay Marina
Tel: 340-774-2255
VHF channels 16 and 11

BUSINESS SERVICES
**Messages, Mail and
More**
340-776-4324
www.mmmvi.com

CHANDLERIES
**Island Marine
Chandlery**
Tel: 340-774-2001

LAUNDRY
Your Choice Laundry
340-715-3277

PROVISIONS
Gourmet Gallery
340-776-1595

RESTAURANTS
Tickles Dockside Pub
340-776-1595
www.ticklesdocksidepub.
com

DIVING
**Blue Island Divers and
Water Sports**
Dive tours, certifications,
and rental of water toys
340-774-2001
www.blueislanddivers.com

CROWN BAY & SUB BASE

BOAT SERVICES
**Sub Base Dry Docks
and Shipyard**
1000-ton dry dock
Machining and fabrication,
paint, fiberglass, rigging,
engine services
340-776-2078
www.subbasedrydock.vi

Island Rigging
340-774-6833

Offshore Marine
Inflatables, diesel
Engines, outboard engines
340-776-5432
www.offshorevi.com

Quantum Sails
340-777-5638

FRENCHTOWN

CHARTER COMPANY
CYOA
340-777-9690
www.cyoacharters.com/
meetcyoa.htm

RESTAURANTS
Bella Blu
Small, restaurant
with delicious
Mediterranean food
340-774-4348
www.bellabludining.com

Craig and Sally's
Delicious
340-777-9949
www.craigandsallys.com

Frenchtown Deli
Open Monday through
Friday from 7am to 8pm
340-776-7211

Hook Line and Sinker
Lovely restaurant with a
harbor view; serving lunch,
dinner and Sunday brunch
hooklineandsinkervi.com

**Oceana Restaurant
and Wine Bar**
Located in Villa Olga
Seafood menu,
great wine bar
340-774-4262
www.oceanavi.com

HULL BAY

RESTAURANTS
Hull Bay Hideaway
Restaurant & Bar
340-777-1898
www.hullbayhideaway.com

THE LAGOON

MARINAS
Boater's Haven (formerly
Compass Point Marina)

ISLAND
CONNECTIONS

Electricity, water, pump
out station
Tel. 340-775-6144

**Independent Boatyard
and Marina**
Water, electricity and
pump-out station
Haul out facility with
repair facilities
VHF channel 16
Tel: 340-776-0466
http://ibyvi.com

Pirates Cove Marina
Water, ice, electricity
VHF channel 16
Tel: 340-774-4655

Saga Haven Marina
Water, fuel, electricity,
small shop
Tel: 340-775-0520

CHANDLERY
Budget Marine
Tel: 340-779-2219
www.budgetmarine.com/
Store.aspx?id=St.%20Th
omas

BOAT REPAIRS
Fiberglass
Mike Sheen
Tel: 340-714-1884

Yacht Carpentry Plus
Jeff Hart
Tel: 340-775-9255

Machine Shop
Bruce Merced
346-513-0671

MAGEN'S BAY

Magen's Bay Authority
340-777-6300
www.magensbayauthority
.com/

REDHOOK

MARINAS
**IGY American Yacht
Harbor**
VHF channel 16
All amenities
Tel: 340-775-6454
www.igy-american
yachtharbor.com

Vessup Point Marina
Water, electricity, ice
Near to Latitude 18
Restaurant & Bar

CHANDLERY
**Island Marine
Outfitters**
Tel: 340-775-6621
www.stcroixmarine.com
/node/2

DIVING
**Red Hook Dive
Center** formerly Chris
Sawyer's
340-777-7804
http://redhookdivecenter
.com

LAUNDRY
Harbor Laundry
Tel: 340-714-7672

BANKING
First Bank VI
Tel: 340-775-5280

RESTAURANTS
Island Time Pub
Pizza
Tel: 340-775-2929

Burrito Bay Deli
Mexican
Tel. 340-775-2944

**Molly Malone's and
Whale of a Tale**
Molly's offers bar food
and drinks; open-air
setting for seafood
Tel:340-775-2080

**Caribbean Steakhouse
and Saloon**
Casual steakhouse
Tel: 340-775-7060
www.caribbeansaloon.com

Duffy's Love Shack
Open 11:30-2am
Across the street from
the marina
Tel: 340-779-2080
www.duffysloveshack.
com/index.asp

PROVISIONS
Marina Market
Across the street from
the marina
Tel: 340-779-2411
www.marinamarketusvi.
com

St. Croix

Charts

NV Charts: Virgin Islands Kit C-17
NIMA: 2561, Imray Iolaire A-23, A234
Admiralty Leisure: 5640-11, 11A,11B,12

 St. Croix lies in splendid isolation 40 miles south of the other Virgin Islands. It is surrounded by the largest island barrier reef system in the Caribbean, and thus has fantastic diving. Rich in history and natural beauty and much less crowded than the other U.S. Virgins, it's definitely worth the trip. The blue water passage takes you over the deep Virgin Island Trough. Allow at least three days—one to get there, one to tour and one to return. Better yet, stay a while. St. Croix is the largest Virgin, more than twice the size of St. Thomas or Tortola. Flatter and more fertile than most islands, it was known as The Garden Spot of the Caribbean during the colonial centuries and it is still relatively unspoiled and undeveloped. There are two charming towns, Christiansted and Frederiksted, and friendly vibes that make the island feel like home. Many cruisers who dropped anchor for a short visit have become permanent residents of St. Croix.

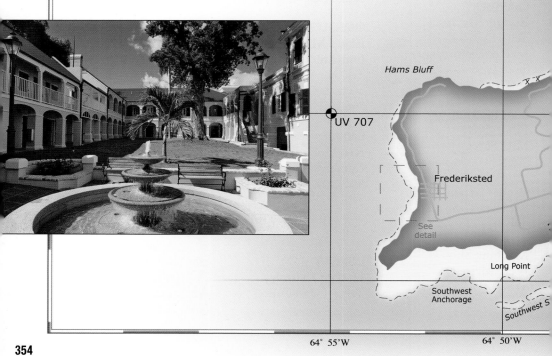

Hams Bluff

UV 707

Frederiksted

See detail

Long Point

Southwest Anchorage

Southwest S

64° 55'W   64° 50'W

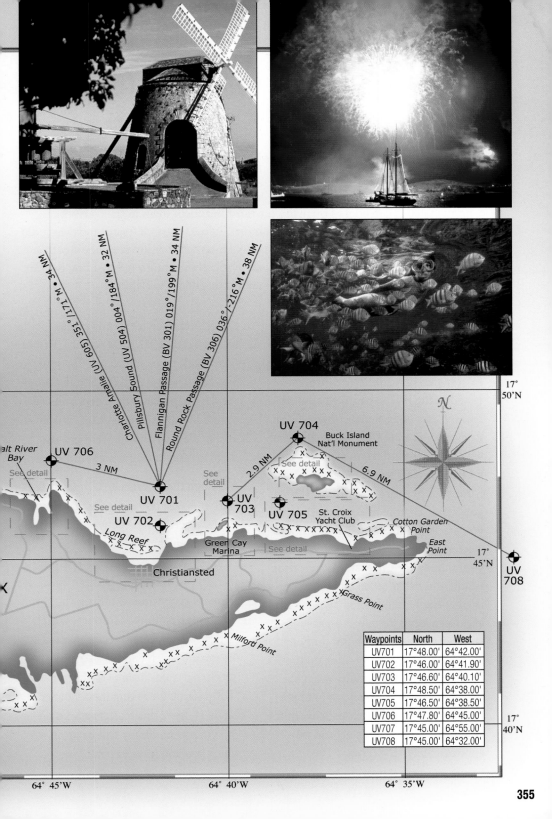

Charlotte Amalie (UV 605) 351°/171°M • 34 NM

Pillsbury Sound (UV 504) 004°/184°M • 32 NM

Flannigan Passage (BV 301) 019°/199°M • 34 NM

Round Rock Passage (BV 306) 036°/-216°M • 38 NM

34 NM

UV 704

Buck Island Nat'l Monument

Salt River Bay

UV 706

3 NM

See detail

UV 701

See detail

UV 702

See detail

2.9 NM

UV 703

UV 705

6.9 NM

Long Reef

St. Croix Yacht Club

Cotton Garden Point

Green Cay Marina

See detail

East Point

17° 50'N

17° 45'N

UV 708

Christiansted

Grass Point

Milford Point

N

17° 40'N

Waypoints	North	West
UV701	17°48.00'	64°42.00'
UV702	17°46.00'	64°41.90'
UV703	17°46.60'	64°40.10'
UV704	17°48.50'	64°38.00'
UV705	17°46.50'	64°38.50'
UV706	17°47.80'	64°45.00'
UV707	17°45.00'	64°55.00'
UV708	17°45.00'	64°32.00'

64° 45'W

64° 40'W

64° 35'W

CHRISTIANSTED

St. Croix

Waypoint: UV702 (17°46.00'N; 64°41.90'W
Navigation: 38nm SSW Round Rock Passage
Services: Full Service Marina, Travel Lift (300-ton), Chandlery, Provisioning, Island Tours

Christiansted is considered by many the most beautiful town in the Caribbean. Formerly the capital of the Danish West Indies, it looks much the same today as it did in colonial days. Entering the harbor is a visual treat, as beautiful old buildings in a bouquet of pastel colors line the waterfront. The harbor is protected by Long Reef to the west and Scotch Bank to the east, the controlling depth is 16 feet.

Navigation & Pilotage

If you are arriving from the other Virgin Islands, try to depart from either the eastern end of St. John or Norman Island in the BVI to gain a close or beam reach. Leave early, no later than 8:00 am, to ensure you enter Christiansted Harbor, which is well-marked, in daylight. If the weather is clear you can see St. Croix from St. Thomas and Tortola. If not, you won't be able to see the hills until you are two hours out. Allow for a westerly 0.5 knot current. If you lay your course for the eastern end of the island you can alter as you near the island. The saddle formed by Lang Peak and Recovery Hill makes an easy landmark. Head for a point midway between them until you pick up the radio tower on Fort Louise Augusta. Pass the first green buoy (#1) to port, then line up the radio tower between the channel markers. This should be approximately 164° True.

Long Reef, which extends across the harbor (and offers good diving), will be seen breaking to starboard. On your port hand is Scotch Bank and, although the charts indicate that parts of it are covered with adequate water, it is wise to stay clear whenever there is a sea running, as it breaks in a ground swell.

Although the entrance to Christiansted Harbor is well buoyed, note that Round Reef, which lies to the west of Fort Louise Augusta and is clearly visible, is a major navigational hazard. There are channels on either side of it but local cruisers recommend taking the "schooner channel" to port, which carries 10 feet. Round reef is marked at the northeastern end by a striped (green/red) mid-channel flashing marker "RR." If you are taking the Schooner Channel, leave this mark to starboard and your second buoy will be green #5 which you will leave to port.

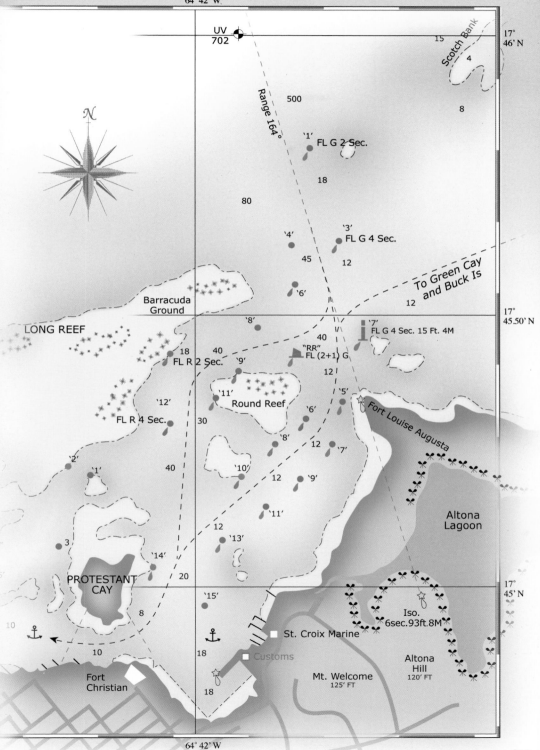

17° 46' N

UV 702

15

Scotch Bank

4

8

500

Range 164°

'1'
FL G 2 Sec.

18

80

'4'

'3'
FL G 4 Sec.

45

12

'6'

To Green Cay and Buck Is

12

Barracuda Ground

17° 45.50' N

LONG REEF

'8'

'7'
FL G 4 Sec. 15 Ft. 4M

40

18

40

"RR"
FL (2+1) G

FL R 2 Sec.

'9'

12

'11'

Round Reef

'5'

Fort Louise Augusta

'12'

'6'

FL R 4 Sec.

30

'8'

12

'7'

'2'

40

'10'

12

'9'

Altona Lagoon

'1'

'11'

3

12

'13'

PROTESTANT CAY

'14'

20

8

'15'

17° 45' N

10

10

18

St. Croix Marine

Iso. 6sec.93ft.8M

Customs

Fort Christian

Mt. Welcome
125' FT

Altona Hill
120' FT

18

ST. CROIX

PROTESTANT CAY

SHOAL

LONG REEF

FL R

GR BUOY

R

GR BUOY

ROUND REEF

GR BUOY

RR
GR BUOY

RED '6'
NUN BUOY

G5

FL G7

ST. CROIX MARINA

FISHING DOCK

G11

G9

G7

TOWER

FORT LOUISE AUGUSTA

ALTONA LAGOON

Anchoring & Mooring

The anchorage in the lee of Protestant Cay is quite crowded with the permanent moorings of cruisers who call this home and seaplanes coming and going to St. Thomas and San Juan from the Seaborne base at the west end of town. Visiting yachts are asked to go to the east side of the harbor, where you can anchor west of St. Croix Marine or pick up a white with blue stripe mooring. These new government moorings are for transient use up to two months. The fee is $3 per foot per month, payable at the Department of Planning and Natural Resources (DPNR) Division of Enforcement in Anna's Hope. The anchorage is off Altona Lagoon, a public beach and fishing area, and has good holding. Do not tie your dinghy to the fishing dock but go to St. Croix Marine, where there is a dinghy dock at the end of Dock C.

Ashore

Vessels sailing from the BVI or other foreign ports must clear customs and immigration at the Gallows Bay Harbor Dock located just west of St. Croix Marine. If your boat is registered in the U.S. you can report your arrival between 8:00am and 4:30pm at 340-773-1011. Foreigners (non US) must visit in person, with passport and visa. After hours, weekends and holidays call 340-778-0216.

There's a lot happening on this quiet island. If you'd like to see what's going on, pick up *St. Croix This Week*, a free tourist magazine with just about everything there is to know about the island and a calendar of events. A comprehensive website is gotostcroix.com and stcroixlime.com.

CHRISTIANSTED

If you're here in the winter months you will probably see the beautiful Roseway at the dock or in nearby waters. A National Historic Landmark schooner, she is the home of the World Ocean School, introducing local middle school students to the wonders of sailing by day and offering short cruises at sunset.

St. Croix Marine, a full service marina and boatyard, is just east of the customs dock. It can dock vessels up to 200 feet and 10-foot draft, and it offers discount fuel, showers and ice. There is a popular restaurant/bar, the Golden Rail, open all day every day. The boatyard offers long and short term storage, a marine railway, 60-ton Travelift, a railway to haul out multihulls, fiberglass repair, USCG and ABS certified welding, custom painting, mechanical and electrical repairs, refrigeration and air conditioning service. Also on the premises is Island Marine Outfitters, a comprehensive chandlery open Monday through Saturday from 7:30am to 5:00pm. The marina is operated by Larry and Ginny Angus and can be reached by phone at (340) 773-0289 or stcroixmarine@hotmail.com. Their website is stcroixmarine.com. They and their staff can help you arrange for car rentals or tours or for delivery from purveyors of food and drink.

A mega-yacht marina is proposed for the Gallows Bay Harbor Dock location. Delays have been ongoing, but the project of Gallows Bay Partners is still on the table.

When operational, the Gallows Bay Marina will accommodate boats up to 375 feet.

Gallows Bay is a convenient location with most services nearby: bank, post office, laundry, hardware store, supermarket, travel agency, pharmacy, ice cream, real estate agents, hair salon, bookstore, boutiques and restaurants. It's also in walking distance of Christiansted town.

In Christiansted Harbor there are two small marinas, Jones Maritime and Silver Bay Dock, both operated by Jones Maritime Co. They have a total of 25 slips accommodating up to 65 feet, a sailing school, yacht management service and charter operation. The marina offers all services but fuel. There are bathrooms with full size showers, laundry service, ice, water, power, courtesy car, 5-dog security and management that lives on the premises. Contact them at 340-773-4709, jonesmaritimeco@gmail.com or jonesmaritime.com.

A boardwalk lined with small hotels, restaurant/bars and shops runs along the entire waterfront, from the seaplane terminal to the town wharf and fort area. (Plans call for continuing the boardwalk all the way to Gallows Bay.) You can tie your dinghy up anywhere along the boardwalk and hit the watering holes or walk to town. Angry Nate's and the Fort Christian Brew Pub are boater hang-outs. Nate's is known for its fresh seafood and the pub hosts crab races Monday during happy hour. There is also a unique bar called Comanche Mill Yacht-Less Club, which has nothing to do with yachts but the drinks are named after local "commodores." On Protestant Cay in the middle of the harbor you'll find Hotel on the Cay. Its Harbormaster Beach Club has a beach barbecue and local music Sunday afternoons and Tuesday nights. In town there are several remarkably good restaurants. This is the place to splurge on a gourmet dinner at Kendrick's, Dashi (sushi) or Savant or the new Thai restaurant, Galangal.

The Town of Christiansted

This gem of a town was built early in the Danish era (1733-1917). Basically neoclassic, the stately architecture was gracefully adapted to the tropics, with arched arcades to protect pedestrians from the sun and rain. The outskirts of town have deteriorated, but restorations are underway.

The Christiansted National Historic Site preserves the wharf area and surrounding buildings much as they were in Danish times. Five yellow buildings are administered by the National Park Service: the imposing Fort Christiansvaern, complete with cannons and dungeons; the Steeple Building, the first church on the island; the Scale House, where merchants weighed their produce before shipping it abroad and where you can find a visitors' center with tourist information; the old Customs House; and the Danish West India & Guinea Company Warehouse, where slaves were auctioned in the courtyard. A museum dedicated to the slave trade is planned for this building. A short way up King Street are two other historic landmarks, imposing Government House, which once was the seat of government and boasts a lovely ballroom upstairs, and the pretty Lutheran Church.

The heart of town is a triangle bound by the waterfront, Queen Street and King Cross Street. Here you can do your duty free shopping in a pleasant, laid back ambiance of charming and uncrowded stores. There are a few really interesting gift shops featuring tropical items and one that carries only locally made arts and crafts: Many Hands. Jewelry stores are abundant but most of them are small and personal, with the designer on the premises. This island is famous for its bracelets, most notably "the St. Croix Hook" originated by Sonya and copied by everyone else and "the Crucian Bracelet" by Crucian Gold. IB Designs has found a niche with jewelry that incorporates chaney, bits of broken old china found on the ground. There are also a number of attractive boutiques selling island fashions. The V.I. Tourism Bureau is in Government House.

The island is home to many artists, and Christiansted has numerous galleries. You can visit them all in one evening during

Art Thursdays, the third Thursday of each month except in summer. Another regular event in Christiansted is First Fridays, a night when restaurants and retailers offer special deals to lure people into town for a night out.

Four nights a year you can join a terrific town party called Jump Up, when the streets are full of bands, vendors and mocko jumbies (stilt dancers), and the shops and restaurants offer special sales. They happen on the Friday night of a special weekend: Thanksgiving, Valentine's Day, a triathlon the first weekend in May, and July 4, in honor of founding father Alexander Hamilton, who spent his boyhood here.

The St. Croix Ironman 70.3 Triathlon draws hundreds of international athletes the first Sunday in May every year. The historic wharf area is the hub of the action, starting at dawn. Other major events in Christiansted include the St. Patrick's Day Parade on the Saturday closest to March 17, complete with water balloons and plenty of green beer. And if you're here any time around the Christmas holidays you can catch some of the action of the Crucian Christmas Festival, which starts in early December and continues past Three Kings Day, January 6. This is the St. Croix version of Carnival and, although most of the major events take place in Frederiksted, there are several others in and around Christiansted.

Island Tour

This beautiful and gentle island is one you will want to drive around in a rental car or tour bus. It doesn't have the precipitous hills and intimidating turns of the other Virgins, but it does have endless beautiful vistas and numerous points of historical or natural interest. Just remember to drive on the left.

St. Croix has been under seven flags, most notably Denmark, which ruled for almost 200 years and divided the island into 375 plantations of about 150 acres each. Sugar cane was the dominant crop. The Danes left a stunning architectural legacy, and the countryside is full of restorations and ruins of the plantation era: greathouses, slave quarters, rum factories and many hurricane-proof windmills, where the sugar cane was ground. They are known locally as sugar mills. The Heritage Trail is a self-guided driving tour that covers many of these historic sites. Follow the brown signs featuring windmills.

The island is 28 miles long by 7 miles at its widest point. Topographically diverse, it is close to desert on the east end and almost rainforest in the west. In between are mountains and valleys and, on the south shore, miles of grasslands grazed by Senepols, a breed of cattle developed by St. Croix ranchers.

A good way to see most of the island and its highlights within a day is to make a circle tour. If you start in Christiansted and head east on Route 82, you will pass the lovely old Buccaneer Hotel; Tamarind Reef Resort with Green Cay Marina; Southgate Coastal Reserve, a bird haven owned by the St. Croix Environmental Association; the St. Croix Yacht Club; Cramer Park, a public beach with picnic facilities; and an 82-foot dish antenna, part of the Very Long Baseline Array of the National Radio Astronomy Observatory.

The island to the north is Buck Island Reef National Monument, a popular sailing and snorkeling destination. Stop at Point Udall, the easternmost point of the U.S., where there is a monument to the millennium. It overlooks beautiful bays on both sides. To the south are Jacks and Isaacs Bays, acquired by The Nature Conservancy as a preserve.

Continuing along the south shore on Route 60, you will see the Divi Carina Bay Resort and across the road its casino, the only one in the Virgin Islands. Turn left on 624 and left again on 62 and pass miles of cattle ranches. Go left on 68 to see St. Croix Renaissance Park, a huge environmentally-oriented industrial and business park on the site of an old alumina refinery. The huge complex near the road is the new headquarters and distillery of Diageo's Captain Morgan Rum.

This road will deliver you to Route 66, the Melvin Evans Highway, the only four-lane road on the island. You'll pass the airport off to your left. Route 64 is a U-shaped road that skirts the airport, first as East Airport Road and later as West Airport Road). Go right at the latter and you're soon at the Cruzan Rum Distillery, for generations a family-run business on the site of an old plantation, where you can tour the factory in half an hour and sample one of their famous flavors. Make a slight departure from your circle tour by turning right on 70 (Queen Mary Highway, also known as Centerline Road), to see St. George Village Botanical Garden, where an excellent collection of native plants and ornamentals is displayed among relics of the pre-Columbian and colonial periods. Back on 70, head west to Whim Museum, a restored sugar plantation. Both the Botanical Garden and Whim Museum are worth touring, and both have attractive gift shops. They are the island's major tourist attractions and both hold numerous popular events during the year—chamber music concerts, Starving Artists fairs, an antiques fair and ruins rambles at Whim; an art exhibit, Christmas gala, moonlight garden walks and a mango festival at the Garden. Also on this road is a KMart, the island's only department store.

Follow 70 into the quaint town of Frederiksted. This is a good stop for lunch and a swim at Coconuts north of town or Beach Side Café south of town. In town, check out Polly's bistro-style restaurant on Strand Street for healthy sandwiches and salads with local produce. Strand Street is on the beautiful waterfront, site of the impressive Caribbean Museum Center for the Arts, and on cruise ship days, the town is hopping with lots of street vendors selling clothing, jewelry, artwork and local fare. At the north end is Fort Frederik where, on July 3, 1848, thanks to progressive governor Peter von Sholten and non-violent slave leader Buddhoe, the slaves of the Danish West Indies were emancipated peacefully. Frederiksted is thus known as Freedom City. If you like paddle boarding, the first beach north of town is where Teres Veho rents boards. The water here is flat and great for beginners.

When you leave the town head north on 63 and take the second turn to the right, Mahogany Road (Route 76). This takes you through the tropical moist forest (there is not enough rainfall to qualify as a rainforest) where you will pass the Lawaetz Museum, a charming old farmhouse built by Danish settlers whose

descendants still live on the island; St. Croix LEAP, a woodworking shop using fallen trees; the turnoff to Mount Victory, an eco-camp, and Creque Dam Farm, a sustainable farm institution, two bright stars in the island's growing eco-tourism field; the Domino Club, a thatch-roofed bar featuring beer-drinking pigs; and the Bottle Museum, a yard full of decorative vignettes made from recycled trash. Turn left on 69, which takes you past the beautiful Carambola Golf Course designed by Robert Trent Jones (one of three golf courses on the island), then down The Beast, a monstrous hill triathletes ride their bikes up in the half ironman competition every May.

You are now back on the north shore. Carambola Hotel is to the left and Route 80 to the right, which takes you past Cane Bay with its famous dive site, the Wall, and a few pleasantly laid-back waterfront bar/restaurants; and Salt River Bay National Historical Park and Ecological Preserve, the only place on U.S. soil where a Columbus party landed and the site of his first hostile encounter with indigenous people. When you reach the end of 80, turn left on 75 and follow it back into Christiansted. You will enter town at Sunday Market Square, a restored block that looks as it did when the slaves gathered there on their day off to visit and buy and sell their own produce and handiwork.

BUCK ISLAND REEF NATIONAL MONUMENT

St. Croix

Waypoint: UV703 (Green Cay) 17°46.60'N, 64°40.10'W
Navigation: 4.6 nm NE Christiansted Harbor
Services: Moorings, Underwater Trail

This is the only offshore sailing destination from St. Croix, but it's so good the locals go back time after time. Several charter boats are National Park Service concessionaires and make day and half-day runs. A small, uninhabited island about a mile off the northeast shore, Buck Island has a gorgeous beach on one end and a snorkeling trail on the other. You're likely to see sea turtles and sting rays here, as well as plentiful reef fish. Schools of Blue Tang abound, swimming through the underwater coral garden and its grottos. The trail has underwater signs guiding snorkelers through the reef and identifying the fish and coral, and there are a couple of floats to rest on so that you won't be tempted to touch the coral. The boundary of the National Monument was expanded in 2001, adding over 18,000 acres of submerged lands to the park. Fishing is prohibited.

Navigation & Pilotage

Departing Christiansted Harbor, there are two options; the first takes you to the west of Scotch Bank, leave the same way you came in until you reach the green sea buoy (#1). Then continue north to waypoint UV701 (1.9nm) marking the central navigation point for the island, then proceed east for 4 miles heading for the prominent point on the south end of Buck Island. An alternate shorter route via the Scotch Bank Channel (12ft) is to proceed north out of the harbor to buoy G7 (15 feet high) just due north of Fort Louise Augusta, leaving it to starboard. Do not go further inshore, as there are two shoal areas. On an approximate bearing of 076°m (4.2nm) leave Green Cay to starboard and head for the white beach on the western end of Buck Island. There are two white buoys that mark the extremities of the park's western patch reef area. If you want to go to the snorkeling trail, proceed eastward along the south shore of the island, keeping the white buoy to port, until you see green and red buoys marking the entrance through the reef into the lagoon. Follow the lagoon passage to the eastern end of the island and pick up one of the Park Service moorings. Depth inside the lagoon varies, averaging only 6 feet. Stay in the middle to avoid shoal areas.

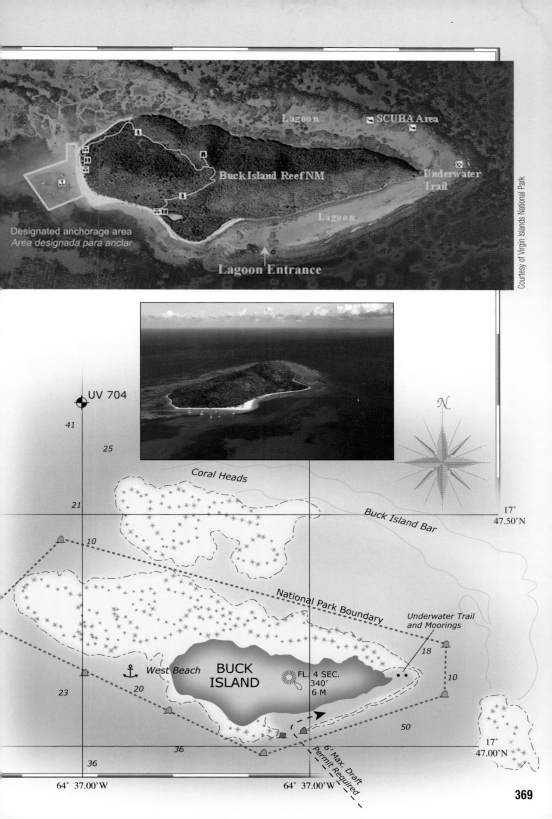

Courtesy of Virgin Islands National Park

Lagoon

SCUBA Area

Buck Island Reef NM

Underwater Trail

Designated anchorage area
Area designada para anclar

Lagoon

Lagoon Entrance

UV 704

41

25

21

Coral Heads

Buck Island Bar

17° 47.50'N

N

10

National Park Boundary

Underwater Trail and Moorings

18

⚓ West Beach

BUCK ISLAND

FL. 4 SEC.
340'
6 M

10

23

20

50

17° 47.00'N

36

36

6' Max. Draft
Permit Required

64° 37.00'W

64° 37.00'W

369

Anchoring & Mooring

There is no anchoring inside the reef. At the underwater trail you're welcome to pick up one of the Park Service moorings for day use only. For the time being anchoring is allowed at the designated area off West Beach. Boaters are requested to obtain a permit (good for one year) from the National Park Service office near the wharf in Christiansted. You can anchor anywhere off the beach in about 15 feet of water in deep sand. Please avoid sea grass areas!

Ashore

Buck Island is a nesting site for four species of endangered or threatened sea turtles. If you anchor overnight between June and December, you are not allowed ashore between sunset and sunrise, and bright lights and loud noise are not permitted. You may see monitors and researchers at work ashore.

There are two picnic areas on Buck Island with pit toilets, picnic tables and barbecue grills, a pavilion east of the small pier on the south shore and one without shelter on the western end. Visit the information kiosk located at each picnic area for park guidelines and information. An overland hiking trail provides a 45-minute walk from beach to beach with a stop at the north side reef overlook. Avoid contact with any plants on the island as many will burn or cause an allergic reaction. There is no collecting in the park.

EAST END MARINE PARK

The entire eastern tip of St. Croix has been designated a marine park to protect and replenish corals and fish by regulating boating, diving and fishing within its boundaries, from Chenay Bay on the north to Great Pond on the south. The local government has placed some single point moorings along the north shore for day use only. Look for 16" yellow mooring balls.

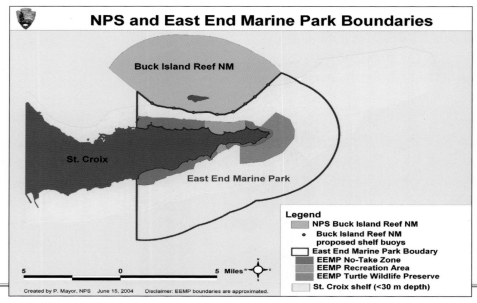

NPS and East End Marine Park Boundaries

Buck Island Reef NM

St. Croix

East End Marine Park

5   0   5 Miles

Legend
- NPS Buck Island Reef NM
- • Buck Island Reef NM proposed shelf buoys
- ☐ East End Marine Park Bouday
- EEMP No-Take Zone
- EEMP Recreation Area
- EEMP Turtle Wildlife Preserve
- St. Croix shelf (<30 m depth)

Created by P. Mayor, NPS   June 15, 2004   Disclaimer: EEMP boundaries are approximated.

Explore

*Tamarind Reef Resort's
Green Cay Marina*

FREE Rental Car* with 2 or 3-day slip
plus privileges at Tamarind Reef Resort

- 154 slips with free WIFI internet ~ Daily, monthly and live-aboard rates.
- Diesel, premium gas, fresh water, ice, showers, laundry, power and cable hook-ups.
- Sanitary pump-out station, storage units and 24-hour security.
- Two restaurants including casual poolside or fine dining.
- Beach, pool, tennis, kayak and spa privileges at Tamarind Reef Resort (38 rooms).
- A great base to explore St. Croix ~ ***Ask about special deals and discounts!***

*FREE Rental car with 2 or 3-day slip is an economy or intermediate car for 1-day. Happy exploring!

St. Croix

Green Cay
Marina

GREEN CAY MARINA

St. Croix

Waypoint: UV703 (Scotch Bank) 17°46.60'N, 64°40.10'W

Navigation: 3nm E of Christiansted Harbor

Services: Marina Slips, Fuel, Pump-Out, Laundry, Showers, Restaurants, Bar, Hotel, WiFi, Pumpout Station

Green Cay Marina is a full service, well protected marina on St. Croix's northern coast east of Christiansted and just south of Green Cay, a small nature preserve. It should be approached from the western side of Buck Island. Look for the yellow buildings with white roofs of Tamarind Reef Resort. The resort and marina are part if the same complex. Visiting yachts enjoy resort privileges including tennis, swimming pool, beach, kayaks, spa and more.

Navigation & Pilotage

From the north, or waypoint UV703, leave Green Cay to port and head for the rock jetties to either side of the entrance. The marina monitors VHF16 and 340-773-1453. If you call ahead, the dock-master will meet you at the fuel dock and lead you to a slip. Depths are 8 to 9 feet. Marina hours are 8am-5pm weekdays and 8am-4pm weekends and holidays. Fuel is available seven days a week. WiFi is free.

Ashore

The marina is well kept and has all the amenities including showers, laundry, water, electricity, pump-out, 24-hour security, fuel and ice. In addition to the 39-room luxury, beachfront resort, beach, tennis courts, kayaks, snorkels, pools and day spa , there are two restaurants, a casual open-air spot (Deep End) on the waterfront and an air-conditioned fine dining establishment (Galleon) overlooking the marina.

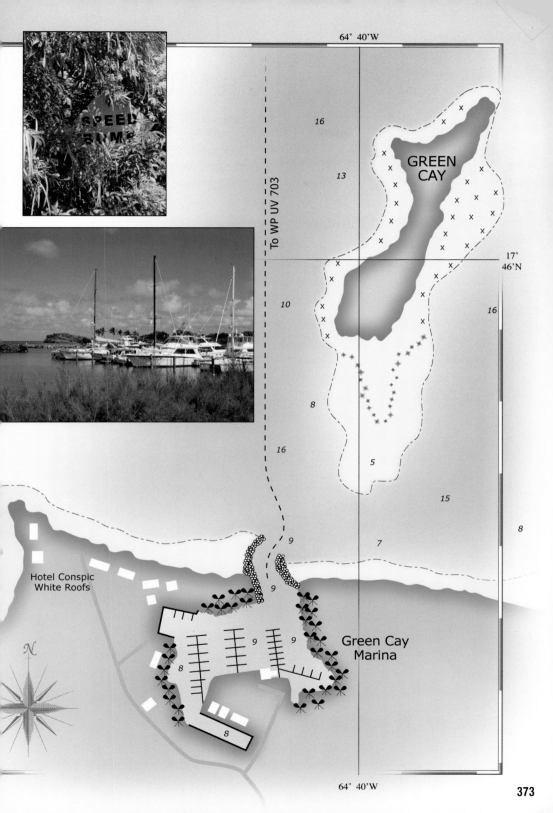

64° 40'W

To WP UV 703

16

13

GREEN
CAY

17°
46'N

16

10

8

16

5

15

8

Hotel Conspic
White Roofs

9

9

7

9

9   9

Green Cay
Marina

N

8

8

64° 40'W

ST. CROIX YACHT CLUB/TEAGUE BAY

St. Croix

Waypoint: UV705 (Coakley Bay) 17°46.50'N, 64°38.50'W
Navigation: 5.2nm E Christiansted Harbor (3.2nm to reef entrance)
Services: Water, Restaurant, Bar, Showers

Navigation and Pilotage

Teague Bay (also marked on the charts as Tague Bay) is 2.5 miles SSW of Buck Island, protected to the north by a continuous reef. Enter from the west at the Coakley Bay Cut where you will see a lighted green marker (Fl.G.4 sec. 15 feet). Leave the marker to port, head well into the bay towards the windmill, then head east, favoring the shore side. The entrance is good for 12 foot depths. The passage is narrow and the prudent skipper will post a lookout on the bow to watch for coral heads. Another opening in the reef, the Cotton Valley Cut, is not recommended except for those with local knowledge as the buoys are privately maintained and there are patch reefs inside the cut. The distance from Coakley Cut to the Yacht Club is approximately 2.7 miles.

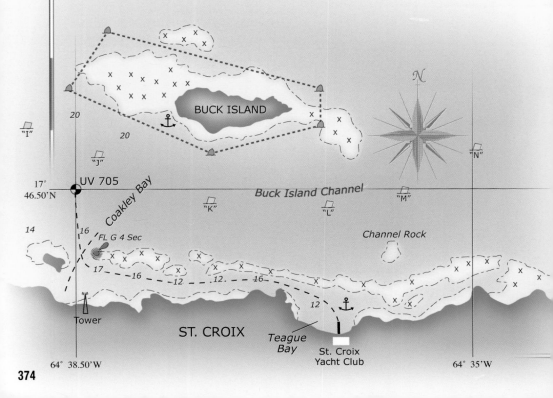

Anchoring

Enter the Yacht Club basin between red and green buoys at coordinates 17°45' 27.7" N & 64°36' 13.3" W. Call the club on VHF16 or 340-773-9531 to find out where to anchor. Slips are rarely available (except in an emergency) and there are no guest moorings. You can tie up your dinghy on the main dock or at a small dinghy dock to the east, both available for a fee.

Ashore

The St. Croix Yacht Club extends a friendly welcome to visiting yachts. Reciprocal use is offered to members of recognized yacht clubs, and others may request a guest pass.

The Club is open Wednesday through Sunday and some holidays. Showers are available, ice may be purchased and garbage may be left in the on-site dumpster. However, no fuel, laundry or provisions are available.

The Club has a bar and restaurant and a full social calendar, with happy hour every Friday and a five-course dinner (by reservation) on Wednesdays. There is an active children's program and frequent races for adults and/or children on weekends. In February, the club kicks off the CORT (Caribbean Ocean Racing Triangle) season the weekend after Presidents Weekend. After 16 years as the St. Croix International Regatta, in 2010 it joined the National Hospice Regatta Alliance and is now known as the St. Croix Yacht Club Hospice Regatta and is a fundraiser for the local hospice. It attracts yachts from all over the Caribbean.

A short dinghy ride from the Yacht Club are two restaurants across the street from each other: Duggan's Reef (773-9800), a waterfront restaurant specializing in seafood open every night for dinner and Sundays for brunch; and Good Spirits (692-4663), a convenience store/deli/barbecue restaurant. It's open every day from 7am.

SALT RIVER
NATIONAL HISTORICAL PARK AND ECOLOGICAL PRESERVE

St. Croix

Waypoint: UV706 (White Horse Rock) 17°47.80'N, 64°45.00'W
Navigation: 3.5nm west of Christiansted Harbor
Services: Marina, Water, Garbage Disposal, Dive Shop, Kayak Rental

Salt River Bay and all the adjacent land surrounding it has been designated a National Park. Ecologically, the bay, with its mangrove forests and sea grass beds, is the heart of a still healthy chain of ecosystems. Historically, this is the only documented Columbus landing site on U.S. soil, and it wasn't a pleasant experience. His armed men went ashore looking for water and were confronted by a canoe full of Carib Indians with bows and arrows. In the altercation that followed, each side had one fatality and all the remaining Indians were taken as slaves.

The Park is managed jointly by the National Park Service and the V.I. Government. In 2004 it acquired the large white house on the western point as a Visitors Contact Station. On the eastern point work has started on the campus of a Marine Education and Research Center that is slated for construction this decade. A project of the Joint Institute for Caribbean Marine Studies, a collective of four universities – Rutgers, North Carolina, the Virgin Islands and South Carolina – it is intended to incorporate the latest green technologies in a design chosen from a competition among architecture and engineering students.

Navigation & Pilotage

Salt River Bay is in the middle of the island on the north shore. It is a very safe anchorage and a popular hurricane hole but is suitable for shallow draft only, a maximum of 6 feet can be carried over the inner sand bar. Local knowledge is advised to enter, as the channel through the reef is narrow, its navigation marker is privately maintained and sandbanks extend from both sides of the bay. Use

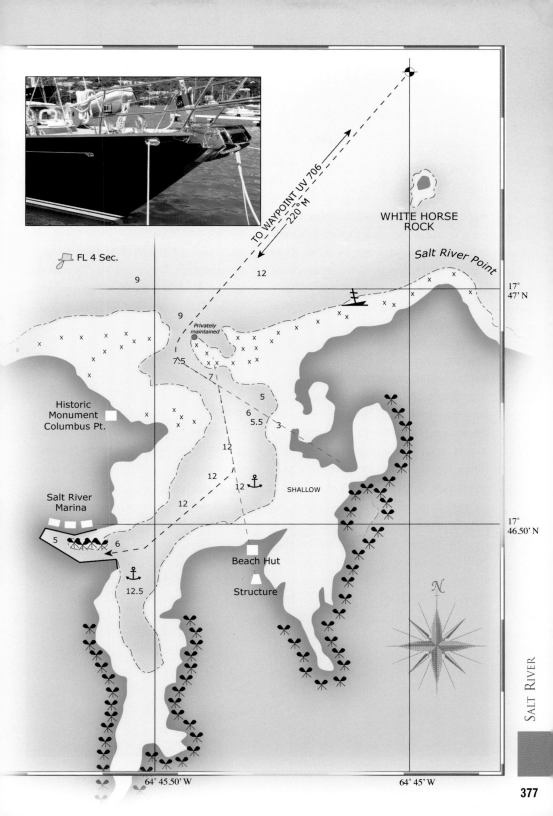

FL 4 Sec.

TO WAYPOINT UV 706
220° M

WHITE HORSE
ROCK

Salt River Point

9   12

17°
47' N

9

Privately
maintained

7.5

7

5

6

5.5   3

Historic
Monument
Columbus Pt.

12

12

12

Salt River
Marina

12

SHALLOW

5   6

17°
46.50' N

Beach Hut

12.5

Structure

N

64° 45.50' W   64° 45' W

of your engine and your depth sounder is advised. Some distance west of the reef entrance, you will see a tall marker. This is a scientific device monitoring various physical attributes of the reef. It is part of a NOAA project called CREWS (Coral Reef Early Warning System).

Approaching Salt River Bay from the east leave White Horse Rock to port. The rock marks the northern extremity of Salt River Point. From waypoint UV705 (north of White Horse Rock), a course of 220°m will bring you to the entrance to the bay. The reef extends from Salt River Point west across the entire bay towards Columbus Landing and Barrons Bluff further to the west. The narrow entrance into the bay is marked by privately maintained green buoy that is only anchored by a weight on the seabed. Do not rely on it being on station. Leaving the green marker to port, follow the reef around to port (until the green buoy at the entrance behind you is abeam); turn southeast until you can see a spire roof on the shore to the south. As soon as you can align the spire with a beach shack in front of it, turn toward it and continue toward that range into the anchorage. Compass bearing 180°m should get you safely between the sand bars. Although the sand bars are constantly shifting it was reported to be able to could carry 5'10" (2 meters) maximum as of January 2010. As soon as you are past the bar the depth will increase rapidly. Salt River Marina monitors VHF16, if you need assistance.

The entrance to the marina is via a narrow channel on the western side of the bay. A sea wall marks the southern side and a mangrove islet will be evident to the north. Do not enter the marina channel without calling the marina first, the marina is small and maneuvering room is very tight once inside.

Salt River Bay

Anchoring & Mooring

You may anchor anywhere you find sufficient water except in the marina channel. You can leave your dinghy at the marina. There is a dinghy dock near the dive shop.

Ashore

Salt River Marina is a small and homey facility tucked into a very protected basin on the west side of the bay. This is a perfect hurricane hole, but as such can be hot and buggy. Space is limited and advance notice is recommended. The marina is open 7 days a week and monitors VHF 16 or 340-778-9650 during daylight hours.

All services are available to dockside customers, with fuel requiring 24-hour notice. There is an open-air restaurant/bar next to the marina office overlooking the boats. Anchor Dive is also on the premises, offering a very short boat ride to the Salt River Canyon, one of the best dive sites in the Caribbean. Kayaks can be rented for touring the mangrove-fringed fingers of the bay. Gold Coast Yachts custom designs and builds 40 to 80-foot catamarans on the property. Otherwise, Salt River is not convenient to shore-based services, but taxis can be called and rides to town can be arranged.

SALT RIVER

FREDERIKSTED

Waypoint: UV707 (West point) 17°45.0'N, 64°55.0'W
Navigation: 3.5nm South of Ham's Bluff (NW point)
Services: Provisions, Restaurants, Bars, Garbage Disposal.

Frederiksted, located on the west coast, is an open roadstead, protected from the prevailing trade winds, but can be dangerous in westerlies, which are extremely rare.

Frederiksted is a quaint, charming and laid-back town with a mixture of Danish Colonial and Victorian architecture framed by beautiful parks along the waterfront. There is an ongoing restoration program evident in Frederiksted as many of the original buildings are painted and renovated in support of the tourism industry. At this time there is no marina in Frederiksted and therefore water and fuel are not available except via dinghy and jerry-cans.

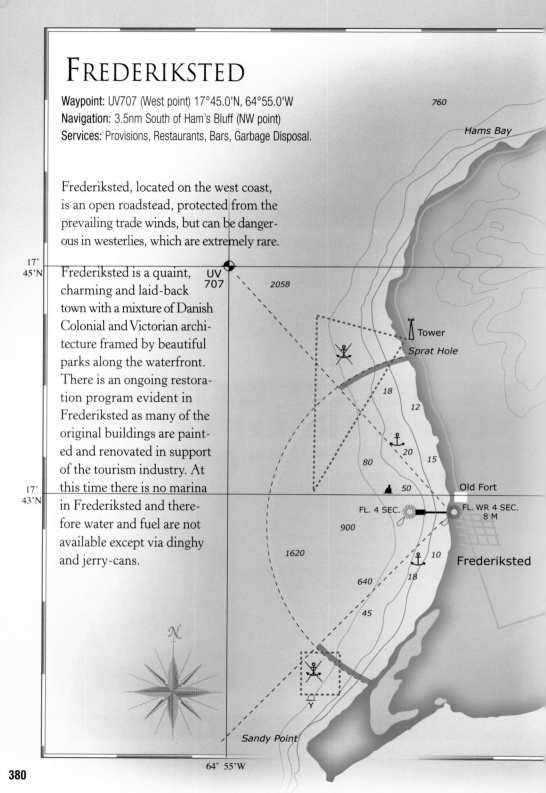

760

Hams Bay

17° 45'N

UV 707

2058

Tower

Sprat Hole

18

12

20

15

80

50

Old Fort

17° 43'N

FL. 4 SEC.

FL. WR 4 SEC. 8 M

900

10

1620

18

Frederiksted

640

45

N

Y

Sandy Point

64° 55'W

Navigation & Piloting

Frederiksted makes a good landfall when sailing from The Spanish Virgin Islands to the west or the Dutch ABC islands to the south. Approaching from the south, give Sandy Point (the SW extremity of St.Croix) a wide berth. A red buoy (R2) at 17°39.40'N – 64°54.37'W is in 60 feet of water outside a shifting sandbar. Approaching from the north you can hug the shore closely at Ham's Bluff on the NW corner of the island, but once around the point stay about 100 yards offshore of the west coast to avoid shoals. At the red destroyer-mooring ball you can head east to the beach (Sunset Grill beach bar) and run close to the beach on into Frederiksted.

Anchoring & Mooring

South of the cruise ship pier the holding is poor with a thin layer of sand over rock. Holding is better on the north side of the

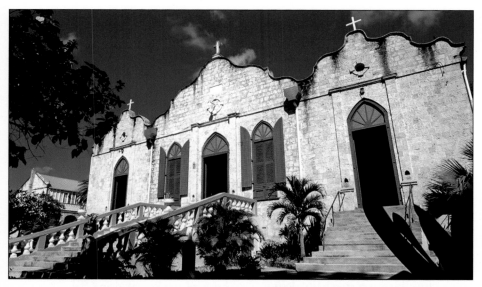

pier and improves as you head north along the beach. The anchorage along the beach away from town is usually quiet but can be rolly if northerly swells are running. Dinghies can be landed on any stretch of the beach or at low docks either side of the cruise ship pier. The prudent skipper will exercise caution leaving the dinghy as some petty theft has been noted in this area.

Ashore

Frederiksted has a long and storied history. The town was established in 1751 and it is the second largest town on St. Croix. It was originally protected by Fort Frederik, which dates back to 1700. Today, the fort houses a museum. Locals often refer to Frederiksted as "Freedom City" because it is the site where then Governor, General Peter Van Scholten, read the proclamation abolishing slavery in 1848.

The town was destroyed by fire in 1878 as a result of a labor revolt. It was later restored during the Victorian era, which is why it now has such lovely blend of "gingerbread" Victorian and Dutch Colonial architecture. The town retains its original seven street by seven street city design.

A visit to Frederiksted will allow you to see several historic buildings including, St. Patrick's Catholic Church, which was built in the 1840s, along with its primary school, the Customs House, the 19th Century Apothecary, as well as many other historic buildings. Unfortunately, many of these have fallen into disrepair due to several major hurricanes and the passing of time.

This small town has all the basics: a post office, banks, drug store, laundry services, small grocery stores and clothing shops, a barber shop, dive shop and coffee shop. It also has some very special attractions notably the Caribbean Museum Center for the Arts, the Crucian Christmas Festival, a loud, colorful and boozy event, and every third Friday of the month Sunset Jazz, a free concert featuring excellent musicians that brings out a diverse family crowd.

Coconuts on the Beach and Bryan's Marine can take careof engine problems and repairs. There are plans to install moorings but not at this time. You can reach them at 340-713-0544.

Several restaurants are worth mentioning such as the Blue Moon Restaurant on the waterfront on historic Strand Street. They have live jazz on Wednesday and Friday nights and at Sunday Brunch. There is also the Beachside Café at Sand Castle on the Beach for something more casual and try Polly's by the pier on Strand Street, the Lost Dog Pub serving Italian American fare. Rhythms at Rainbow Beach serve burgers, wings, salad and fish.

A Millennium Vision

January 1, 2000

Since the dawn of consciousness, time has been measured by the sun. This marker, in the year 2000, is a continuum between all who have come before and all who are yet to come. The design concept started with the Roman numeral "M"=1000, "MM"=2000. The stone piers represent the abstraction of alignment of the shadow pole, and the marker pin designates the azimuth of the sun on January 1, 2000. The shadow of the pole on the true north line designates local noon daily.

"Past, Present, Future:
A Millennium Vision"

The Millennium Monument, East End, St. Croix

CHRISTIANSTED

AUTO RENTAL
Olympic Rent-A-Car
Tel: 340-773-8000
www.olympicstcroix.com

BANKS
Banco Popular
Tel: 340-693-2777
www.popular.com

Bank of St. Croix
Tel: 340-773-8500
www.bankofstcroix.com

First Bank
Tel: 340-775-7777
www.firstbankvi.com

ScotiaBank
Tel: 340-773-1013
www.scotiabank.com

DIVE SHOPS
Cane Bay Dive Shop East
Tel: 340-773-4663
www.canebayscuba.com/

Dive Experience
Tel: 340-773-3307
www.divexp.com

SCUBA
Tel: 340-773-5994
www.divexp.com

ELECTRONICS
Mike's Electronics
Tel: 340-778-6655

Radio Shack
Tel: 340-778-5667

SHOPPING
Cache of the Day Gifts
Tel: 340-773-3648

DesignWorks
Tel: 340-713-8102

Gone Tropical
Tel: 340-773-4696
www.gonetropical.com

IB Designs Jewelry
Tel: 340-773-4322

Island Tribe
Tel: 340-719-0936
Batik dresses

Many Hands
Tel: 340-773-1990
http://manyhands.
stcroixtravelusvi.com

Royal Poinciana
Tel: 340-773-9892

Tesoro
Tel: 340-773-1212
www.tesorostcroix.com

Violette's Boutique
(cosmetics, perfumes)
Tel: 340-773-2148

LIQUOR, BEER, WINE*
BACI Duty Free
Tel: 340-773-5040

Kart East
Tel: 340-719-9190

S&B Liquor
Tel: 340-772-3934

LAUNDRY SERVICES
Neighborhood Laundry
Tel: 340-778-6138

Sunny Isle Laundromat
Tel: 340-778-6606

Du-N-Save Laundry
Tel: 340-778-8699

La Reine Laundry
Tel: 340-778-2801

EMERGENCY/MEDICAL
Ambulance/Fire/Police
Tel: 911

Acute Alternative Medical Group
340-772-2883
Urgent care center

Juan Luis Hospital
Tel: 340-778-6311
Frank T. Bishop, M.D.
Tel: 340-778-0069

Rodney A. Fabio, Jr.,Dentist
Tel: 340-778-6900

Daniel T. Kenses, Dentist
Tel: 340-692-9770

Arakere Prasad, M.D.
Tel: 340-778-7788

LODGING
Holger Danske
Tel: 340-773-3600
www.holgerhotel.com

ISLAND CONNECTIONS

Buccaneer Hotel
Tel: 340-712-2100
www.thebuccaneer.com

Carrington's Inn
Tel: 340-713-0508
www.carringtonsinn.com

Chenay Bay Beach Resort
Tel: 340-773-2918
www.stcroix-chenaybay.com

Club Comanche Hotel
Tel: 340-773-0210

Hibiscus Beach Hotel
Tel: 340-718-4042
hibiscusbeachresort.com

Hotel on the Cay
773-2035

King Christian Hotel
Tel: 340-773-6330
www.stcroix-kingchristianhotel.com

Tamarind Reef Resort
Tel: 340-718-4455

The Palms
Tel: 340-778-8920

PROVISIONS
Cost U Less
Tel: 340-692-2220

Foodtown
Tel: 340-718-9990

Plaza Extra East
Tel: 340-778-6240

Pueblo Supermarket
Tel: 340-773-0118

Schooner Bay Market Place
Tel: 340-773-3232

MARINA
St. Croix Marine
Tel: 340-773-0289
www.stcroixmarine.com

RESTAURANTS
Café Christine
Tel: 340-713-1500
Lunch only, Monday-Friday, closed in summer. Reservations

Dashi
Tel: 340-773-6911
Excellent sushi and Vietnamese specials served in a quaint courtyard – often with live music

Galangal
Tel: 340-773-0076
A new Thai restaurant near the wharf, open every night but Sunday.
www.galangalstx.com

The Golden Rail
Tel: 340-719-1989
At St. Croix Marine in Gallows Bay, a casual, breezy spot open all day every day.

Kendricks
Tel: 340-773-9199
This is one of the island's best restaurants. Open Mon-Sat, 5-9:30 pm. Reservations requested.

Lalita
Tel: 340-719-4417
Specializes in vegan and raw/live cuisine, juices, smoothies and organic wines. Open all day every day.

Luncheria
Tel: 340-773-4247
Moderately priced Mexican food in a casual outdoor setting.
Open 11am-9pm daily except Sunday.

Namaste Café
Tel: 340-772-2529
Coffees and teas, light breakfasts and lunches and free WiFi are served daily from 7 am to 6 pm.

Rumrunners
Tel: 340-773-6585
Right on Christiansted Harbor, this restaurant serves three meals a day, seven days a week.
rumrunnersstcroix.com

Savant
Tel: 340-713-8666
Dine in or out every evening but Sunday on a fusion of Thai, Mexican and Caribbean cuisines. Reservations suggested.
www.savantstx.com Reservations.aspx

The Pickled Greek
Tel: 340-713-1868
An authentic Greek restaurant just east of Christiansted & Gallows Bay. Open Mon-Sat 4-10 pm.
www.pickledgreek.com

Tutto Bene
Tel: 340-773-5229
Good Italian food in a spacious upstairs setting. Open for dinner every night from 6-10. Reservations suggested.
tuttobenerestaurant.com

SAILMAKERS/REPAIRS
Wesco Awning & Marine Canvas
Tel: 340-778-9446
www.wescoawning.com

Wilson's Cruzan Canvas
Tel: 340-773-0694
www.doylecaribbean.com /locations/usvi.html

MARINE REPAIR & SUPPLIES
St. Croix Marine
Tel: 340-773-0289
www.stcroixmarine.com

Blue Mountain Purified Water
Tel: 340-778-6177

D&V Onestop Locksmith
Tel: 340-778-5211

The New Paint Locker
Tel: 340-718-0105

TAXI
Antilles Taxi Service
Tel: 340-773-5020

Caribbean Taxi Service
Tel: 340-773-9799

Cruzan Taxi
Tel: 340-773-6388

St. Croix Taxi
Tel: 340-778-1088
www.stcroixtaxi.com

FREDERIKSTED

AUTO RENTAL
Avis Rent-A-Car
Tel: 340-778-9355

Budget Rent-A-Car
Tel: 340-778-9636

Centerline Car Rental
Tel: 340-778-0450

Hertz Rent-A-Car
Tel: 340-778-1402

BANKS
First Bank
Tel: 340-712-1020
www.firstbankvi.com

ScotiaBank
Tel: 340-772-0880
www.scotiabank.com

DIVE SHOP
Cane Bay Dive Shop West
Tel 340-772-0715
www.canebayscuba.com

LIQUOR, BEER, WINE*
Kmart West
Tel: 340-692-5848

LODGING
Frederiksted Hotel
Tel: 340-772-0500
www.frederikstedhotel.dk

Sandcastle on the Beach
Tel: 340-772-1205
www.sandcastleonthe beach.com

PROVISIONS
Plaza Extra West
Tel: 340-719-1870

RESTAURANTS
Beachside Café
Tel: 340-772-1266
At Sand Castle on the Beach Hotel south of Frederiksted, serving lunch/brunch and dinner. Live jazz Saturday nights. Reservations recommended.

Blue Moon
Tel: 340-772-2222
Right across from the waterfront park in Frederiksted town, it's famous for its jazz or blues

on Friday nights and during Sunday brunch. Reservations suggested.

Coconuts
Tel: 340-719-6060
A fun beach restaurant/bar with live music and casual food for breakfast, lunch and dinner.

Lost Dog Pub
Tel: 340-772-1205
www.lostdogpub.biz

Motown
Tel: 340-772-9882
Serves local West Indian food, specializing in seafood. It is on the waterfront Strand Street.

Polly's at the Pier
Tel: 340-719-9434
Located on Strand Street right across from the cruise ship pier, this new enterprise has become much more than an internet café. Light meals are available all day.

Rhythms at Rainbow Beach
Tel: 340-772-0002

Turtles Deli
Tel: 340-772-3676
A unique deli and coffee shop, with gourmet sandwiches served on homemade bread in a setting right on the beach.
www.turtlesdeli.com

GREEN CAY

LODGING
Tamarind Reef Resort
Tel: 340-718-4455
www.tamarindreefhotel.com

MARINA
Green Cay Marina
Tel: 340-718-1453

RESTAURANTS
Cheeseburger in Paradise
Tel: 340-773-1119
Near Green Cay Marina. A popular, friendly spot open from 11am to 10pm daily. Live music Thu-Sun starting at 7pm.

Deep End Bar
Tel: 340-718-7071
Part of the Green Cay Marina/Tamarind Reef Resort complex. A casual open-air restaurant, it is open every day for breakfast, lunch and dinner.

Galleon
Tel: 340-718-9948
Overlooking Green Cay Marina, in Tamarind Reef Resort, an air-conditioned setting for dinner daily. Reservations suggested.
www.galleonrestaurant.com

SALT RIVER

DIVE SHOP
Anchor Dive Center
Tel: 340-778-1522

Cane Bay Dive Shop
Tel: 340-773-9913
www.anchordivestcroix.com

LODGING
Cane Bay Reef Club
Tel: 340-718-2966

Carambola Beach Resort
Tel: 340-778-3800
http://carambolabeach.com

Waves at Cane Bay
Tel: 340-778-1805
www.canebaystcroix.com/scuba.html

MARINA
Salt River Marina
Tel: 340-778-9650

TEAGUE BAY

St. Croix Yacht Club
340-773-9531
www.stcroixyc.com

LODGING
Divi Carina Bay Resort & Casino
Tel: 340-773-9700
www.divicarina.com

LIQUOR,BEER,WINE*
*Also available in grocery stores and supermarkets.

DISCOVERING
the VIRGINS
BELOW SEA LEVEL

BRITISH VIRGIN ISLANDS

Visitors come to the Virgin Islands to savor the magnificence of the area's natural resources –the steady, gentle trade winds, glorious sunshine, crystalline waters, the splendor of the coral reefs and abundant sea life. This is a fragile area, however, which must be protected if it is to be enjoyed for many years to come.

The anchors of the charter boats have taken their toll in broken coral, destroying the incredible beauty below the sea that once housed many different forms of sea life. In an effort to defend the reefs against the carelessness of yachtsmen, the National Parks Trust has taken a firm stand and has installed mooring buoys developed by Dr. John Halas of the Key Largo National Marine Sanctuary. This mooring system is being used worldwide to protect reefs and prevent damage from anchors. It calls for a stainless steel pin cemented into the bedrock and a polypropylene line attached to a surface buoy. The system is very strong and extremely effective in eliminating damage when used properly.

MARINE PARK REGULATIONS

- Do not damage, alter or remove any marine plant, animal or historic artifact.
- All fishing – including spearfishing – is strictly prohibited. Lobstering and collecting live shells are also illegal.
- Use correct garbage disposal points; do not litter the area. Water balloons are prohibited.
- Water skiing and jet skiing are prohibited in all park areas.
- No anchoring in the restricted area in and around the Wreck of the Rhone. When the mooring system is full, vessels should utilize the Salt Island Settlement anchorage and arrive by tender, using the dinghy mooring system provided.

MOORING USAGE REGULATIONS

- Vessels must legally have met BVI Customs and Immigration requirements, and have in their possession valid clearance forms and cruising permits.
- The buoys of the reef protection system are color-coded:
  Red: Non-diving, day use only.
  Yellow: Commercial dive vessels only.
  White: Non-commercial vessels for dive use only on first-come, first served basis (90-minute time limit).
  Blue: Dinghies only.
  Large Yellow: Commercial vessels, or day sailing boats or vessels over 55' in length.
- Vessels must attach to the buoy pennant, making sure to avoid chafing of the pennant against the vessel. If the configuration provided is not compatible with your vessel, an extension line must be attached to the pennant eye.
- All buoys are used at user's risk. While the moorings are the property of the BVI Government and are managed by the BVI National Parks Trust, neither bears

NATIONAL PARKS TRUST
MOORING BUOYS IN THE BVI
For day use only with National Parks Permit

Norman Island
1. Angel Fish
2. The Caves
3. Ring Dove Rock
4. Black Forest
5. Santa Monica Rock
6. Water Point
7. Spyglass Wall
8. Brown Pants
9. Pelican Island &
   The Indians

Peter Island
10. Carrot Rock
11. Shark Point
12. Black Tip
13. Rhone Anchor
14. Fearless
15. Great Harbour

Dead Chest
16. Painted Walls
17. Coral Gardens
18. Blonde Rock

Salt Island
19. The Rhone
20. Rhone Reef

Cooper Island
21. Dry Rocks East & West
22. Haulover Bay
23. Mary L.
24. Incannes Bay
25. Cistern Point
26. Thumb Rock
27. Markoe Point

28. Devil's Kitchen
29. Carvel Rock

Ginger Island
30. Ginger Steps
31. Alice in Wonderland
32. Ginger Patch
33. Alice's Backside

Virgin Gorda
34. Fallen Jerusalem
35. The Baths
36. Fisher's Rocks

The Dogs
37. Great Dog South
38. George Dog
39. Bronco Billy
40. Cockroach Island
41. The Chimneys
42. Wall to Wall
43. Joes Cave
44. Flintstones
45. Dolphin Rocks
46. Seal Dogs
47. Mountain Point
48. Cow's Mouth
49. Paul's Grotto

Necker Island
50. The Invisibles

Scrub Island
51. Scrub Island
    Point
52. Scrub Island
    West

Great Camanoe
53. Diamond Reef

Guana Island
54. Monkey Point
55. The Chikuzen

Tortola
56. Brewers Bay
57. Green Cay
58. Great Tobago
59. Great Thatch

BVI MARINE PARK MOORINGS

the responsibility for any loss or injury resulting from the use of the system. Charterers may purchase permits through their charter companies, and visiting private yachts may purchase permits through customs. The fees are nominal and go directly to the Parks Trust for the installation and maintenance of the buoys.

The BVI National Parks Trust Maintains Moorings on the Following Islands

- Norman
- Pelican
- The Indians
- Peter Island
- Dead Chest
- Salt Island
- Cooper
- Ginger
- Guana
- George Dog
- Great Dog
- Cockroach
- Tortola
- Virgin Gorda

VIRGIN ISLANDS NATIONAL PARK, ST. JOHN, US VIRGIN ISLANDS

By Carol Bareuther

Coral reefs reflecting sapphire seas, pristine beaches rimmed with palm trees and lush green hills unmarred by resorts or residences. The paradisiacal beauty of the Virgin Islands National Park is like a movie scene that makes you want to jump in and instantly become immersed. But slow down. To really appreciate the charms of this southernmost U.S. park, you have to add some new lingo to your vocabulary. *Limin'*, meaning to "hang around idly", as defined by the late Virgin Islands historian and park ranger, Lito Valls, is a verb best carried out by forgetting time, setting aside the to-do list and enjoying your surroundings in a lazily, leisurely, limin' sort of way.

MARINE SCENE

Secluded coves, dazzling beaches and wondrous coral reefs have lured pleasure boaters to park waters. In addition, the Virgin Islands rank as one of the Caribbean's premier diving and snorkeling locations. Several dive shops rent snorkel and scuba gear and run trips to offshore reefs. Park waters are open to sports fisherman with hand-held rods, and bone fishing along the flats by Leinster Bay is excellent.

Over the last two decades, however, the sheer number of visiting boats has accelerated damage to sea grass beds and coral reefs due to anchor damage. To protect these natural resources, the park has installed 182 moorings – 154 on the North Shore and 28 on the South Shore, and established protected zones around several of the more sensitive sea grass and reef areas. Starting in 2002, the park implemented a fee for the overnight use of these moorings. To pay the mooring fee several "iron rangers", (small kiosks) are located in several of the bays. Envelopes are provided for enclosing the fee, with a place to note your vessel's name and the date. Rangers patrol the bays regularly to insure compliance.

ANCHOR ZONE

Park regulations require vessels 17 to 60 feet to pick up a mooring if one is available. However, there is an anchoring zone in the park, designated by four GPS coordinates, where anchoring is permitted. Vessels 60 to 125 feet, who are prohibited from using moorings are encouraged to use this anchor zone.

USVI National Park

There is no reservation system for moorings, but one may be developed in the future. Moorings are in high demand from December to March, while September and October usage is low because of the threat of hurricanes. Boaters may only stay in park waters for a maximum of 30 nights in a 12 month period and no longer than seven consecutive nights in one bay.

Using the National Park Mooring System

Park moorings are safe, easy to use and identified as white balls with blue stripes. Moorings are fixed to the sea bottom with either a sand screw or a stainless steel eyebolt, which is cemented directly into coral pavement. To pick up a mooring, grab the floating mooring line, or painter, and tie it to a short bowline on the vessel. Don't raft boats together or set anchors while on a mooring. All moorings are checked and maintained by Park Service personnel, however please do report any safety defects to a park ranger so they can be promptly repaired. The moorings are not designed for rough weather use. In high wind or heavy sea conditions, it is recommended that vessels anchor in a protected bay.

Park Activities

The Cruz Bay Visitor Center is a short walk from the public ferry dock, and is open daily from 8 am to 4:40 pm. The center contains exhibits, a park video, brochures, maps, and books. Park rangers can help you plan your visit, which may include island hikes, historical tours, snorkeling, cultural craft demonstrations, and evening campground programs.

Throughout the year, the park plays host to two to three day events. A commemoration of Black History Month is held at the Annaberg Sugar Plantation the latter part of February and includes crafts, storytelling, and cooking demonstrations. St. John's Carnival on July fourth includes parades and island cultural activities during the week prior. The park presents interpretive programs during the winter season at Cinnamon Bay campground. From January through April, the non-profit Friends of the National Park offer seminars with topics ranging from outdoors photography to archeology, natural history and traditional West Indian cooking. Hurricane season extends from June through November. The park provides ongoing information for visitors including where to go in the event of a serious storm.

PARK RULES & REGULATIONS

Vessels & Water Operations:

* Vessels with a overall length greater than 210 feet, and commercial vessels over 125 feet, are prohibited from anchoring or mooring within Park waters.

* Private vessels with a length overall between 125 and 210 feet shall only anchor in sand seaward of mooring areas and at depths greater than 50 feet in Francis Bay shoreward of a line from Mary Point to America Point.

* Vessels with a length overall between 60 and 125 feet shall anchor in north shore bays, in sand at least 200 feet seaward of mooring fields only if there are no moorings available.

* Vessels less than 26 feet length overall may access NPS beaches where channels have been designated by a red and green buoy to drop-off or pick-up passengers.

* Motorized vessels or vessels under sail shall not enter or anchor in areas identified as Boat Exclusion Areas.

ANCHORING AND MOORING

* Anchoring is prohibited within beach access channels marked by red and green buoys.

* Vessels less than or equal to 16 feet length overall may anchor within park waters on the south side of St. John. The only exception is that anchoring is permitted for the specific purpose of fishing for Blue Runner in the area due south of Cabritte Horn Point extending to Virgin Islands Coral Reef National Monument boundary. Vessels over 16 feet length overall must use NPS provided moorings on the south side of St. John.

* Vessels with a length overall of 60 feet or less are required to use NPS moorings if available; if moorings in a specific bay are fully occupied, vessels may anchor 200 feet seaward of mooring fields except for the south side. However, commercial day charter vessels and those vessels not staying overnight, may only anchor in Salomon Bay which is adjacent to Honeymoon Beach and Cinnamon Bay adjacent to Little Cinnamon Beach.

* Setting of anchors is prohibited while on NPS moorings. Vessels using NPS moorings may not use additional ground tackle.

* Rafting of vessels is prohibited while on moorings provided by the NPS.

* Securing vessels to moorings using stern cleats is prohibited.

* NPS moorings shall be vacated if sustained winds exceed 40 mph.

* NPS moorings shall not be modified by any user.

* Vessels anchoring or mooring within park waters may not exceed 30 nights in a calendar year and no more than seven consecutive nights in one bay.

* The National Park water area in Cruz Bay Creek in the vicinity of the

Little Iobago

U.S. VIRGIN ISLAND NATIONAL PARK
MOORINGS BY BAY

$15.00 per night for overnight usage

St. Thomas

Tortola

Great Thatch

Pete

Norman Island

St. John

Durloe Cays

St. John – North Shore Bays

1.	Lind Point	-	21 overnight moorings
2.	Salomon Bay	-	26 overnight moorings
3.	Honeymoon Bch	-	21 overnight moorings
4.	Caneel Bay	-	22 overnight moorings
5.	Durloe Cays	-	2 day use moorings
6.	Hawksnest Bay	-	13 overnight moorings
7.	Trunk Bay	-	4 overnight moorings
8.	Cinnamon Bay	-	8 overnight moorings
9.	Maho Bay	-	28 overnight moorings
10.	Francis Bay	-	29 overnight moorings
11.	Whistling Bay	-	3 overnight moorings and 3 dive moorings
12.	Leinster Bay	-	20 overnight moorings

South Shore Bays Anchoring is prohibited on the south shore of St. John

13.	Reef Bay	-	2 day use moorings
14.	Little Lameshur Bay-		5 overnight moorings
15.	Great Lameshur Bay-		14 overnight moorings
16.	Salt Pond Bay	-	2 dive moorings at Textite off Cabritte Horn Pt. 1 dive mooring
Other South Shore Bays	-		8 overnight moorings

two day use moorings each in Ram Head Bay and the Textite site

PARK REGULATIONS

boat ramp is authorized for only vessels 60 feet or less to anchor no longer than three hours, to utilize local public services.

* Recreational kite surfing is prohibited in boat exclusion areas and moorings areas. Commercial kite surfing activities are prohibited within park waters.

* Operating a vessel in excess of five mph or creating a wake in mooring fields or within 200 feet of a mooring field is prohibited.

* Trash being disposed of from vessels may not exceed two 10-gallon bags and must fit inside NPS trash containers identified for vessel trash in Cruz Bay, Francis Bay, Leinster Bay, Salt Pond and Little Lameshur Bay.

* Each vessel is required to pay an overnight fee of $15.00 per night when mooring or anchoring in the park between 5:00pm and 7:00am. Failure to pay the overnight fee is prohibited.

* Coral is very fragile and easily damaged by anchors, human touch, feet and flippers. Coral damaged by one person can take hundreds of years to re-grow. Remember, "If it's not sand, don't stand." Coral and other sea life can also cause injury to people when touched.

* It is illegal to dump litter in park waters or on land. Dispose of litter in designated receptacles throughout the Park.

* No dumping of waste from vessels, use your storage tanks.

* Water skiing and jet skiing are not permitted in Park waters.

* Kayaks, dinghies, rafts or any other motored or rowed vessels must stay outside demarcated swim areas. Boats 26 feet or less may access the beach using channels marked by red and green buoys, but may not anchor in this channel. Boats may pick up NPS moorings.

* Boat anchoring is prohibited in Park waters on the south shore and boats must use moorings provided. This includes all the bays from Cocolobo Point to Ram Head and the new Coral Reef Monument.

* Boats are limited to 30 nights per calendar year in Park waters. Moorings are provided on a first-come, first-served basis.

* Boats 125 feet to 210 feet (length on deck) may anchor only in Francis Bay, in sand, and must be in depths greater than 50 feet.

* Fishing is allowed outside of swim areas, but not in Trunk/Jumbie Bay. Spear guns are prohibited anywhere in Park waters.

* Caribbean spiny lobster catch is limited to two per person per day and the season is October 1-March 30. Whelk must be larger than 2.5" and take is limited to one gallon per person per day, and 3/8" lip thickness.

* Collecting plants and animals – dead or alive – or inanimate objects, includ-

PRIVATE VESSEL SIZE LIMITS

ing cultural artifacts, coral, shells, and sand is prohibited. Metal detectors are not allowed anywhere in the Park.

* Camping is allowed only at Cinnamon Bay Campground.

* Fires are permitted only on grills at designated picnic areas.

* Feeding marine and terrestrial wildlife is prohibited and may be dangerous to you.

* Pets are not allowed on Park beaches, in the campground or in picnic areas, but may be walked – leashed – on trails.

* Glass bottles are not permitted on Park beaches.

CONTACT INFORMATION

It is highly recommended you look at these websites before boating in the Park to get any updates to the current information, and to familiarize yourselves with the Park rules and regulations. The National Park Service offers a wealth of fascinating information on the underwater sea life and above water flora and fauna.

Virgin Islands National Park
1300 Cruz Bay Creek
St. John, USVI 00830
Tel: 340-776-6201
Email: virg@us-national-parks.net
www.nps.gov/viis
www.virgin.islands.national-park.com

Friends of the VI National Park:
www.friendsvinp.org

Mooring & Anchoring Guide for the Virgin Islands National Park:
www.usviinfo.com/infousvi/npmooring

ST. JOHN NATIONAL PARK		
Length on Deck	**North Shore**	**South Shore**
16ft or less	May anchor only in sand and not within 200ft of a mooring field	May anchor only in sand and not within 200ft of a mooring field
17 to 60ft	Must use moorings if available	Must use moorings if available
61 to 125ft	Prohibited from using moorings – must anchor in sand 200 feet seaward of mooring field	Prohibited from mooring or anchoring
126 to 210ft	Prohibited from using moorings – must anchor in sand at Francis Bay 200 feet seaward of mooring field (at depths greater than 50 feet) and shoreward of a line drawn from Mary Point to America Point	Prohibited from mooring or anchoring
Greater than 210ft	Prohibited from mooring or anchoring	Prohibited from mooring or anchoring

DIVING THE VIRGIN ISLANDS

The Virgin Islands are one of the best sailing and cruising areas in the world. They are also recognized as one of the top dive destinations.

The wreck of the R.M.S. Rhone has become synonymous with the BVI in dive circles, regarded by many as the best wreck dive of the Western Hemisphere.

Superb reefs for both snorkeling and diving are found in and around most of the anchorages. The U.S. Virgin Islands have a series of underwater parks: Trunk Bay, St. John, Buck Island, St. Croix and Coki Beach, St. Thomas. In the British Virgin Islands, the island of Anegada has over 300 documented shipwrecks.

Servicing the needs of the visiting yachtsmen, many professional dive shops and dive tour operators have set up businesses, providing complete services from equipment rental and air tank refills, to tours and instruction.

For the non-diver, a resort course will enable you to explore the underwater world with the aid of an instructor. Full certification courses are available from the individual dive shop operators conveniently located throughout the islands.

The rules and regulations of the marine parks of both the U.S. and British Virgins are similar.

DIVING IN THE BRITISH VIRGIN ISLANDS

Dive operators of the Virgin Islands, through a cooperative effort, have pooled information to give you these brief but picturesque descriptions of 20 of their favorite locations:

Painted Walls: Long canyons, a cave, a sponge-encrusted tunnel, barracudas, rock beauties, angelfish and a variety of pelagic fish make the Painted Walls an exciting and picturesque dive with 28 to 50-foot depths.

The Rhone: Just about everyone in diving has heard of the classical wreck, the RMS Rhone. Even those who have not visited the BVI have seen the Rhone in Columbia Pictures' treasure diving epic, *The Deep*. An ocean steamer, 310 feet in length, this magnificent vessel sank off Salt Island during an extremely violent hurricane in 1867. After over 140 years of silent slumber in 20-80 feet of water, this great ship remains remarkably intact with much of her decking, rigging, steam engine and propeller still visible. Gilded with colorful sponges and flourishing corals, the Rhone is perhaps the most impressive shipwreck in the entire Caribbean.

Rhone Reef: Two coral-encrusted caves are located in less than 25 feet of water at Rhone Reef, Salt Island. A variety of hard and soft corals, fish, turtles and the occasional shark can be found here. Due to its proximity to the Rhone, it is a protected area.

Great Harbour: Directly across the channel from Road Town Harbour lies a large, protected bay on the north side of Peter Island. At the center of this bay is a shallow coral reef less than 20 yards offshore, beginning in 8 feet of water. Loaded with colorful sponges and a marvelous array of small marine life, the reef slopes gently to approximately 18 feet, then drops vertically to a depth of 40 feet.

Indians: The Indians are four large rock formations that rise from the ocean floor to a height of about 90 feet. Deepest depth is 50 feet on the westward side. The Indians have just about everything for the snorkeler as well as the scuba diver; brain, finger, star and elkhorn corals are abundant, as are gorgonians and sea fans.

Caves: The caves at Norman Island can provide many hours of fun for snorkelers.

There is a large variety of subjects for the underwater photographer such as schools of dwarf herring or fry. These fish provide food for the many pelicans in the area. The reef in front of the shallow caves slopes downward to a depth of 40 feet.

Angelfish Reef: One of the best sight-seeing dives is a sloping reef located off the western point of Norman Island. Depths here range from 10–90 feet. The high point of your dive will be a visit to the bottom of the channel where a large colony of angelfish resides. There is plenty of fish action at this particular site because of the swiftly flowing currents in the nearby channel and the close proximity to the open sea.

Cooper Island: The southeastern shore of Cooper Island, called Markoe Point, is a sheer rock wall that plunges some 70 feet to the ocean floor. Nurse sharks are frequently encountered lying on sandy floors at the base of small canyons formed by the rugged walls of the island.

Scrub Island: The south side of Scrub Island is a splendid reef with depths of up to 60 feet.

Little Camanoe: The northeastern tip of Little Camanoe offers a 30-foot reef dive. The coral overhangs in this area are exceptionally good. Caution: ground seas.

Seal Dog Rock: Plenty of pelagic fish. Depth of 80 feet. Caution: may have a current. This dive is recommended for experienced divers.

George Dog: The rocky point in the anchorage at George Dog is an easy 25-30 foot dive for beginning divers.

BVI DIVE SITES

Invisibles: (East of Necker Island) Spectacular soaring peaks from 4-70 feet from surface. Flashing schools of every kind of fish, sleeping nurse sharks and all forms of sea life abound.

Visibles: (Southwest underwater pinnacle off Cockroach Island) Caves, canyons, resident 8-foot green moray and nurse shark. Depths to 70 feet. Spawning area for many species of jacks, snappers, groupers.

Chimney: (West Bay of Great Dog) Winding canyon goes to a colorful underwater arch. Many coral heads with an unbelievable variety of small sea creatures.

Joe's Cave: (West Dog Island) Cathedral-effect cave with schooling glassy-eyed sweepers. Clouds of silversides overshadow a variety of eels, pelagic fish and other species, with an occasional school of bulky, splashing tarpon.

Van Ryan's Rock: (Off Collison Point, Virgin Gorda) Huge lobsters, turtles, and plenty of fish among brilliant corals and swaying sea fans.

Ginger Island: Mushroom coral heads 15-20 feet high, great visibility. Graduated shelves ending at 70-90 feet in a huge sand patch. You will see stingrays and huge goliath grouper.

Southside of Great Dog Island: Reef runs east and west, 100 yards of island coral, butterfly fish. Exciting dive locations, each more unusual than the next. Expect to see just about anything!

Anegada Reef: Graveyard of some 300 documented shipwrecks dating from the 1600s to the present. Spanish galleons and English privateers with uncountable treasure.

The Chikuzen: This 245-foot ship was sunk in 1981 and provides a fantastic home for all varieties of fish, including big rays and horse-eye jacks. The depth here is less than 80 feet. Located about 5 miles north of Camanoe Island.

Diving in the U.S. Virgin Islands

Cartenser Sr.: (Off St. Thomas, near Buck Island) A spectacular dive on the intact, coral-encrusted hull of a World War I cargo ship in 50-foot depths. Tours easily arranged.

Cow and Calf: Two rocks between Christmas Cove and Jersey Bay, 5 feet below the surface. The lee side of the western rock provides intricate arches, ledges and caves. Many angelfish and beautiful coral.

Christmas Cove: Good beginner's dive on the northwest side of Fish Cay in 40 feet of water. Swim amongst the coral heads. Plenty of fish.

Dog Rock: For advanced divers on the northwestern side of Dog Island in 40-50 foot depths. Rock and coral ledges and caves. Caution: This one can be rough.

Coki Beach: A good place to snorkel off the beach. Coral ledges.

Little Saint James: A 40-foot dive on the lee side has some deep ledges to explore, sheltering various schools of fish.

Twin Barges: Located off Limetree Beach lie two wrecks sunk approximately in the 1940s. Although visibility is limited outside the wrecks, the clarity improves inside the ships' chambers.

Carvel Rock: Off of the northern side of this rock, near St. John, in depths to 90 feet, big schools of pelagic fish pass through colorful, sponge-encrusted caves.

Thatch Cay: Divers at the Tunnels here explore 8 different arches and tunnels.

Scotch Bank: Off St. Croix, this popular dive spot is a favorite for spotting stingrays and manta rays.

Long Reef: A 6-mile-long reef which provides dives at depths from 30–50 feet. A forest of coral, including pillar and elkhorn colonies.

Salt River: This area has 2 distinct walls. The East Wall plunges from depths of 50-100 feet, revealing many caves and caverns. The West Wall peaks at 30 feet and tumbles to 125 feet. The colors of the sponges grasping the crevices and pillars are awesome.

Buck Island: Off St. Croix, this national monument features abundant tropical fish and a jungle of huge staghorn and elkhorn coral. An absolute must for anyone visiting St. Croix.

Frederiksted Pier: (St. Croix) 30-foot-deep pilings offer splendid diving day or night. The pilings provide a home for bright sponges and algae, as well as sea horses, crabs and octopus.

Cane Bay, Davis Bay and Salt River: All have walls of coral from 20 feet to over 1000 feet. Several anchors have been discovered along the wall. One of the most-photographed anchors is nestled in sand at 60 feet on the Northstar Wall.

MEDICAL EMERGENCIES

In the event of diving related emergencies, contact the U.S. Coast Guard Search and Rescue on VHF 16 or telephone 340-776-3497 for immediate assistance. There is a recompression chamber in St. Thomas at the Hospital Chamber telephone (340) 776-2686, Divers Alert Network (919) 684-8111, 24 hours or call collect 919-684-4DAN.

Your charter company also can be of great assistance, and should be contacted if you run into a problem.

10 Ways to Protect the Coral Reef

1. Realize that coral reefs are systems of slow-growing animals that have taken many centuries to develop into what we see today. They are not rocks and standing on them or kicking them will cause substantial damage. Corals have very limited ability to recover from damages; breaking off a piece of coral is usually fatal, killing hundreds of years of growth.

2. Don't drop anchors or anchor chains on corals. Know what is below before you drop your anchor. If you aren't sure that you are over sand jump in the water with a mask to take a look. Dropping anchors and chains on coral crushes, pulverizes and dislodges the corals from the bottom. This destructive practice can be easily avoided by using a mooring to secure your boat or snorkeling to see what lies below your keel before you drop the hook.

3. Don't touch, kick or stand on coral. Don't drag dive equipment or cameras across it. Don't kick sand on it. Fins, cameras, dive gauges, and regulator second stages can crush coral polyps, or break off entire sections of coral. Sand kicked up by fins, feet or boat engines can smother corals, depriving them of sunlight and food they require for growth and life. And while small contacts may not be life-threatening, the additional stress may prove too much and become fatal. Abrasions also provide locations for infections in the coral, or places for invasion by marine micro-organisms.

4. Don't drive boats into reefs. While running aground is a nightmare for the cruiser, it is also fatal for the reef. Know where you are cruising. Pay attention to charts and navigation and limit distractions. Don't leave the helm while operating a boat and don't (or limit) cruising at night.

5. Don't pump-out holding tanks/bilges and don't add chemicals to these places. Pollutants in the form of sewage and oils are harmful to reefs. Nutrients in the sewage promote algal growth that out-compete coral for space on the reefs. (This is also why you should avoid urinating while snorkeling or diving. Use your boat's marine heads; that is why they are there.) Chemicals that are put into holding tanks and bilges are harmful to reefs and can interfere with the treatment of these wastes when they are properly pumped-out on shore.

6. Know where and how you can fish. Many cruisers love trolling and fishing, but before doing so, make certain you are in compliance with local regulations (either US or British).

7. Once you are aware and in compliance with fishing regulations, catch only what you will eat. Local reef fisheries are over-exploited, and fish play an important role in the ecology of the reef.

8. Take only pictures, leave only bubbles. Collecting shells and coral/live rock is illegal in the British and US Virgin Islands; even the "dead" rubble on shorelines. Shells, even ones that appear "empty" are illegal to collect. Photography or sketching is a non-destructive way to turn these finds into lasting memories.

9. Littering kills. Cruisers love Caribbean trade winds, but care must be taken so articles don't blow off the boat into the water. Towels and wet clothes will blow off safety lines, sinking to entangle in the reef. Solid waste such as cups, napkins and plates that blow overboard are unsightly and destructive to marine life. Plastics smother reefs and harm turtles. Use proper trash facilities for solid waste, and don't let towels or trash blow off your boat into the water.

10. Avoid fuel spills. Use extreme care when fueling your boat and dinghy. If you do spill gas, don't use any dispersants such as detergents or soap. This causes oils to sink to the bottom and smother corals. Oil spills are an environmental and safety hazard, and legal violation.

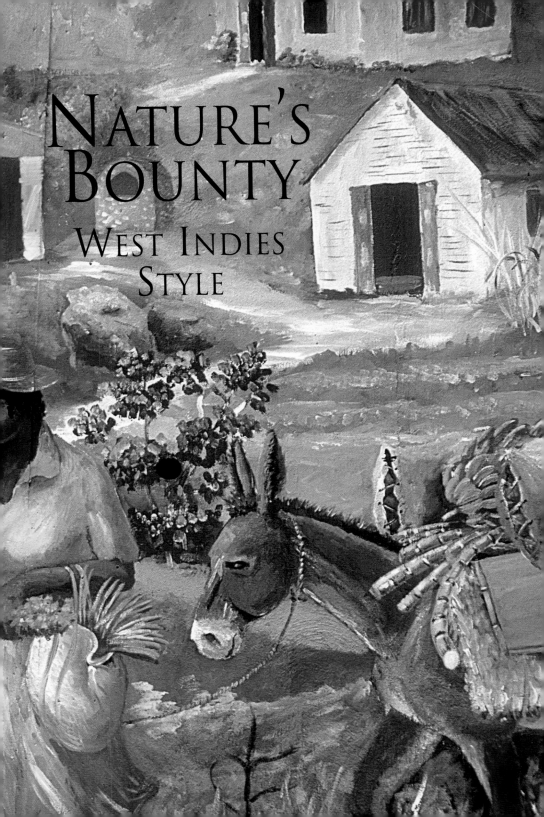

Nature's Bounty

West Indies Style

Fabulous Island Fruits & Vegetables

A collection of some of the most delicious tropical produce to be found in the Virgin Islands.

Sugar Apple

A favorite throughout the islands, the sugar apple looks like it wears a coat of armor! Actually when ripe, it breaks open easily and the delicious, custard-like interior can be scooped out by the spoonful or by eating it by the mouthful, taking care to spit out the shiny seeds inside. It is well worth the effort, as the inside is sweet, with a wonderful sort of soft texture.

Guava

This colorful fruit is used for making jams, jellies, and is scrumptious in pies and tarts. The guava is a small, usually round fruit that grows on a tree. The skin is green to yellow-green, and pulp inside is pink or peach to an almost red colour, with lines of seeds. Guava ice cream is a delicacy not to be missed.

Passion Fruit

Despite the connotation of the name, this fruit may be rather baffling to the first time taster. It is actually quite unattractive with a tough, wrinkly, brownish skin and is about the size of a lemon. The interior has a yellow green jellyish pulp with edible brown seeds. When the seeds are removed, the passion fruit essence is used to flavor exotic drinks, ices, tarts and pies, becoming an interesting, perfumey addition to many recipes.

Genip

Looking like a bunch of green grapes, these small, round fruits are a bit more challenging to eat! First the somewhat tough skin encasing the pulp must be pulled off (usually with your teeth). Once the skin is gone, the inside is yours to tug the sweet, sometimes tart pulp from the rather large pit. Although not easy fruits to eat, genips can keep you busy for quite awhile!

Ugli Fruit

Resembling an ugly version of a grapefruit the ugli fruit is light green to a yellowy orange colour, and can be the size of an orange to the size of a large grapefruit. Succulent and dripping with juice it is best eaten the same way as a grapefruit or an orange (the skin is easily peeled). If you have an opportunity to try this wondrous fruit, be sure to enjoy its blessings.

Tamarind

Growing from large, lovely shade trees are the pods of the tamarind tree. Used in many sauces such as Worcestershire, chutney, and piccalilli, tamarind is also used for sweet candies, and jams. One has to develop a taste for this often tart fruit, but, once acquired, it is hard to stop the attachment. To eat you must first crack open the pod, remove the threads and then consume the sticky paste attached to the large seeds.

Papaya

Growing from a tall, slender umbrella-shaped tree, the fabulous "paw-paw" varies from an eggplant shape to an oval or round shape. The colors vary from a green to orange or yellow, but the fruits must be tested by squeezing to ascertain whether it is ripe or not. The texture of the lovely orange, melon like interior of the fruit is almost as heavenly as the taste, especially when sprinkled with a bit of fresh lime. Green papaya still hard to the squeeze, is used as a cooked vegetable in many delectable recipes.

Sapodilla

About the size of a medium apple, the sapodilla should be eaten only when very ripe and almost mushy like a plum. The skin is a pale tan or beige colour with shiny black seeds inside that should not be eaten. This fruit is used in making many dessert dishes, and is delicious when eaten with other fruits in a fruit salad.

Soursop

A very unlikely looking delicacy this fruit is large (often weighing several pounds), with a green, spiny exterior. The shape is like that of a large pine cone irregularly formed. Only very few are eaten fresh, as most are used in flavoring other dishes with it's sweet fragrance, like soursop ice cream, or in tropical fruit drinks with a healthy measure of rum!

Mango

The mango grows from a large, leafy tree that during mango season becomes heavily laden with its scented fruit. Mangos come in many varieties, but are usually best eaten at the beach, where one can jump into the sea to clean off the delicious stickiness. Grafted mangos are less fibrous, and when peeled are a delight. One may see children and adults sucking on mangos to extract the juicy, orange flesh from the fibers and bulky seed in the middle.

Breadfruit

The breadfruit tree is a
common sight on many
Caribbean islands. Mature fruits
have dimpled green skins and grow to
6 inches or larger in clusters on
magnificent trees of up to 60 feet in
height with huge, long-fingered leaves.
Inside, the soft, fleshy fruits are yellowish-
brown to white in color and rich in
carbohydrates and vitamins A, B and C.
Breadfruit can be cooked as a starchy vegetable
side dish or in breadfruit breads, puddings and
pies. Try it baked with salt, pepper and butter.

Dasheen

This versatile plant grows to a height of four to six feet. The large, handsome, arrow-shaped leaves, sometimes called elephant ears, are similar to spinach. The young, tender leaves are used in callaloo soup, while the tubers, shown here, are generally stubby and similar in size to potatoes. Also called cocoyam, taro, eddo and kalo, the dasheen tubers are usually boiled, roasted or baked and eaten like potatoes.

Christophene

The pear-shaped christophene originated in Mexico where it is known as chayote, and is a member of the gourd family. It can be eaten raw or cooked and is crisp, juicy and nutty flavored, with a taste like fresh, young squash. Large christophenes may be stuffed with a mixture of bread crumbs, meat, cheese, onions, herbs and seasonings and broiled or baked.

Aubergine

This egg-shaped member of the potato family is a common plant throughout the Caribbean, as it relies on the warm climate and plentiful rain supply to support its growth. The large, glossy fruits are known by various other names, including Chinese eggplant, Jew's apple, egg fruit, melongene, garden egg and mad apple. The skin colors range from dark purple to mottled purple-and-white. Served as a vegetable, the ripe aubergines may be cubed and boiled or cut into strips or slices, battered and fried. Comprised of over 90 percent water, aubergines are low in both calories and nutritional value.

THE ORIGIN OF GROG

True "grog" had its beginning in the Royal Navy in the 18th century – specifically on August 21, 1740. It is the most traditional of all sea drinks.

Prior to 1740, Pusser's Rum was issued to the men "neat" – that is without water. But Admiral Vernon, the hero of Porto Bello and Commander-in-Chief West Indies was to change all this by the issuance of his infamous Order to Captains No. 349, given on board his flagship HMS Burford on August 21, 1740.

His order refers to the:
"...unanimous opinion of both Captains and Surgeons that the pernicious allowance of rum in drams, and often at once, is attended with many fatal effects to their morals as well as their health besides the ill consequences of stupefying their rational qualities.

...You are hereby required and directed... that the respective daily allowance... be every day mixed with the proportion of a quart of water to a half pint of rum, to be mixed in a scuttled butt kept for that purpose, and to be done upon the deck, and in the presence of the Lieutenant of the Watch, who is to take particular care to see that the men are not defrauded in having their full allowance of rum."

The tars had already nicknamed Vernon "Old Grog" from the grosgrain cloak he often wore when on the quarterdeck. The watered rum gave great offense to the men, and soon they began referring to it contemptuously as "grog" from the name they'd already provided Vernon.

Vernon's order provided that every man's half-pint Pusser's Rum allowance be diluted with one quart water. This was later changed to two parts water and one rum. In 1756, the daily ration was increased to one pint per man! Just before the end in 1970, it was reduced to one-eighth pint.

On board another ship of Vernon's squadron, the HMS Berwick, and just after the issuance of Vernon's order, one of the men wrote this poem that became famous throughout England:

"A mighty bowl on deck he drew
And filled it to the brink.
Such drank the Burford's gallant crew
And such the Gods shall drink.
The sacred robe which Vernon wore
Was drenched within the same,
And Hence its virtues guard our shore
And Grog derives its name."

LIMEY

Tall glass or old-fashioned glass
filled with ice cubes
2 ozs. Pussers Rum
Soda water

Squeeze the juice from one half lime. Add
sugar to taste (optional, but not traditional). Top
off with soda water, stir, and float the expended
lime peel on top.

ROYAL NAVY FOG CUTTER

Ice cubes to fill shaker
2 ozs. Pusser's Rum
1/2 ounce gin
1/4 cup lemon juice
2 tbsps. orange juice
1 tbsp. orgeat syrup
1 tsp. dry sherry
Fruit slices for garnish

THE BIG DIPPER

Ice cubes to fill shaker
1 oz. Pusser's Rum
1 oz. brandy
1 tbsp. lime juice
1/2 tsp. sugar
dash of Cointreau
Club soda

Shake well rum, brandy, lime juice, sugar and
Cointreau. Strain into an old-fashioned glass
with several ice cubes, fill with club soda and stir
slightly. This is a popular drink on Atlantic
crossings just before star time.

EMPIRE TOP

2 parts Pusser's Rum
1 part French Vermouth
1 part Grand Marnier
1 dash Angostura bitters
Crushed ice

Shake all the ingredients well and serve.

DIFFERENT DRUMMER

3 cups orange juice
3/4 cup coffee liqueur
6 orange or lemon slices (garnish)
3/4 cup Jamaican or dark rum
2 dozen ice cubes

Combine ingredients and shake well. Garnish
with orange or lemon slices and serve immediately.
Serves 6.

PLANTER'S PUNCH

1 cup cracked ice
3 ozs. Pusser's Rum
1 oz. lime juice
1 oz. sugar syrup
3-5 dashes Angostura bitters
soda water

Shake all ingredients together well and pour
unstrained into tall glass with several ice cubes.
Top off with soda water, stir, garnish with lime
slice and serve with a straw.

THE DEEP SIX

Tall glass filled with crushed ice
2 ozs. Pusser's Rum
1 tbsp. lime juice
1/2 ounce sugar syrup
Champagne

Combine rum, lime juice and sugar, and stir well.
Fill glass with champagne and stir gently.
Garnish with a slice of lime. This is an unusual
drink — smooth, flavorful & powerful.

FORCE 12

Ice cubes to fill shaker
1/4 cup Pusser's Rum
1 oz. vodka
1 tbsp. lime juice
1 tbsp. grenadine
1/4 cup pineapple juice

Shake well and pour into tall glass. Garnish with
fruit slices. This drink is a good test for sea legs.

"The Origin of Grog" and the above recipes are provided courtesy of Pusser's Ltd., Road Town, Tortola, BVI.

Cruising Guide Publications

CRUISING GUIDE TO THE VIRGIN ISLANDS

By Nancy &
Simon Scott
16th Edition,
2013-2014
ISBN 978-0-944428-95-5
6 x 9, 350 pp. **$32.95**

Completely re-designed
and updated style, with
more Virgin Island pho-
tography and full color
detailed anchorage charts, these guides have been
indispensable companions for sailors and visitors
to these islands since 1982. Includes a free 17 x 27
color planning chart, with aerial photos of some of
the anchorages. Covers the Virgin Islands including
all the U.S. and British Virgin Islands!

- GPS co-ordinates for every anchorage
- Anchoring and mooring information and fees
- Customs, immigration and National Park regulations
- Particulars on marina facilities and the amenities they offer
- Water sports-where to go and where to rent equipment
- Shore-side facilities, restaurants, beach bars, shops, provisions, internet connections

Everything you will need to help make your vacation an enjoyable and memorable experience in a concise easy-to-use format.

CRUISING GUIDE TO THE LEEWARD ISLANDS

Chris Doyle
2012-2013
ISBN 978-0-944428-93-1
6 x 9, 529 pp
$34.95

This twelfth edition covers
the islands from Anguilla to
Dominca, and is an essential
tool for all cruisers sailing this region. Chris Doyle
spends months sailing these islands to update each
edition. Included are over one hundred up-to-date
color sketch charts, full color aerial photos of most
anchorages, island pictures, and detailed shore-side
information covering services, restaurants, provisioning, travel basics and island history. Information is
linked to the author's website where you can download the GPS waypoints given in the sketch charts,
learn of essential updates, print town maps, and
obtain links to local weather, news, and businesses.

VIRGIN ANCHORAGES

By Nancy & Simon Scott
2012 Edition
ISBN 978-0-944428-84-9
8.5 x 11, 96 pp. **$29.95**

Virgin Anchorages features
stunning color aerial pho-
tography of 46 of the most popular anchorages in the
Virgin Islands. Graphic overlays aid in navigating
to safe anchorages. This is an excellent companion
to Cruising Guide to the Virgin Islands.

WATERPROOF PLANNING CHART OF THE VIRGIN ISLANDS
COLOR WITH AERIAL PHOTOS

Color, 17 x 27 **$9.95**

Printed on two sides this new chart includes the
U.S. & B.V.I. from St. Thomas to Anegada, including anchorage and mooring locations as well as GPS
co-ordinates, sailing routes and distances between
waypoints. The waterproof chart is excellent for
the cockpit and attractive enough to hang on the
wall when you get home. Designed for use with The
Cruising Guide to the Virgin Islands

LEEWARD ANCHORAGES

By Chris Doyle
ISBN 0-944428-82-7
8.5 x 11, 91 pp **$29.95**

Leeward Anchorages shows
aerial photographs of all
the favorite anchorages from Anguilla through
Dominica with graphic overlays to illustrate dangerous and safe passages from a bird's eye view.
Carefully researched and recorded by Chris Doyle,
safe passages, markers, buoys and hazards are all
marked to guide you to safe, enjoyable anchorages.
This is a companion book to use with The Cruising
Guide to the Leeward Islands.

SAILORS GUIDE TO THE WINDWARD ISLANDS

By Chris Doyle
16th Edition,
2013-2014
ISBN 978-0-944428-94-8
6 x 9, 430 pp. **$32.95**

Revised and updated for 2013-2014, this guide features detailed sketch charts based on the author's own surveys, and aerial photos of most anchorages. It also includes clear and concise navigational information. By far the most popular guide to the area, it covers the islands from Martinique to Grenada, with dazzling scenic photography, unsurpassed onshore information, sections on exploring, provisioning, water sports, services, restaurants and photography. Information is linked to the author's website where you can download town maps, GPS waypoints from the sketch charts, and obtain links to local weather, news and more.

CRUISING GUIDE TO VENEZUELA & BONAIRE

By Chris Doyle
2006
ISBN 0-944428-78-9
6 x 9, 290 pp. **$27.95**

This is the latest updated version of the only seriously researched guide to this area. The book includes color aerial photos of many anchorages, clear and concise navigational charts, with information on things to do and places to go while on shore. The guide is linked to the author's website where you can download updates, town maps and much more.

CRUISING GUIDE TO TRINIDAD, TOBAGO PLUS BARBADOS AND GUYANA

By Chris Doyle
2013
ISBN 978-0-944428-96-2
6 x 9, 256 pp. **$27.95**

This updated edition has been expanded to include Guyana. Including 55 sketch charts, aerial photographs, dazzling scenic photography throughout, unsurpassed onshore information with sections on exploring, provisioning, services and restaurants. The guide is linked to the author's website where you can download town maps, GPS waypoints given in the sketch charts and much more.

WINDWARD ANCHORAGES

By Chris Doyle
ISBN 0-944428-83-5
8.5 x 11, 96 pp
$29.95

Windward Anchorages is the third in the Anchorages series and a companion book to the Sailors Guide to the Windward Islands by Chris Doyle. Stunning aerial images depict anchorages from Martinique south through Dominica. These aerial images are overprinted to show the hazards to avoid, as well as markers and buoys to guide you to the safe passages and anchorages of the Windward Islands.

CONCISE GUIDE TO CARIBBEAN WEATHER

1997 ISBN 0-9652476-1-9
6 x 9, 72 pp.
$19.95

The safest way to navigate this popular cruising area - David Jones, founder of the most successful weather net in the Caribbean, garners praise all around for his unique knowledge and clear explanations.

CRUISING GUIDE TO THE FLORIDA KEYS

By Captain Frank Papy
12th Edition, 6 x 9, 208 pp. **$19.95**

This 12th ed. is laid out in easy reference form, with a chapter devoted to each Key with color aerial photographs, 42 detailed sketch charts, along with navigational secrets. Covers Ft. Lauderdale down through the Keys and up to Tarpon Springs on the West Coast of Florida and includes facts on marinas, anchoring spots, artificial reefs, fishing information and much more.

TRICKS OF THE TRADES

By Bruce Van Sant
2001 ISBN 0-944428-62-2
6 x 9, 182 pp. **$14.95**

The author of Gentleman's Guide to Passages South widens the scope of his book to include stratagems and tips for sailors cruising aboard for the first time. Not how to sail, but how to live safely and comfortably while aboard - in short tricks he has learned during his many years of cruising.

Toll free 800-330-9542 or 727-733-5322
Fax 727-734-8179 or info@CruisingGuides.com

ABOUT THE AUTHORS

Simon and I met while cruising in the British Virgin Islands during the mid '70s where some years later, we were married at St. George's church in Road Town. Simon, a native of the UK, spent time in New Zealand as a teenager, where he raced dinghies and fell in love with sailing and the cruising lifestyle. A career in international marketing took him back and forth between London and New York before a sabbatical to the Virgin Islands aboard the classic John Alden cutter *Tomorrow* introduced him to the charms of the islands. He later returned to manage a major charter fleet where he was ideally positioned to listen to the needs and concerns of sailors from around the world discovering the delights and challenges of Caribbean cruising.

As my father was a U.S. naval officer we lived in many places. Japan was where he taught me to sail dinghies and several moves later we lived in Hawaii where sailing became a major focus in my life. I cruised extensively in the Bahamas in an old, wooden Tahiti Ketch, *Ichiban*, before sailing into the British Virgin Islands where I met Simon. We moved aboard *Zephyrine*, our Saxon class sloop, and began what would become our lifetime commitment to the sailing industry.

The first **Cruising Guide to the Virgin Islands** was published in 1982 and since that time we, along with our daughters, have continued annual surveys of the cruising area. I continue to oversee the daily operations of publishing guides at the offices of Cruising Guide Publications with my team in Dunedin, Florida.

We thank our readers for their loyalty, suggestions and criticism. It is for you that we write the books, and it is because of you that we are encouraged to improve.

We look forward to seeing you in Virgin waters.

Nancy & Simon Scott

ADVERTISERS INDEX

PUSSER'S® WEST ENI
Restaurant, Bar & Pusser's Co. Sto

The Pusser's Landing at Soper's Hole, Tortola, across from the Customs Dock, West E

Dockage, Fuel, Water, Ice & Moorings availabl
The best place to clear in and out of the BVI.

- Deck dining at sensible prices, or just enjoy the day's sunset with a Pusser's Painkiller in a take-home mug.

- Two dining choices; The Deck or the Crow's Next restaurant overlooking the anchorage.

The Pusser's Painkiller Mug

- Shop at our **PUSSER'S CO STORE** The Caribbean's m complete line of Tropical & Nautical clothing & unique gifts and accessories for women & men.

- A Full marina next door: Fuel, Ice, Water, Slips & Moorings.

FREE RUM & BIG SAVINGS IN THE BV

Typical BVI Bottle Price $9.95 vs. the U.S. $27. Buy 5 Bottles in a PUSSER'S STORE and get the 6th bottle FREE, a savings of $112.25 over the U.S. price on 6 bottles.

Pusser's Landing, Channel 16 or 495-4554
No better food, drink, fun & value on Tortola!
You may also shop with us online at www.pussers.com